REVOLUTION REASSESSED

Revolution Reassessed

Revisions in the History of Tudor Government and Administration

EDITED BY

CHRISTOPHER COLEMAN

AND

DAVID STARKEY

CLARENDON PRESS · OXFORD
1986

Oxford University Press, Walton Street, Oxford OX2 6DP

Oxford New York Toronto
Delhi Bombay Calcutta Madras Karachi
Kuala Lumpur Singapore Hong Kong Tokyo
Nairobi Dar es Salaam Cape Town
Melbourne Auckland

and associated companies in
Beirut Berlin Ibadan Nicosia

Oxford is a trade mark of Oxford University Press

Published in the United States
by Oxford University Press, New York

British Library Cataloguing in Publication Data

Revolution reassessed: revisions in the
history of Tudor government and
administration.
1. Great Britain—History—
Tudors, 1485–1603
I. Coleman, Christopher II. Starkey, David
942.05 DA315

ISBN 0-19-873064-0
ISBN 0-19-873063-2 Pbk

Set by DMB (Typesetting)
Printed in Great Britain
at the University Printing House, Oxford
by David Stanford
Printer to the University

CONTENTS

ABBREVIATIONS

All documents cited are in the Public Record Office, London, unless otherwise stated.

APC	*Acts of the Privy Council*, ed. J. R. Dasent (32 vols., London, 1890–1907).
BIHR	*Bulletin of the Institute of Historical Research*
BL	British Library
BL Add. MSS	British Library, Additional MSS
BL Cott. MSS	British Library, Cottonian MSS
BL Eg. MSS	British Library, Egerton MSS
BL Harg. MSS	British Library, Hargrave MSS
BL Harl. MSS	British Library, Harleian MSS
BL Lansd. MSS	British Library, Lansdowne MSS
Bod. Lib.	Bodleian Library, Oxford
Camb. Univ. Lib.	Cambridge University Library
CCR	*Calendar of Charter Rolls*
CJ	*Commons Journals*
CPR	*Calendar of Patent Rolls*
CSPD	*Calendar of State Papers, Domestic*
CSPF	*Calendar of State Papers, Foreign*
Derby. Archaeol. J.	*Derbyshire Archaelogical Journal*
DNB	*Dictionary of National Biography*
EcHR	*Economic History Review*
EHR	*English Historical Review*
Essex RO	Essex Record Office
Guaras	*The Accession of Queen Mary: the contemporary narrative of Antonio de Guaras, a Spanish merchant resident in London*, trans. and ed. R. Garnett (London, 1892).
HC 1509–58	*The House of Commons 1509–1558*, ed. S. T. Bindoff (3 vols., History of Parliament Trust, London, 1982).
HC 1558–1603	*The House of Commons 1558–1603*, ed. P. W. Hasler (3 vols., History of Parliament Trust, London, 1981).
HJ	*Historical Journal*
HMC	Historical Manuscripts Commission
J. Med. Hist.	*Journal of Medieval History*

LP	*Letters and Papers, Foreign and Domestic, of the Reign of Henry VIII, 1509–47*, ed. J. S. Brewer, J. Gairdner, and R. H. Brodie (21 vols. and Addenda, London, 1862–1932).
Northants RO	Northamptonshire Record Office
P&P	*Past and Present*
PRO	Public Record Office
Span. Cal.	*Calendar of Letters, Despatches, and State Papers, relating to the negotiations between England and Spain, preserved in the archives at Vienna, Simancas, and elsewhere*, ed. Royall Tyler (vols. xi–xiii, London, 1916, 1949, 1954).
Staffs. RO	Staffordshire Record Office
Stat. Realm	*Statutes of the Realm*, ed. A. Luders *et al.* (11 vols., London, 1810–28).
St. Pap.	*State Papers Published under the Authority of His Majesty's Commission, King Henry VIII* (11 vols., London, 1830–52).
Trans. Camb. Bibliog. Soc.	*Transactions of the Cambridge Bibliographical Society*
TRHS	*Transactions of the Royal Historical Society*
Ven. Cal.	*Calendar of State Papers and Manuscripts relating to English affairs existing in the archives and Collections of Venice, and in other libraries of northern Italy*, ed. Rawdon Brown (vols. v, vi, London, 1873, 1877, 1881).
Vita Mar. Reg.	'The *Vita Mariae Angliae Reginae* of Robert Wingfield of Brantham', ed. and trans. Diarmaid MacCulloch, *Camden Miscellany* xxviii (Camden 4th series, xxix, London, 1984).

INTRODUCTION

PROFESSOR ELTON'S 'REVOLUTION'

CHRISTOPHER COLEMAN

THE 'revolution' with which Professor Elton's name is usually associated is, of course, the subject of his first book, *The Tudor Revolution in Government*.[1] But he deserves to be associated with another. For the influence of this seminal work, and the author's continuing energy and activity within his chosen field, have revolutionized Tudor studies. Not only has he provided us with a brilliant and imaginative interpretation of the crowded events of the 1530s, but he has transformed our view of the century as a whole, and shaped our perceptions of the way in which it ought to be studied. Not satisfied with telling us what happened and why, and simplifying it all in two splendid volumes of general history, he has also taught us what history is and how to practise it. To make matters easy for us, he has taken on the tedious, but necessary, chore of providing an annual bibliography of historical literature, which has included even works not related to the sixteenth century. And when we have published our own views, he has corrected them, in over two hundred and fifty trenchant reviews.[2] It is thus hardly surprising that so much of the published work of recent years bears the unmistakable imprint of his mind and personality.[3]

[1] G. R. Elton, *The Tudor Revolution in Government* (Cambridge, 1953).

[2] For a comprehensive list of his publications between 1946 and 1981, including the works alluded to here, see D. J. Guth and J. W. McKenna, eds., *Tudor Rule and Revolution: Essays for G. R. Elton from his American Friends* (Cambridge, 1982), 393–407. Since 1981 he has published, among other things, a second edition of *The Tudor Constitution: Documents and Commentary* (Cambridge, 1982); a third volume of his collected essays, *Studies in Tudor and Stuart Politics and Government*, vol. iii, *Papers and Reviews 1973–1981* (Cambridge, 1983); another statement of his views on the practice of history, in G. R. Elton and R. W. Fogel, *Which Road to the Past? Two Views of History* (Yale, 1983); and two reports on his continuing work on parliament, 'The English Parliament in the Sixteenth Century: Estates and Statutes', in A. Cosgrove and J. I. McGuire, eds., *Parliament and Community* (Dublin, 1983), 69–95, and 'Parliament', in Christopher Haigh, ed., *The Reign of Elizabeth I* (London, 1984), 79–100.

[3] The general debt is a personal one in the case of five of the six contributors to this volume, and one of which they are deeply aware.

However, it is not with the second of these revolutions that this book is concerned, but the first. To summarize very briefly what has often been summarized before, *The Tudor Revolution* presented a new and exciting vision of the 1530s and of its place in English history, a vision that was expanded subsequently in *England Under the Tudors*.[4] According to Professor Elton, Thomas Cromwell, whom he has elsewhere described as 'the most remarkable revolutionary in English history',[5] seized the unique opportunity presented by Henry VIII's marital problems to turn England into a unified, independent sovereign state, ruled by a constitutional monarch through national and bureaucratic institutions. By using statute—the law made by parliament—to solve a variety of complicated legal and constitutional problems, and by exploiting the powers devolved upon him by the monarch, Cromwell was able to shift the burden of government from the personal servants of the royal household to properly organized departments of state. Thanks to his work, the king was recognized as the (divinely appointed) supreme head of an independent, but still Catholic, Church of England, with the power not only to regulate its laws and courts, but also to determine its doctrine and ritual. Royal authority was extended into the dark corners of the realm, by the abolition of the liberties and franchises, the provision of royal justice and shire administration for all England and Wales, and the strengthening of the Councils in the North and the Marches. Government and administration—very much Professor Elton's central concerns— were transformed in a number of ways: by the creation of a complex bureaucratic system (eventually comprising six separate revenue courts) to manage the royal finances; by the reorganization of the haphazard medieval Council into a more formally constituted board of government; and by the promotion of the principal secretary (Cromwell himself) to the position of chief executive and co-ordinating minister. Moreover, Parliament's share in these dramatic events had, as Cromwell intended, important consequences

---

[4] See, for instance, Elton, *England Under the Tudors* (2nd edn., London, 1974), 160–92; Penry Williams, 'Dr. Elton's Interpretation of the Age', *P & P* xxv (1963), 3–8. Many aspects of the summary presented here will be described at greater length in the relevant chapters of this book.

[5] Elton, *England Under the Tudors*, 127. He has more recently assessed him as 'the most remarkable English statesman of the sixteenth century and one of the most remarkable in the country's history', in 'Thomas Cromwell Redivivus', *Studies*, iii. 373–90.

for its own institutional development. The Lords and the Commons now clearly established their identity as Houses *of* Parliament, separate institutions within one body, and as necessary partners, albeit subordinate and occasional ones, in the business of government; statute law was shown to be universally binding, all-embracing, and free of the restrictions of natural and divine law; and a new concept of sovereignty—the sovereignty of king-in-Parliament —was established by Parliament's provision of the laws which alone made the Henrician Reformation enforceable. In short, even though the minister's reforming career was terminated prematurely by his execution, leaving much of his work incomplete, Cromwell had done sufficient by 1540 to engender a revolution in government, in administration, and in the church, which continued after his death.

Professor Elton has, needless to say, developed and modified his views considerably in the thirty-odd years which have elapsed since *The Tudor Revolution* was published. For one thing—to adopt a metaphor of which he is fond—he has built substantially upon the foundations he laid down in 1953. If he was originally open to the charge that he was too concerned with what a small number of people did, argued, or enacted at Westminster, rather than what actually happened in the localities, with institutions rather than ideas, with abolition and destruction rather than construction, he is no longer. For in *Policy and Police* he introduced us to Cromwell the manager and propagandist, and showed us how the minister *persuaded* southern England to accept the policies which in fact provoked a rebellion in the north in 1536; in *Reform and Renewal* he revealed Cromwell the constructive statesman, the patron of a circle of reforming intellectuals who were Protestant and humanist in inspiration, battling, not altogether successfully, with the social and economic problems of the day—depopulation, grain-hoarding, urban decay, prices, and so on; and in *Reform and Reformation* he presented Cromwell the evangelical Protestant, a man influenced by the Bible as well as Aristotle and Marsiglio of Padua, viewing the construction of the sovereign state not as an end in itself, but as a means to another end—the purification of religion and the regeneration of society.[6] For another, he has accepted, and

[6] G. R. Elton, *Policy and Police: The Enforcement of the Reformation in the Age of Thomas Cromwell* (Cambridge, 1972); *Reform and Renewal: Thomas Cromwell and the Common Weal* (Cambridge, 1973); *Reform and Reformation: England 1509–1558* (London, 1977).

incorporated into the grand theory, a number of the criticisms which have been levelled at his work, though often in such a way as to diminish their force considerably. To cite but a few examples, he now agrees that the antecedents of the 'revolution of the 1530s' were more important than he thought, but maintains that Cromwell brought together many existing strands and made a new thing out of them. Indeed, he congratulates the minister on his grasp of 'the roots and long established realities of the polity he wished to transform' and on his recognition of the political advantages of introducing radical transformation under the guise of continuity.[7] He accepts that he probably ascribed too much planned consistency to Cromwell's reforms, which were necessarily designed to solve immediate problems, but still asserts that the minister's solutions demonstrate the application of general principles.[8] He concedes that Cromwell was less successful than he originally thought in rooting out household government, but still holds that the later demise of the Privy Chamber had more to do with the developments of the 1530s than with subsequent historical accidents.[9] He admits that he underestimated the degree to which the two-house structure and business organization of Parliament had developed before the Tudor period began, but still thinks that the long and vital sessions of the Reformation Parliament gave that institution 'a new air', even changed it 'essentially into its modern form as the supreme and sovereign legislator.'[10] And so on. In effect, therefore, the consequence of his work subsequent to the publication of *The Tudor Revolution* has been to expand the original vision, to purge it of what he has modestly referred to as its simplicities, and to reassert the essentials of his initial analysis and description of Cromwell's activities in the 1530s.[11]

However, if Professor Elton has become more, rather than less, convinced of the correctness of his views on this subject, he has also had to accept the fact that many historians have reservations about some of them, and some, serious ones.[12] His ideas have been criticized, sometimes extensively, by, among others, R. B. Wernham,

[7] Elton, *Reform and Renewal*, 160; *England Under the Tudors*, 479; *Reform and Reformation*, 172, 220. This defence is entirely consistent with his earlier veiws in *England Under the Tudors*, 160.

[8] Elton, *England Under the Tudors*, 480; *Reform and Reformation*, 214.

[9] Elton, *Reform and Reformation*, 211–20; *Tudor Constitution*, 132–3.

[10] Elton, *England Under the Tudors*, 482–3; *Tudor Constitution*, 233–4.

[11] See esp. Elton, 'Cromwell Redivivus'; *Reform and Reformation*, 211–20; *Tudor Constitution, passim.*   [12] Elton, *Reform and Renewal*, 166.

who, in a forthright review of *The Tudor Revolution*, argued that the author had exaggerated both Cromwell's influence over events and the novelty of the 1530s;[13] by G. L. Harriss, P. H. Williams and J. P. Cooper, who engaged Professor Elton, in the pages of *Past and Present*, in a memorable debate on a wide range of issues 'which predictably ended without either side feeling defeated';[14] by J. J. Scarisbrick who, by implication, rejected Professor Elton's interpretation of the relationship between Henry VIII and his minister;[15] by B. W. Beckingsale, who argued that 'the revolution of the 1530s did not consist in a decisive move to establish a despotic or a secular or a bureaucratic state, that it did not entail any radical change in the social or economic structure and that its political inspiration was in favour of a traditional mixed polity and its religious aim was the moderation of a middle way';[16] and, more recently, by Brendan Bradshaw, who, though prepared to concede that Cromwell was the originator of 'a gigantic project of structural reorganisation designed to transmute the Crown's (medieval) jurisdiction into a unitary—i.e. fully integrated and absolutely sovereign—state', argued that there were no convincing grounds for seeing the 1530s as a great age of social reform or Cromwell as an evangelical.[17] Furthermore, the *other* authors of recent general histories of the Tudor period have been, on the whole, reluctant to endorse Professor Elton's views. Some have been less so than others, but it would not be too gross a simplification to say that, while there has been a confusing range of responses to the concept of 'Tudor Revolution', it has only extended from the dismissive to the guardedly and selectively supportive.[18] It is all too

[13] *EHR* lxxi (1956), 92–5.

[14] G. L. Harriss and Penry Williams, 'A Revolution in Tudor History?', *P & P* xxv (1963), 3–58; J. P. Cooper, 'A Revolution in Tudor History?', ibid. xxvi (1963), 110–12; G. R. Elton, 'The Tudor Revolution: a Reply', ibid. xxix (1964), 26–49; G. L. Harriss and Penry Williams, 'A Revolution in Tudor History?', ibid. xxxi (1965), 87–96; G. R. Elton, 'A Revolution in Tudor History?', ibid. xxxii (1965), 103–9. The quotation is from *England Under the Tudors*, 479.

[15] J. J. Scarisbrick, *Henry VIII* (London, 1968).

[16] B.W. Beckingsale, *Thomas Cromwell: Tudor Minister* (London, 1978), 152–3.

[17] Brendan Bradshaw, 'The Tudor Commonwealth: Reform and Revision', *HJ* xxii (1979), 459–69.

[18] Conrad Russell, *The Crisis of Parliaments: English History 1509–1660* (Oxford, 1971; reprinted with corrections from 1974), postscript to p. 103, 110–11; D. M. Loades, *Politics and the Nation 1450–1660: Obedience, Resistance and Public Order* (London, 1974), 172–9; C. S. L. Davies, *Peace, Print and Protestantism 1450–1558* (London, 1977), 195–6, 226–8; Penry Williams, *The Tudor Regime* (Oxford, 1979), 457–8; A. G. R. Smith, *The Emergence of a Nation State: the Commonwealth of England 1529–1660* (London, 1984), 91–2.

likely, therefore, that the one conclusion those who study the sixteenth century at second hand will reach is that, thirty years after
the publication of *The Tudor Revolution in Government*, historians
are as far as ever from agreeing with either Professor Elton or with
each other on the extent to which its central ideas are, or are not,
valid.

Such a situation might be considered sufficient on its own to justify a searching re-examination of the subject. But the editors of
Revolution Reassessed did not only have the difficulties of students
in mind when they began to think of the possibility of publishing
this volume. For one thing, they were convinced that their own
research had led them to conclusions about the history and the
nature of Tudor government and administration which were fundamentally incompatible with some of the views Professor Elton had
expressed in *The Tudor Revolution*, and they thought it important
to publish their findings. For another, they felt that the (continuing) work of a number of fellow historians in adjacent fields had
added considerably to our knowledge and understanding of the
subjects with which Professor Elton was principally concerned, but
that, for lack of opportunity, it had not yet been as carefully
related to his ideas as was desirable. But they also shared the belief
that the *Past and Present* debate of the 1960s had been largely an
unproductive one, and not simply because it ended 'without either
side feeling defeated'. If the editors now confess that they are much
more aware of the difficulties of co-operative scholarship than they
were in 1981, when they first began to think about this book, they
may be forgiven for saying that the earlier critics of Professor Elton
made a tactical mistake: they concentrated too much of their fire
on the antecedents to the alleged revolution, and too little on what
actually happened in the sixteenth century. In particular, they failed
both to remedy Professor Elton's own, relative, neglect of the
Household, whose supposed eclipse in the 1530s was the essential
corollary to the establishment of bureaucratic government, and to
scrutinize his (understandably) sketchy account of the fortunes of
Cromwell's 'departments of state' after 1540. In short, they
neglected the essentials, and it was for this reason that the editors
finally decided to reopen the whole issue.

However, they also decided to adopt a rather different approach
to it. The first of the decisions that they took in this respect was not
to return to the pages of the learned journals, but to produce a

book whose core would consist of six chapters on the central themes of government and administration, each contributed by a specialist in the appropriate field. The second was that the book's principal—but by no means only—aim should be to remedy the shortcomings of the earlier debate by giving careful attention to the neglected areas of sixteenth-century history. The third was that the keynote of the book should be originality: in other words, that no part of it (other than this Introduction) should be used simply to debate again over the ground covered in *Past and Present*, or to summarize the publications of the last thirty years, or to challenge received ideas without offering any others in their place. Rather, every chapter should be solidly grounded on new material, and should, as far as possible, offer important new insights into the period. The fourth, and last, decision taken at this stage was that the editors should attempt neither to impose a uniformity of approach on the contributors, nor to conceal any differences that might arise between them (though of course they would try to resolve them), nor to insist on their arriving at any predetermined conclusions: in other words, they should firmly turn their back on any temptation to use the book as a vehicle for the introduction of a new orthodoxy. It is principally to these decisions, and to the willingness of the contributors to work within the loose framework of rules created by them, that *Revolution Reassessed* owes its shape and highly individual character.

Thanks, in part, to a late editorial initiative which the contributors agreed to endorse, the book opens with a short chapter on the fifteenth century. In it, David Starkey reminds us that Professor Elton's vision of the sixteenth century as a reforming era depended (in part) on the perception of its predecessor as an unreformed age in which the need for reform was not even recognized, and argues that such a view of the fifteenth century is no longer tenable. Synthesizing the work of a number of historians, he shows that, in the time of the so-called Wars of the Roses, the revenue basis of the crown was transformed and methods of revenue administration were radically altered, largely in response to the influence of reforming ideas about the nature of the monarchy and the efficient functioning of govenment, ideas which were debated in Parliament, demonstrated for by the commons of England, and adopted by the parties engaged in the political conflicts of the day. But he does more than this. Drawing on his own research, he argues that, in the same period, the language of politics was transformed, and that by the 1460s, the vocabulary of 'commonweal' argumentation, so familiar in Tudor discourse, was a fully developed feature of political debate. So Yorkist England was not simply an age in which there *were* reforms: it was an age in which the need for reform was widely recognized and was justified in language that prefigured the sixteenth-century usage.

David Starkey also provides the second chapter, which deals with the Court and its contribution to royal government in the first half of the sixteenth century. He begins, as Professor Elton did not, by examining the history of the Household, devoting particular attention to the process by which one of its relatively insignificant subdepartments—the Privy Chamber of Henry VII—developed into the third and most important of its departments under Henry VIII, before the end of 1519. In so doing, he offers a fundamentally different account of Household reform from that presented in *The Tudor Revolution*. He then applies the insights provided by this approach to a re-examination of the Household's contribution to government, focusing, in particular, on the offices of the treasurer of the Chamber and the king's secretary, whose fortunes, he maintains, have become test-cases for our understanding of administrative development. This enables him to show that, contrary to Professor Elton's views, the decline of the Chamber had nothing to do with structural changes in the theory and practice of government; that the functions of the declining Chamber were not transferred to bureaucrats or bureaucratic departments, but taken over by the Privy Chamber; and that the latter's governmental activity was still flourishing at the end of Henry VIII's reign.

The third and fourth chapters of the book are devoted to the Council. In the third, John Guy tests Professor Elton's claims that Thomas Cromwell created the Privy Council 'between 1534 and 1536, as a conscious act of administrative reform designed to modernize the existing King's Council as inherited from Wolsey's regime', and that the minister relieved the new executive board of the burden of judicial work, by vesting the principal responsibility for conciliar justice in institutionally separate courts of Star Chamber and Requests. This he does by examining the way in which the structure of the Council changed between 1485 and 1540. There is no doubt, he concludes, either that the new-style Privy Council existed by 10 August 1540, or that the Courts of Star

Chamber and Requests had acquired a separate institutional identity by this date, or that Cromwell had made some contributions to these developments. But the Privy Council was probably structured —on lines planned by Wolsey—during the tense months of the Pilgrimage of Grace, as a pragmatic response to crisis, not as a conscious exercise in statecraft, and Wolsey, not Cromwell, was the founding father of the mature Courts of Requests and Star Chamber, whose venue, business, and court procedure were virtually untouched by the changes of the 1530s.

In the fourth chapter, Dale Hoak adopts an altogether different approach to the subject, and presents the reader with a case-study rather than a survey, one which challenges Professor Elton's notion of 'revolution' and suggests an apposite redefinition of the word. Making full use of the recently published *Vita Mariae Angliae Reginae* of Robert Wingfield of Brantham, he offers an entirely new history of the Council in the reign of Mary I—and in so doing casts much-needed light on the politics of the period. His chapter explains how Elizabeth I inherited the system of government-by-Council established in the time of the duke of Northumberland, and makes it clear how large a part in the process was played by historical accident. Mary's first Council owed nothing to 'Cromwellian principles'. It was a war Council, composed of her own servants and those peers and gentlemen of East Anglia who were prepared to take the considerable risk of directing a rebellion against Queen Jane. This 'extraordinary band' won her England but was incapable of governing it, so she had to reinforce it with experienced councillors, who had served not only her father and brother, but also Queen Jane. In a hitherto undetected coup, the 'professionals' who had been active under Northumberland took over the direction of the most important matters of state. Philip's departure from England rendered them indispensable for the rest of the reign, and so enabled them to maintain the continuity of the programme of governmental reform initiated in 1550.

In the fifth chapter, Jennifer Loach deals with the subject of Parliament, and reminds us that we should not let Professor Elton's insights into the development of the institution in the century after 1530 obscure his own emphasis on the continuity of parliamentary history. There were important changes in the 1530s, and Cromwell's part in them was significant, but Parliament remained the same body as its medieval predecessors, and contemporaries continued to perceive it as such for decades. Though the size of the House of Commons increased considerably in the sixteenth century, it was not as a consequence of a *new* enthusiasm for membership, stimulated by dramatic events in the 1530s and a subsequent pressure on the monarch to create new seats: the expansion of the Lower House had begun in Henry VI's reign. It was principally a result of the crown's need to have sufficient 'useful' men in the Commons to ensure that 'this amateur and often aimless body' should deal satisfactorily with the business put before it, and therefore of the crown's deliberate creation of large numbers of new seats for its own agents in areas under firm royal control—for instance, in the Duchies of Cornwall and (especially) Lancaster. Things began to change in the late 1570s, but it was not until the early seventeenth century that the notion of parliamentary representation as being a privilege, rather than an expensive duty, began to prevail, and serious competition for seats begin.

The sixth and seventh chapters are concerned with financial administration. In the sixth, Jim Alsop does two things. He explains, first of all, why it is that historians have so signally failed to agree in their interpretations of the character and significance of the developments of the first half of the sixteenth century, and shows that their work has been vitiated by serious misunderstandings of the essential nature of financial administration. (Not even the editors of *Revolution Reassessed* escape the occasional glancing blow here.) He then applies his own insights to a reappraisal of the period. The transition from 'undifferentiated household administration to the management of crown revenue within departments of state' which took place between the death of Henry VII and the accession of Elizabeth I was, he agrees with Professor Elton, a crucial development: but the change took place without an associated 'revolution' in administrative procedures, and for reasons far more complicated than can be explained in terms of one man's genius.

Christopher Coleman uses the seventh chapter to examine the history of the Receipt of the Exchequer between *c*.1554 and 1572, and to show that there is little to justify Professor Elton's belief that the amalgamation of the revenue courts completed Cromwell's work, or terminated a period of 'change and experiment', or provided 'a solution of enduring effectiveness' to the long-standing problems of financial administration. He demonstrates, among other things, that Cromwell's supposed pupil and heir, the marquess of Winchester, was an arch-conservative who did his best to re-establish what he thought was the constitution of Henry II in the Receipt; that, in the course of a protracted and acrimonious dispute, the Receipt was reorganized no fewer than four times, and not in one consistent direction; and that the late 1560s and early 1570s witnessed a series of major disasters in the tellers' office. More importantly, perhaps, he shows that the (very complicated) process of change owed nothing to a Cromwellian reforming ideology, consistently applied.

Finally, David Starkey concludes the volume by drawing together its major themes, relating them to Professor Elton's views, and suggesting a number of important reinterpretations of the developments of the period. What these are it would be illogical to reveal here, but it should perhaps be remarked that he maintains to the last the editors' commitment to originality, by making an illuminating comparison of the fiscal strategy of the earlier Tudors with that of their contemporaries in Valois France. That said, it only needs to be added that if, as the editors think, they now see some aspects of the sixteenth century a little more clearly than Professor Elton did thirty years ago, it is only because they have the advantage of standing on the shoulders of a giant.

CHAPTER 1

WHICH AGE OF REFORM?

DAVID STARKEY

PROFESSOR Elton has made the sixteenth century his own, and he has made it an age of reform, in church, society, and above all in government. In his first and most important book, *The Tudor Revolution in Government*, he argued that between 1530 and 1550 the government of England changed decisively: medieval 'household' methods were abandoned and modern 'bureaucratic' ones were adopted. The changes were inspired by Thomas Cromwell and largely carried through under his direction. They clustered so thickly and were so fundamental that only the term revolution will describe them. Elton defended this position vigorously in the *Past and Present* debates of the 1960s; subsequently he has conceded on particular points whilst yielding nothing of the whole.[1]

But a reformed sixteenth century implies an unreformed fifteenth. Elton went even further. Not only was late medieval England unreformed; the need for reform was not even perceived. Instead there was resignation to man's inevitable lot. In 1953, when *The Tudor Revolution* appeared, such a position was just about tenable. Since then, however, the publication of the work of K. B. McFarlane together with the labours of a host of other scholars have made it absurd. Far from 'helpless resignation' and 'leaving it all to God',[2] the fifteenth century displayed a lively and effective concern for the things of this world. This concern is now familiar stuff to medievalists. But too many students of Tudor history follow Professor Elton in being, in Conrad Russell's phrase, 'profoundly uninterested in the middle ages'.[3] So it seems advisable to preface our reappraisal of Cromwellian reform with an account of how the

[1] See, for example, G. R. Elton, *Reform and Reformation* (London, 1977), 211 n. 13, 220 n. 19.

[2] Ibid. 16.

[3] Conrad Russell, 'On the side of the winners', *Times Educational Supplement*, 4 Nov. 1977.

age before Cromwell put its own governmental house in order. Most of this account will only synthesize and systematize the work of others. But on the language of politics, in particular the origins of the term 'commonwealth', it will have something more original to say.

The duke of York, the dominant figure of the 1450s, has been described by implication as a man of 'arrested intellectual development'.[4] The verdict is often extended to his age. Thought and action had separated to their mutual detriment. Philosophers chopped logic; politicians chopped heads. This judgement is a travesty of both the duke and the decade. York was no mere dynastic dinosaur but the spokesman for a sophisticated programme of reform. And the programme drew on the work of political theorists who were as concerned as any Marxist with the marriage of theory and practice.

Doyen of these theorists was Sir John Fortescue, lawyer, councillor and, for most of his career, Lancastrian loyalist. His most important and characteristic work was *The Governance of England*.[5] This begins with the famous distinction between two types of monarchy; the *regnum regale* or absolute monarchy of France, and the *regnum politicum et regale* or limited or mixed monarchy of England. In the first, a king can pass laws and raise taxes at will; in the second, he cannot. Fortescue then goes on to diagnose the current disease of the English body politic. He identifies this as royal poverty. A poor king was a weak king, who struggled in vain to impose his will on subjects richer and therefore mightier than himself. Finally, Fortescue puts forward a programme of reform that would cure the English disease without altering the peculiar balance of the English constitution.

Two things are particularly noteworthy in all this. The first is how very untheoretical Fortescue's theory is. What he has seen is more important than what he has read; and the real views of the authors he cites are ruthlessly bent to fit the facts as he observes them. The second is the reform programme itself. The royal finances should be restored through the royal lands. These were in a sorry state as more and more had been granted away to favourites.

---

[4] Cf. K. B. McFarlane, *The Nobility of Later Medieval England* (Oxford, 1973), 229.

[5] Sir John Fortescue, *The Governance of England*, ed. Charles Plummer (Oxford, 1885).

Now the time had come to reverse the process. What had been granted away should be taken back. And once back in hand the lands should be made inalienable. Thus the king would, in Fortescue's own words, make 'a new foundation of his crown'.[6] But the means were as important as the end. The taking back of the royal lands could only be, Fortescue thought, 'by general resumption, made by authority of parliament'; while the inalienability of the restored lands could only be guaranteed by a standing Great Council which would vet all future royal grants.[7] This Council would be more than a fiscal watchdog, however. Its status, independence, and permanence would transform political debate and action alike. It would discuss:

How the going out of money may be restrained; How bullion may be brought into the land: How also plate, jewels, and money late born out may be gotten again; . . . and also how the prices of merchandise growen in this land may be held up and increased, and the price of merchandises brought into this land abated. How our Navy may be maintained and augmented . . . How also the laws may be amended in such things as they need reformation in; where through the Parliament shall [be able to] do more good in a month to the mending of the law than they shall be able to do in a year if the amending thereof be not debated and by such Council ripen to their hands.[8]

The nice turn of that last sentence is the work of a man who wrote English prose as easily as he spoke it. The content of the *Governance* likewise shows its author at home in a sophisticated political culture. Its proposed reforms were proffered as a contribution to a reasoned and open debate; they were to be enacted by Parliament and judged against constitutional propriety and a developed conception of the common good. They also corresponded very closely to what was actually done. The credit cannot directly go to Fortescue, however. By the time he—at last reconciled to Yorkist rule—presented a revised version of the treatise to Edward IV in the 1470s, its recommendations were old hat. But, almost certainly, he had first formulated them thirty years before in the 1440s, when, as newly made king's sergeant and chief justice, he had joined the royal Council and experienced the problems of government at first hand.[9] The *Governance* was thus originally a

6 Ibid. 154–5.
7 Ibid. 143.   8 Ibid. 148.
9 Cf. B. P. Wolffe, *The Crown Lands 1461–1536* (London, 1970), 26.

bold and loyal proposal for reform from within the Lancastrian regime. As such, given the character and court of Henry VI, it was doomed to failure.

But this was a beginning not an end. Originally the reform programme incorporated in the *Governance* had been formulated by the gentlemen-bureaucrats like Fortescue who ran the governmental machine. Now it was being taken up by their cousins, colleagues, and friends amongst the knights, gentlemen and substantial citizens. These, the best educated, most responsible, and richest section of the population, were the nearest thing to a fifteenth-century public opinion. And it was an opinion that was becoming increasingly alienated from the government. As taxpayers they were weary of supporting a government that cost more and more for doing less and less. As local magistrates and men of property they were appalled at the breakdown of public order. And as patriotic Englishmen they were shocked at the crumbling of the king's French dominions. The reform programme might have been designed for them. The resumption of crown lands would lift the burden of taxation; conciliar reform promised better government; and finally, Parliament—the chosen instrument of reform—was their special province. Give or take some magnate intervention, they were able to swing the electorate in the constituencies, while the MPs themselves were drawn from their ranks.[10]

So balked at Court, reform resurfaced in Parliament. The first Parliament of 1449 demanded resumption so vigorously that it had to be dissolved. A year later, with resolve further stiffened by the débâcle in France and the fall of the favourite, the duke of Suffolk, the Commons forced through an Act of Resumption. But the Act was frustrated by the king's councillors and favourites who had most to lose. Reports of their delaying tactics combined with other grievances to trigger off Cade's Rebellion. Resumption of crown lands was high on the agenda of the rebels' demands. At this juncture the duke of York returned to England from Ireland. He did the obvious: partly to gain popularity and partly to weaken his opponents, he put his weight behind reform. The combined pressures of the heir presumptive, popular revolt, and parliamentary opposi-

---

[10] For this and what follows, see B. P. Wolffe, 'Acts of Resumption in the Lancastrian Parliaments, 1399–1456', *EHR* lxxiii (1958), 583–613, reprinted in *Historical Studies of the English Parliament*, ed. E. B. Fryde and Edward Miller (2 vols., Cambridge, 1970) ii. 61–91.

tion overwhelmed resistance at Court, and in 1451 the first effective Act of Resumption received the royal assent. Two years later came the reward. Fortescue had argued that in return for the king's agreement to a real general resumption, a grateful Parliament would 'be willing to grant him a subsidy'.[11] And so it proved, for the Parliament of 1453 made Henry VI an almost unprecedented life grant of the customs and tonnage and poundage.

The Parliament of 1453 was the nearest the Lancastrian government came to putting its own house in order. Several things had helped: the government's own gestures towards financial reform; reaction against York's resort to force at Dartford in 1452; and, above all, Henry's own unwonted activity in affairs of state.[12] But the effort proved too much. That same year the king suffered the first of his bouts of prostrating insanity. And with the king's mind went the last chance of reform from within. Leadership of the Lancastrian cause passed to the new favourite, the duke of Somerset, and Queen Margaret. But they were mere power-brokers and left the field free for York to make the cause of reform his own.

York had returned to English politics as a reformer; now he turned reform into his party slogan. His propaganda harped relentlessly on good governance, and in his brief moments of power he was careful to turn his words into action. In his first protectorate he supressed the worst of the local feuds in person and issued reforming ordinances for the royal household;[13] in his second, he attempted unsuccessfully to force through a stringent act of resumption.[14] His sincerity was never of course subject to the long-term test of kingship. But his son's was. And it does not emerge badly. The reform programme, espoused in opposition, became the blueprint for Yorkist government. Edward IV's very declaration of the royal title incorporated a form of resumption, and further formal Acts of Resumption were passed in 1465 and 1467.[15] This last is particularly important, since before the Commons began their discussions King Edward addressed them in person. His speech was recorded in the

[11] Fortescue, *Governance*, 136–7.

[12] There is an admirably clear account of these events in B. P. Wolffe, *Henry VI* (London, 1981), 254–66.

[13] Ibid. 281 ff. and A. R. Myers, *The Household of Edward IV* (Manchester, 1959), 9.

[14] R. A. Griffiths, *The Reign of King Henry VI* (London, 1981), 757.

[15] B. P. Wolffe, *The Royal Demesne in English History* (London, 1971), 150.

Parliament roll and sets out forcibly his personal commitment to reform:

> The cause why I have called and summoned this my present parliament is that I purpose to live upon mine own and not to charge my subjects but in great and urgent causes, concerning more the weal of themselves, and also the defence of them and of this my realm, rather than mine own.[16]

What reality underlay these fine phrases? Certainly two disaffected members of his own government took a dim view, and, in the manifesto they issued from Calais in 1469, Clarence and Warwick flung Edward's commitment back in his teeth. Quoting the king's very words, they demanded an effectual act of resumption, so that taxation would be unnecessary, 'unless it were for the great and urgent causes concerning as well the wealth of us, as of our said sovereign lord.'[17] The implication, of course, was that Edward's resumptions of the 1460s were a sham. That is a charge which will not stick, although modern research certainly confirms that there had been some back-sliding. Usually the king's fickleness and uncertainty of purpose are blamed.[18] But more important was political instability—seen at its worst in the Readeption crisis which followed immediately in the wake of the Calais manifesto. The precariousness of Edward's power forced him perpetually to use the royal lands for patronage: that is, to sacrifice long-term financial goals to short-term political ends. When the political question was settled—partly by Edward's restoration in 1471 and partly by the removal of Clarence seven years later—Edward was able to commit his energies and resources whole-heartedly to financial reform. No longer were forfeited lands (in More's phrase) dispensed in 'large gifts [to] get . . . unsteadfast friendship';[19] instead they were used to augment a consolidated royal domain whose revenues were gathered by a network of surveyors and receivers, and garnered by the treasurer of the chamber.[20]

So the political struggles of the mid-fifteenth century were not merely obscure and sterile dynastic conflicts, in which 'the Barons

---

[16] *Rotuli Parliamentorum, 1278–1504*, ed. J. Strachey *et al.* (6 vols., London, 1767–77) v. 572.

[17] *A Chronicle of the First Thirteen Years of King Edward the Fourth*, ed. J. O. Halliwell (Camden Society, old series, x, London, 1839), 50–1.

[18] See in particular Charles Ross, *Edward IV* (London, 1974), 376.

[19] Sir Thomas More, *The History of King Richard III*, ed. R. S. Sylvester, *The Yale Edition of the Complete Works of St Thomas More* (New Haven and London, 1963), ii. 8.   [20] Wolffe, *Royal Demesne*, 154, 166 ff.

now made a stupendous effort to revive the old Feudal amenities of Sackage, Carnage and Wreckage, and so stave off the Tudors for a time.'[21] Instead, the intensity of the struggle stimulated open and vigorous debate on the nature of monarchy, fundamental reform of the governmental machine, and even, I shall now argue, a new language of politics: I mean the term 'commonweal'.

The word seems to have made a modest entry into the language in the middle of Henry VI's reign. In 1447, for example, Parliament lamented the paucity of schoolmasters in London, 'against all virtue and order of well public'.[22] Here the phrase means simply 'general welfare'; it is not a political slogan. It emerged as such, rather tentatively, in 1450. This year was the climacteric of Henry VI's reign, in which the loss of Normandy abroad triggered a massive crisis at home. Parliament impeached the king's minister and favourite, the duke of Suffolk, and Kent rose in rebellion. 'Commonwealth' played a part in both events. The Commons' original charges against Suffolk included the article that he had traitorously disclosed the business of the Council to the French, 'as well of this your realm for the common weal of the same, as of the governance of Franc';[23] while in their riposte to the duke's answer to the accusations against him, the Commons inveighed against his plundering of the royal resources, without any regard for the king's necessary expenses 'for the common weal, increase and profit of all the land and for his honourable household.'[24] But though the term 'commonwealth' is used, it is hardly dominant. Cade's Rebellion tells a rather different story. *Gregory's Chronicle* describes how the rebels entered London 'as men that have been half beside their wit, and in that furiness they went, as they said, for the commonwealth of England.'[25] This section of the *Chronicle*, it is argued, was written by Gregory himself, and more or less at the same time as the events he describes.[26] So 'commonwealth' was the rebels' slogan. But not on paper, since it occurs in none of Cade's own manifestos.[27]

[21] W. C. Sellar and R. J. Yeatman, *1066 and All That* (Harmondsworth, 1960), 54.

[22] *Rotuli Parliamentorum*, v. 137.

[23] Ibid. 178.

[24] Bod. Lib. MS Eng. Hist. b. 119, HMC *Third Report* (London, 1872), 279–80.

[25] *The Historical Collections of a Citizen of London*, ed. J. Gairdner (Camden Society, new series, xvii, London, 1876), 191.

[26] Ibid. iii ff.

[27] John Stow, *The Annals of England* (London, 1631), 388–92; HMC *Eighth Report* (London, 1881), Part I, 266–9.

Nor at first was the duke of York any faster to pick the phrase up. In neither of the two 'bills' which he issued after he returned to English politics in 1450 was the term 'commonweal' used.[28] Two years later, however, in 1452, York went into open opposition and the notion, and probably the phrase itself, became one of his slogans. It seems to have been used for the first time in his articles against the royal favourite, the duke of Somerset, which talk of 'the great welfare and the common avail and interest of your majesty royal and of this your noble realm' and 'the great and singular weal of this your said realm'.[29] The royalist counter-propaganda is even more explicit, when it refers to the 'great labour and business . . . done . . . under untrue, feigned and pretenced colours of intending to the commonweal of this our land, whereas God knoweth the intent of those that so labour is to the subversion thereof.'[30] York's bid for power failed in 1452. But he soon returned to the attack and once more used the 'commonweal' slogan. The word itself appears in the articles to be opened to the king on behalf of the lords and Parliament in March 1454;[31] and again in York's letter of 20 May 1455 there is very similar phraseology. He is advocating, he claims, 'such things as of reason must most speedily grow to the said honour and weal and the good public, restful and politic rule and governance of his said land and people.'[32] But on balance, in David Morgan's careful weighing of the evidence, the phrase and even the idea is 'not very obtrusive' in the political debate of the mid-1450s.[33] It was only one of the planks of the Yorkist platform, and it often tended to be obscured in the welter of specific charges of malice and misgovernment directed against the king's favourites and ministers.

All this changed in 1459, however. Then the Yorkists moved decisively first to take over and finally overthrow the government of Henry VI. At the same time 'commonweal' 'crashes to the fore . . . with insistent, repetitive force.'[34] It was prominent in the mani-

[28] R. A. Griffiths, 'Duke Richard of York's Intentions in 1450 and the Origins of the Wars of the Roses', *J. Med. Hist.* i (1975), 187–210.

[29] *The Paston Letters*, ed. J. Gairdner (6 vols., London, 1904) i. 103–8.

[30] *Proceedings and Ordinances of the Privy Council of England, 1386–1542*, ed. N. H. Nicolas (7 vols., London, 1834–7) vi. 90–2.

[31] *Rotuli Parliamentorum*, v. 241–2.   [32] Ibid. 280–1.

[33] Letter to the author, 27 July 1984. I should like to thank David Morgan for his generous help in the preparation of this Introduction. This discussion of the origins of 'common weal' is a mere appetizer to his forthcoming account.

[34] Loc. cit.

festo issued by the earls of March, Warwick, and Salisbury on their way to the Yorkist rendezvous at Ludlow castle;[35] and it dominated the definitive manifesto issued from the castle. York and his allies began by protesting to Henry VI that their only intent was 'to the prosperity and augmentation of your high estate, and to the common weal of this realm'; and they ended by reiterating their 'truth and duty to your said highness, and to the said common weal.'[36] Faced with this, royalist counter-propaganda had to move on to its opponents' ground, and the *Somnium Vigilantis*, the Lancastrian tract also issued in 1459, harps obsessively on 'commonwealth'.[37]

So the 1450s marked the birth of a new political language. The word 'commonwealth' first appeared in the crisis of 1450; it was experimented with in York's increasingly desperate forays for power in the mid-1450s; and it was fully developed in the grand upheaval of 1459. The notion was not, of course, entirely novel. Rather, a new word was used to express an old idea. Probably from the earliest times, and certainly since Magna Charta, Englishmen had drawn on a distinction between the king and his kingdom. They were separate, not fused as in Louis XIV's supposed dictum of '*l'état c'est moi*'. This meant that the obligations between king and subject were mutual. The subject did not only have a duty to obey his king; the king also had a duty to pursue his subjects' welfare. And what went for the king applied *a fortiori* to his councillors, who were sworn to do their best 'to the king's worship, profit and behalf, and to the good of his realms, lordships and subjects',— more succinctly, to act 'for the universal good of the king and of his land.'[38]

All this has the air of commonplace. But the commonplace was roused into life by the mounting difficulties of Henry VI's majority. Fortescue made the distinction the foundation of his *Governance of England*. In the *regnum regale* (France) king and kingdom are one; in the *regnum politicum et regale* (England) the king and the 'polis' or community are separate. In the former the king has no duty to his people, and indeed the French are poor and oppressed;

[35] BL Add. MS 48031, fos. 137v–138.

[36] *An English Chronicle of the Reigns of Richard II, Henry IV, Henry V, and Henry VI*, ed. J. S. Davies (Camden Society, old series, lxiv, London, 1856), 81–3.

[37] H. P. Gilson, 'A Defence of the Proscription of the Yorkists in 1459', *EHR* xxvi (1911), 515, 518–20.

[38] J. F. Baldwin, *The King's Council in England during the Middle Ages* (Oxford, 1913), 353–4.

in the latter the king has such a duty and the English are rich and free.[39] But the English balance of 'royal' and 'political' was in danger of toppling over into either absolutism or anarchy. To preserve it Fortescue put forward his programme of reform. And every item of that programme of reform was tested against the double benefit, to which Fortescue the councillor had sworn, of 'the universal good of the king and his land.' The re-endowment of the crown with land would make the king rich without making his subjects poor (as would a shift to a tax-based monarchy like the French);[40] the reconstructed Council would protect the king's long-term interests and give him disinterested advice; it would also facilitate a public welfare programme to the benefit of all.[41] And so on. Fortescue was writing to save the Lancastrian regime; its opponents found the same body of ideas just as useful. When the Kentish rebels had settled into their fortified camp on Blackheath, Henry VI sent a delegation of lords to discover their aims. Captain Cade replied that they had come together 'for the weal of him our sovereign lord, and of all the realm, and for to destroy the traitors being about him, with divers other points.'[42]

A fortnight later the rebels burst into London, crying out the slogan of 'commonwealth', as we have seen. What they had done was to condense the ideology at the heart of Cade's reply to the lords into a single phrase. The 'commonwealth' was the national interest, 'common' or shared between king and people. It was also 'common' or popular because ordinary folk had a claim—staked out by the Peasants' Revolt, acknowledged by Fortescue, and reiterated by Cade—for their needs to be taken into account in the government of the country. Finally the 'weal' was 'common' because its custodians under the king were the Commons assembled in Parliament. 'Commons' in this sense were not to be identified with the commons as proletariat. But the rebels were not simply proletarian either. Just how many of the gentry—the parliamentary class—had rebelled is now in dispute.[43] That some did, however, is certain. Cade's standard-bearer was a gentleman and future MP,[44]

---

[39] Fortescue, *Governance*, 109–16.

[40] Ibid. 131–4.

[41] Ibid. 147–9.

[42] *Historical Collections*, ed. Gairdner, 190.

[43] Griffiths, *Henry VI*, 619.

[44] See Wolffe, *Henry VI*, 233, who presents the opposite view of the rebels to Griffiths.

while the rebels' national demands echoed in detail the proposals of the gentry-led Commons for resumption, the removal of evil councillors, and the restructuring of the Council. Also, the rebels showed a strong interest in freeing parliamentary elections from undue magnate influence.[45] Taken together, all this suggests that the commons of Kent saw the House of Commons as the proper and usual spokesmen for the commons of England. Increasingly the Commons were taking a similar view of themselves. From being a collection of individual representatives of particular localities, they were becoming a body of delegates of all the commons of the land. The idea first appears in a petition of 1414. The petition, asking that the Commons' requests might be granted or rejected but not altered, was presented in the name of 'your humble and true lieges, that be come for the common of your land.'[46] The phrase reappears in the 1450s and then becomes frequent.[47] It was used by Edward IV in his address to the Commons in 1461 and again in 1467. On that latter occasion the king told the speaker, 'John Say, and ye Sirs, coming to this my court of parliament for the commons of this my land', that out of regard for the 'weal' of his subjects he proposed to forgo taxation and depend instead on his lands, augmented by an act of resumption which they, the Commons, would be requested to pass.[48] The interweaving of Commons, commonweal, and reform is thus complete.

But despite the proud insularity of both Fortescue and the men of Kent, 'commonweal' was not simply English. It drew on broader European origins, or at least was grafted on to them. In the latter part of the *Somnium Vigilantis* the writer moves from English into French. As he does so 'commonweal' gives way to 'le bien publique', 'la chose publique', or 'le bien commun'.[49] This is not merely translation, but a reflection of an independent and earlier French tradition (carefully ignored by Fortescue) of 'la reformation du royaume'. Both the past and future of the French tradition were impressive. It went back at least to the beginning of the fourteenth century, while in the next decade it was to supply the ideology of the civil war known as the 'Guerre du bien publique' against Louis

[45] See n. 28 above.
[46] S. B. Chrimes, *English Constitutional Ideas in the Fifteenth Century*, (Cambridge, 1936), 131–2.
[47] Ibid. 131–2.
[48] See n. 16 above.
[49] Gilson, *EHR* xxvi. 524–5.

XI.[50] More important, however, was an older tradition still: the Latin *res publica*. The term and the complex of associated ideas were enjoying a full-scale revival at the hands of the Italian civic humanists.[51] The first trace in England seems to come with the *Boke of Noblesse*. The *Boke* was revised in the 1470s, but it had first been written in the 1450s. The probable author was William Worcester, a gentleman clerk of modish, if not very deep, learning. He flourished Latin tags in his letters, and played with Greek in his commonplace book.[52] And the *Boke of Noblesse* is certainly modish. Within its pages *res publica*, the key word of the new humanism, is translated as the 'common profit', the key phrase of the new and still unfinalized English political language. Then a full-blown humanist definition is given.

And as well the term of *res publica*, which is in English tongue cleped a common profit, it ought as well be referred to the provision and wise governance of messuage or household as to the conduct and wise governance of the village, town, city, country or region.[53]

But this avant-garde language was used to present a case that seems reactionary to us (and would have done so too to a later generation of humanists like Erasmus and More): the resumption of war with France. It was a failure in governance and the commonweal that had brought England to defeat; while reluctance to restart the war was due to the putting of the private above the public good.[54] The second version of the *Boke* was made for presentation to Edward IV on the eve of the campaign of 1475; while it had first been written for—of all people—Henry VI in 1453. At that moment Henry had re-established his authority in his kingdom of England;[55] now he was urged to put on his father's armour and reconquer his other kingdom of France. The moment was shortlived. Thereafter the duke of York was the only hope for men like Worcester. York

[50] Raymond Cazelles, 'Une exigence de l'opinion depuis saint Louis: la réformation du royaume', *Annuaire-bulletin de la Société d'Histoire de France* (1962–3), 91–9.

[51] Hans Baron, *The Crisis of the Early Italian Renaissance: Civic Humanism and Republican Liberty in an Age of Classicism and Tyranny* (2 vols., Princeton, 1966).

[52] *DNB*; K. B. McFarlane, 'William Worcester: A Preliminary Survey', in *Studies Presented to Sir Hilary Jenkinson*, ed. J. C. Davies (Oxford, 1957).

[53] *Boke of Noblesse*, ed. J. G. Nichols (Roxburghe Club, lxxvii, London, 1860), 68.

[54] Ibid. 51 ff.

[55] See p. 17 above.

was making the language of commonweal his party slogan; and, while not exactly offering to lead a crusade across the Channel, he was using the loss of international prestige—the 'derogation, . . . lesion of honour, and villany'—which had flowed from defeat in France as a wickedly effective tool in his attack on his rival, the duke of Somerset.[56] Moreover, if York had seen the *Boke* he would, contrary to some historians' judgements, have been well able to understand it. He was not of course in the same class as the erstwhile great patron of both humanism and the war party, Humphrey of Gloucester. But the man who commissioned a bilingual version of Claudian's poem '*De Consultatu Stilichonis*' to mark his five years of public office and high command as the king's lieutenant in France was surely up to Worcester's hand-me-down classicism.[57]

It was in this borrowed toga of *res publica* that commonweal was to play its central role in Tudor discourse. In the fifteenth century, though, it did well enough without fancy dress. There are two particularly telling examples: Fortescue's writings, and the preambles to the Acts of Resumption. Fortescue—like most intellectuals turned politicians—was an intellectual as well as political trimmer. The main text of the *Governance*, belonging essentially as it does to the 1440s, is innocent of the term 'commonweal'. But when Fortescue came to rewrite crucial sections of the *Governance* for the unexpected Lancastrian restoration of 1470, it is a very different story. In substance the 'Advertisements sent by the Lord Prince [that is Edward, the Lancastrian Prince of Wales] to the Earl of Warwick' is a boiled-down version of the *Governance*: part précis part *morceaux choisis*.[58] There are no new ideas, and whole sections are lifted bodily from the earlier work. Yet there is one consistent innovation: throughout the book the new language of 'commonweal' is interpolated in the text. The 'Advertisements' were for 'the good public of the realm'; the king was not to be 'counselled by men of his chamber, of his household, nor other which cannot counsel him';[59] instead there was to be a standing Council of twenty-four, through whom 'the good public shall . . . be conducted to the prosperity and honour of the land'. Such a Council would be expensive

---

[56] Griffiths, *Henry VI*, 694.
[57] C 54/288, m. 20.
[58] Fortescue, *Governance*, Appendix B, 348–53.
[59] Ibid. 349, 350.

to maintain, yet its labours 'for the good politic weal of this land'—
as by increasing stocks of bullion and augmenting the price of ex-
ports and lowering that of imports—would more than pay for
itself.[60] And so on.

The Acts of Resumption show a similar pattern. In the first Act
of 1450 there is an elaborate two-pronged justification for the mea-
sure. The sufferings of the Commons, brought about by the depre-
dations on the royal lands, are described; at the same time the
king's financial plight is documented by statement of debts and expenses.[61] In 1467, however, all this is swept away. Instead, and
following closely on the words of Edward's keynote speech of that
year, the Act begins with a short and simple formula:

For divers causes and considerations concerning the honour, estate, and
prosperity of the King, and also of the commonweal, defence, surety, and
welfare of the realm.[62]

The uncertain neologism of the 1450s had become the established
commonplace of the sixties and seventies.

Which age of reform indeed? In the fifteenth century, to look no
further than finance, the revenue base of the crown was transformed
and the method of revenue administration radically altered—all
within the last decade of Edward IV's reign. On Professor Elton's
own criteria, therefore, Yorkist England was no less an age of
reform than the Cromwellian era of the following century. Changes
were fundamental, and they clustered thickly. But they went further. What is most striking is the context of the change. The
reforms were formulated theoretically; they were debated in Parliament and demonstrated for by the 'commons'. They were tossed
around in a pamphlet war and became a badge of party allegiance.
Everybody knew what was happening, and most were enthusiastically behind the changes. So reform was no mere private matter for
the king and his councillors. The nuances of language alone make
that plain. Reform was the precondition for 'good governance'.
And 'good governance' was not only good government—rule that
was economical, efficient, and effective—but also government in
the wider interests of the king's subjects—in short, of the 'commonweal'. All this suggests a new, or at least an expanded

[60] Ibid. 350–1.
[61] *Rotuli Parliamentorum*, v. 183–4.
[62] Ibid. 572.

criterion. It is, it seems to me, this self-consciousness of change, as much as change itself, that is the hallmark of the true age of reform. The fifteenth century had it in abundance. But did the sixteenth, in matters of secular reform, at any rate?

We will be better able to answer that question at the end of our volume. In the meantime we must shorten our sights to the sixteenth century, and the current debate on the Cromwellian revolution.

CHAPTER 2

COURT AND GOVERNMENT

DAVID STARKEY

ON 20 October 1529, 'in a certain inner chamber next to the king's closet' at Windsor, Henry VIII applied the great seal to a few documents with his own hands. Among the witnesses were not only the officials of Chancery, who normally handled the business of the great seal, but also 'Henry Norris, Thomas Heneage and others of the Privy Chamber of the said Lord King.'[1] The sealing, carefully recorded on the close roll, was a calculated drama. It put to rest the claims of the fallen Wolsey to hold the chancellorship and the great seal for life. And it reaffirmed the absolute dependence of the great seal, the most formal and public instrument of government, on the mere will of the personal sovereign, Henry VIII. The king applied the seal in person, in a secret chamber of the palace and in the presence of his private servants.

But as well as providing an epilogue to Wolsey's ministry, the scene at Windsor in 1529 is also a set-piece illustration of Professor Elton's view of medieval government as 'household' government, in which the driving force was the king and his immediate entourage. In the next ten years, however, Professor Elton claimed in *The Tudor Revolution in Government*, there was fundamental change: 'in every sphere of the central government, "household" methods and instruments were replaced by national bureaucratic methods and instruments.' At the same time the household itself, 'driven from the work of administration', became 'a department of state concerned with specialized tasks about the king's person'; in short, it changed from 'medieval household to modern court'.[2] Subsequently Professor Elton has conceded on specific issues. But he has given no ground on the broad principles. Here, therefore, I shall consider the thesis as a whole, but with one important change

[1] *Foedera, Conventiones, Litterae*, ed. T. Rymer (15 vols., London, 1704–35), xiv. 349.
[2] G. R. Elton, *The Tudor Revolution in Government* (Cambridge, 1953), 414–15.

of approach. In *The Tudor Revolution* Professor Elton tackled the household last, almost as an afterthought. In contrast, I begin with the history of the household; only once that is established do I examine the fate of 'household' government.

THE HOUSEHOLD: FROM CHAMBER TO PRIVY CHAMBER

The servants of the Privy Chamber who attended on the king at the sealing of 1529 were a novelty. The office held by Norris and Heneage was only ten years old; the department itself no more than thirty. Yet in these few decades the Privy Chamber had become the 'principally and most highly to be regarded' department of the household.[3] So our story is not recessional, as the corpse of the medieval household is embalmed into the early modern Court, but a progression, as a household of two departments—Household and Chamber—is replaced by a household of three departments—Household, Chamber and Privy Chamber.

The initial impetus for change was architectural. The two departments of the medieval household had corresponded to the two main areas of the royal house (or rather houses, for there were at least a dozen). 'Downstairs' was the Hall, where the king's servants ate, and where the service quarters of kitchens, buttery, and the rest, were situated; 'Upstairs' was the king's private apartment or Chamber. The 'Downstairs' servants formed one department, the Household, under the lord steward; the 'Upstairs' servants the other, the Chamber, under the lord chamberlain. This two-department household assumed its characteristic form under Edward II and Edward III; a hundred years later the *Black Book* of Edward IV, which perpetually harks back to 'the statutes of noble Edward III', gave it final polish and systematization.[4]

The apogee was short-lived, however. For the layout of the palace, the rationale of the two-department household, was changing. The king's original apartment, the Chamber, had been—as its

---

[3] Bod. Lib., Laudian MS Misc. 597, fo. 24 (printed from an inferior MS in *A Collection of Ordinances and Regulations for the Government of the Royal Household* (Society of Antiquaries, London, 1790), 154.

[4] Mark Girouard, *Life in the English Country House* (New Haven and London, 1978), 30 ff; H. M. Colvin, ed., *The History of the King's Works* (6 vols., London, 1951–82) iv/2. 1–40; H. M. Baillie, 'Etiquette and the Planning of the State Apartments in Baroque Palaces', *Archaeologia*, ci (1967); A. R. Myers, *The Household of Edward IV* (Manchester, 1959), 19, 128, 298–9.

name implies—just one room. It was handsomely proportioned, but it was still a bedsit, in which a whole range of often conflicting functions took place. The solution was to add on separate specialized chambers and by the mid-fifteenth century the greater palaces, at least, contained a suite of three rooms. The first two were more or less public reception rooms, but the third, the Secret or Privy Chamber, was the king's own private room, to which in time a whole complex 'privy lodging'—of bedroom, library, study, and so on—was added.[5] The effect of this was to create a division within the Chamber itself as important as the original distinction between Hall and Chamber: on one side of the door of the Privy Chamber lay public ceremonial; on the other, private life. For some time organization lagged behind the changed layout; then Henry VII took the first steps to bring things into line. He restricted the lord chamberlain's direct authority to the outer chambers and their routine ceremonies; and he turned the Privy Chamber into a largely autonomous sub-department of the Chamber, with its own staff.[6]

Henry VII, we are told on all sides, 'was not an original mind; he was no great innovator'.[7] Yet in the history of the household the setting up of the Privy Chamber is arguably the greatest innovation of all. Its full implications, however, lay in the future. At the time it was small beer, a minor adjustment in the inner recesses of the Court that was unknown to most and unremarked by all. It left correspondingly little trace in the record. The personnel of the new department are listed in the accounts of the Wardrobe, which supplied them with clothing; while their activities can be traced through payments to them by the treasurer of the Chamber. The only coherent account of the department, however, is given in the household Ordinances of about 1495. Of these, no contemporary copy survives, but their text can be recovered thanks to their reissue in 1526, complete with, by then, quite anachronistic clauses, which in turn establish the original date of publication.[8] Round the clauses of the Ordinances the other fragments of information arrange themselves into a reasonably full picture.

[5] Colvin, loc. cit.

[6] David Starkey, 'The king's Privy Chamber, 1485–1547' (unpublished Cambridge Ph.D. thesis, 1973), 17 ff.

[7] S. B. Chrimes, *Henry VII* (London, 1972), 319.

[8] College of Arms, Arundel MS XVII[2], printed from a later MS copy in *The Antiquarian Repertory*, ed. E. Jeffrey (4 vols., London, 1807–9), ii. 184–208; Starkey, Privy Chamber, 17 ff.

The new sub-department was small and modestly staffed. At its head was the groom of the stool, whose original and continuing task was to wait on the king when he used the close stool (the contemporary form of lavatory). Under the groom were about half a dozen other grooms and a handful of pages, almost all of whom, in so far as they are traceable, were from modest gentry families. This staff, which was a far cry from the pompous establishment of knights and esquires which the Chamber had supplied (at least in theory) to dance attendance on the royal person, carried out the whole range of the king's private service: they dressed and undressed him; waited on him at table; watched over him at night, and kept him supplied with everyday necessaries.

This modest kind of Privy Chamber was adequate for a king like Henry VII. Indeed it might very well have been the result of deliberate choice. Its servants could exercise none of the direct political pressure of the Court aristocracy; nor was their service surrounded by the time-consuming ceremonial necessarily entailed by the attendance of the high-born. Instead Henry was free to rule and work as he desired.[9] But his son, Henry VIII, though he was determined to rule, was far less eager to work. A different king needed a different sort of Privy Chamber.

So to architecture we must add the royal personality as a force for change. It is important, however, to be clear about both the pace and the nature of what now happened. And the more so since the Privy Chamber of Henry VIII, in contrast to his father's, is almost too richly documented, with two major sets of household regulations: Wolsey's Eltham Ordinances of 1526,[10] and the Cromwellian Ordinances of 1539–40.[11] The natural temptation, abetted by the fact that the text of the Eltham Ordinances has been available in print since 1790, is to see the Ordinances as instituting the changes. This fits well both with our modern attitude to legislation and with our general assumption that it was the ministers, Wolsey and Cromwell, who were the fount of all policy. But the evidence tells another story.

The first decade of the reign saw little structural change in the Privy Chamber. On the other hand, there was a revolution in the

    [9] See the rather fuller speculation in David Starkey, 'From Feud to Faction: English Politics *c.*1450–1550', *History Today*, xxxii (November 1982), 16–22.
    [10] See n. 3 above.
    [11] BL Add. MS 45,716 A, of which extracts were printed in *The Genealogist*, new series, xxix–xxx (1913–14).

style of the Court, as Henry VIII's openness and fondness for sport led to the reappearance of a creature missing since Edward IV's reign at least, the court favourite. Only one of the favourites, however, Sir William Compton, was put into the Privy Chamber as groom of the stool. For the rest the department remained much as before.[12] Then in 1518 things began to change. At home, the king's attention had shifted to a new and markedly younger group of favourites, known as the 'minions'; while abroad, a *renversement d'alliances* brought England into friendship with France. In France there had been parallel developments at Court which had gone further and resulted in actual institutional change. The foreign and the domestic came together with the grand *entrée* of the French embassy into London on 23 September. To give the English minions parity of status with their French colleagues they too needed office. So the French office of 'Gentleman' was added to the Privy Chamber's establishment and conferred on the minions in a body.[13]

Up to this point there is no trace of Wolsey. The changes arose in the long term from the altered demands of Henry VIII's personality and life-style; they were triggered by foreign relations and given shape by the King's tendency to imitate slavishly French fashions. But the creation of the office of Gentleman of the Privy Chamber altered the rules of the game. Until then, with the exception of Compton, the officers of the Privy Chamber were men of no consequence; now the department included the minions. They were high-spirited and high-born and intervened as of right in politics (to support France) and patronage (to challenge Wolsey).[14] The minister, who had been used to no rival in influence, now had one. The following May he struck back and procured the exile from Court of the leading minions. To replace them 'men of greater age, and perhaps of greater repute, but creatures of Cardinal Wolsey' were brought in.[15] This presented something of a problem. Hitherto, office in the Privy Chamber had carried no separate salary, since formally the Privy Chamber remained a mere sub-department of the Chamber, with most of its staff on secondment from the senior

---

[12] Starkey, 'Privy Chamber', 64 ff.

[13] Ibid. 80 ff; Edward Hall, *The Union of the Two Noble and Illustrious Families of Lancaster and York* (London, 1809), 593–4.

[14] Starkey, 'Privy Chamber', 112 ff. and 50–1 below.

[15] R. L. Brown, trans. and ed., *Four Years at the Court of Henry VIII* (2 vols., London, 1854) ii. 269 ff.

department. However, the new appointees were successful careerists, who reasonably expected cash as well as a title. And their
claims were reinforced by personal circumstances. Sir William
Kingston had received no substantial appointment hitherto, and
was clearly in line for something (Wolsey had already thought of
him as standard-bearer in 1517);[16] Sir Richard Jerningham had just
lost his major existing post with the return of Tournai (where he
had been governor) to France in February 1519;[17] while most press-
ing was the case of Sir Richard Wingfield, who had resigned the
governorship of Calais to take up his Privy Chamber office.[18] So
first Wingfield, the elder statesman among the new recruits, was
feed (on the very day he surrendered his Calais office);[19] then came
fees for his three fellow appointees;[20] and finally all the rest of the
department were put in wages at amounts carefully graduated
according to rank.[21]

The changes of 1518–19 were merely *ad hoc*. There is no evidence
whatever of planning before the event, and not much of co-ordin-
ation after it (even Wolsey had struck first for political motives and
only wakened up to the problem of fees later). Yet however
piecemeal the reforms were, their effect was to transform the Privy
Chamber from a shadowy sub-department into the fully-fledged
third department of the royal household: much smaller and newer
than the Chamber and Household; yet outranking both in prestige,
the distinction of its staff, and the level of their remuneration. A
Cinderella had become a *corps d'élite*. After all that, there was not
much left for the Ordinances of 1526 and 1539–40 to do with the
structure of the royal household. They conferred the retrospective
sanction of legislative respectability on what had already taken
place and they dotted i's and crossed t's. Which is not to deny that
they had a wider significance. But their importance is fiscal and
political, not institutional. Moreover, 1526 and 1540 do not stand
in a tradition, with Cromwell delivering what Wolsey had merely
promised; rather they are mirror images. In 1526, in the aftermath
of war, Wolsey was struggling for retrenchment and economical

---

[16] SP 1/232, fo. 41 (*LP*, Addenda I, i. 196).
[17] C. A. Cruickshank, *The English Occupation of Tournai, 1513–19* (Oxford, 1971), 264.
[18] *LP* III. i. 229.
[19] C 66/633, m. 9 (*LP* III. i. 231).
[20] Ibid. mm. 11, 12, 15 (*LP* III. i. 247–9).
[21] Starkey, 'Privy Chamber', 115 ff.

reform;[22] in 1539–40, however, the royal coffers were stuffed with the spoils of the monasteries, and Cromwell and his master could afford to be bountiful. Not only was a new royal bodyguard, the band of gentleman pensioners, set up (which Elton himself characterizes as 'useless and spendthrift' and blames on the king),[23] but also supernumeraries were absorbed into the regular establishment and feed; while wages themselves, for the first and last time in the sixteenth century, were brought into line with inflation, with a one-third increase all round.[24]

Politics presents a similar contrast. The Eltham Ordinances were Wolsey's cover for a renewed attempt to purge and neutralize the Privy Chamber. In 1539–40, on the other hand, Cromwell, far from neutralizing the Court, completed its politicization. He had already packed the Privy Chamber with his own supporters and made himself its honorific head as chief nobleman-in-waiting; now, it seems, he intended to consolidate his grip on the whole upper household, Chamber as well as Privy Chamber, by Frenchifying its structure and assuming the ancient office of lord great chamberlain. The powers of this position had usually slumbered in the hands of its more or less hereditary occupants, the de Veres, earls of Oxford. Held by Cromwell, however, its dormant authority would have wakened into an absolute grip on the Court.[25] In 1526 Wolsey's control of the Court was just as absolute. But he had exercised it remotely and quasi-judicially by giving himself as 'the Lord Cardinal and Chancellor of England' powers to conduct a quarterly inquisition into the observance of the Eltham Ordinances.[26] The contrast with Cromwell's direct assumption of high court office could not be plainer.

Thus neither the substance of household reform, nor its chronology, nor the reasons for it fit with Professor Elton's arguments. The main theme of the household history of these years is the formation of the Privy Chamber. This begins in the 1490s and is complete in essentials by 1519—long before Wolsey, let alone Cromwell,

[22] A. P. Newton, 'Tudor Reforms in the Royal Household', in *Tudor Studies*, ed. R. W. Seton Watson (London, 1929), 238 ff.

[23] Elton, *Tudor Revolution*, 388.

[24] Starkey, 'Privy Chamber', 212 ff.

[25] This account of the great chamberlainship is more 'political' than the treatment in my dissertation (Starkey, 'Privy Chamber', 281 ff). I hope to discuss more fully the whole question of great offices of state shortly.

[26] Bod. Lib., Laudian MS Misc. 597, fo. 33ᵛ (*Household Ordinances* 161).

gave any systematic attention to the household. And the reasons for change are just as unyielding. An astonishing diversity was involved: fashion in building and life-style; the royal personality; international affairs; political self-interest; and fiscal necessity. These do not of course exclude broader strategic considerations (though they do not leave a great deal of room for them either). And, indeed, some more or less coherent attitudes can be discerned behind ministerial policy. But they are the opposite of what Professor Elton would lead us to expect. It is Wolsey who displays systematic hostility to the Privy Chamber, and Cromwell who packs it with his supporters, assumes its headship in person and crowns his career with the great chamberlainship.[27] It remains to be seen whether the attitudes of the two ministers to 'household' government follow the same pattern.

HOUSEHOLD GOVERNMENT

'Household' government was the king's government *par excellence*, and the king naturally chose its agents from the men closest to him. And this, at the beginning of our period, meant that he chose from the Chamber. The Household had more skilled accountants and administrators, but the Chamber's proximity far outweighed mere professionalism. So when first Edward IV and then, after some hesitations, Henry VII decided on the slap of firm government, many, though not all of the instruments, were officers of the Chamber. In finance the treasurer of the Chamber quickly became dominant; in the secretariat the king's secretary, who was also a member of the Chamber, acquired a more erratic importance. The contrasting fates of these two officers have become test-cases for our understanding of administrative development. For Professor Elton the decline of the treasurer and the rise of the secretary were the surest testimonies of the administrative revolution. But his account of 'household' government left out the history of the

---

[27] As well as the exhaustive account of the institutional history of the Privy Chamber in my dissertation, two shorter and more accessible studies may prove useful: David Starkey, 'Representation through Intimacy' in Ioan Lewis, ed., *Symbols and Sentiments* (London, New York, and San Francisco, 1977), 187–224; and David Starkey, 'Intimacy and Innovation: the rise of the Privy Chamber' in David Starkey, ed., *The English Court from the Wars of the Roses to the Civil War* (forthcoming).

household itself, in particular the formation of the Privy Chamber. When that is put back a very different picture emerges.

From Chamber to Privy Purse

The years 1465 to 1509 were the golden age of the treasurer of the Chamber. By the end of Henry VII's reign he had reduced the Exchequer, the ancient national treasury, into a satellite. The Exchequer handled only a fifth as much revenue as the Chamber and handed over its surplus to the treasurer at the year's end. The treasurer had gained this pre-eminence largely because he had been made receiver-general of the crown lands. These lands had been massively expanded in the 'land revenue experiment', begun by Edward IV and accomplished by Henry VII, which had turned the crown estates into the chief anchor of national finance.[28] But the treasurer's importance went further. The move from Exchequer to Chamber meant the replacement of decentralized debit finance with a highly centralized, wholly cash-based fiscal system. This system, the great achievement of the Chamber, survived (as I argue in my Conclusion) the decline of the Chamber in the years after 1529. Here, though, it is the decline itself which must be anatomized. The attack on the Chamber came from two different directions: from without, by the agencies of 'national' finance, and from within, by the royal household. The Exchequer launched its first counter-attack in 1509; this narrowly failed,[29] but in the 1530s the Chamber fell before the assault of Cromwell's own personal treasury on the one hand, and the series of formal revenue courts he set up on the other. Finally, in 1554, the new courts of the 1530s in turn were absorbed into an expanded Exchequer, which thus reasserted its supremacy over the whole field of finance (save for the surviving outposts of the Duchy of Lancaster and Court of Wards and Liveries).

This external attack provides both the thread of Professor Elton's narrative and the key to his explanation of financial change. But at the same time there was another, insidious undermining

---

[28] B. P. Wolffe, *The Crown Lands* (London, 1970).

[29] Here I differ from Dr Alsop (below chapter 6). He is right to argue that there was no fundamental difference in administrative method between Exchequer and Chamber. But there was a difference none the less: a legal one. The Exchequer's activities were grounded in common law; the Chamber's were not. It was on these grounds that the Chamber was attacked and was vulnerable to attack. Cf. Wolffe, *Crown Lands*, 76 ff.

of the Chamber from within, or rather from behind. Originally the treasurer's household department, the Chamber, had provided the king's most private service. But in the 1490s, as we have seen, it lost this task to the Privy Chamber. The consequences for financial administration were immediate. Long before I found an actual reference to the fact, I guessed that one Hugh Denys must have been groom of the stool and head of Henry VII's Privy Chamber. This was because of a unique series of entries in the Chamber books of payments. These entries, numbering hundreds, show Denys handling almost the whole financial side of the king's everyday life: he paid out the king's alms, rewards and gambling debts, and bought minor items of clothing and domestic utensils. At first he was reimbursed item by item; later he tended to present a consolidated bill three or four times a month. The sums involved were insignificant, averaging only about £220 a year. (The Chamber was handling over £100,000 p.a.) But they have an importance out of all proportion to their size. The treasurer of the Chamber's original function—and the foundation of all his subsequent importance—was the handling of just this class of expenditure. But now another official, the groom, had interposed himself between the king and the treasurer.[30]

This was inevitable. The Chamber itself had become relatively distant from the king; at the same time the treasurer's national responsibilities kept him at Westminster, in his office in the sanctuary,[31] rather than at Court, which might be anywhere. Nor at first was the treasurer's control really compromised. Not only was the groom's account small-scale; it was also a mere sub-treasury, drawing all its funds from the Chamber. But towards the end of the reign that changed. In September 1508 Sir Edward Belknap was appointed surveyor of the king's prerogative, with the task of exploiting to the utmost the king's financial rights as head of the feudal and judicial systems.[32] In the course of the following six months he raised about £450, all of which he paid over (more or less as the money came into his hands) 'to Hugh Denys by the commandment of our said Sovereign Lord.'[33] At the same time Denys's

30 Starkey, 'Privy Chamber', 357 ff.

31 Chrimes, *Henry VII*, 128.

32 The exact date (8 Sept.) when 'the said Edward received his patent for surveying divers prerogatives' *CPR* (1494–1509), 591 is established by his accounts (E 101/517/15, fo. 2).

33 Ibid. fo. 5.

receipts from the Chamber fell sharply, and after January 1509 he was paid nothing at all.[34] In other words, Denys had ceased to be a mere sub-treasurer; and instead of being funded through the Chamber he was now drawing his receipts directly from Belknap.

The independence of the groom's account, sketched out in the last years of Henry VII, was powerfully advanced in the first years of Henry VIII, with a new king and a new groom, the favourite William Compton. Four-figure sums were paid from the Hanaper (which dealt with the fees collected by Chancery) 'to the use of the King for the time being Henry VIII, in his Chamber that is to say to the hands of William Compton';[35] together with similar amounts from the land revenues administered by the general surveyors.[36] At the same time Chamber payments fell to £27,000 in 1510–11, which was the lowest total since 1495–6, and whole classes of expenditure, like building and jewels, almost vanished.[37] Compton clearly was going far beyond Denys. He was tapping revenue sources which had gone in their entirety to the Chamber for the last twenty years; while his payments (it has to be guessed in the absence of accounts) expanded to take in the types of conspicuous expenditure that disappeared from the Chamber.

But this sudden development was equally suddenly checked— probably by Wolsey's rise to power. He feared Compton's influence and could not let him become a major national treasurer. So from 1513 the revenues which the groom had poached were restored to the Chamber, and the groom once more drew his funds from the treasurer. But, despite Wolsey's pruning, the groom's account clearly remained on a much larger scale than it had been under Henry VII. Between 1514, when payments from the Chamber resumed, and 1519 Compton's receipts varied between £18,000 and £20,000 a year.[38] These amounts were too large and too fluctuating for comfort. So Wolsey decided on a more systematic treatment, and put the groom's account at the head of the programme of government reform he drew up in 1519. First, a ceiling was imposed on Compton's account: he was to receive £10,000 a year from the Chamber, payable in quarterly blocks of £2,500. Second, a line of

[34] E 36/214, fo. 157^v.

[35] E 101/220/1 (*LP* I. i. 579/1).

[36] E 101/517/16 (*LP* I. ii. 2766).

[37] F. C. Dietz, *English Public Finance, 1485–1641* (2 vols., London, 1964) i. 85, 88, 90.

[38] Starkey, 'Privy Chamber', 370 ff.

demarcation between the Chamber and Privy Chamber accounts was laid down: in future, ambassadorial expenses and building costs (many of which had been diverted to Compton) were to be paid only by the Chamber. Finally, provision was made for proper accounting: Compton was to keep duplicate account books, which were to be audited monthly in the king's presence.[39] In one aspect, the 1519 reform programme was merely a cover for Wolsey's expulsion of the minions from the Privy Chamber in May of that year. But there was substance as well. Even Palsgrave, one of Wolsey's bitterest enemies, admitted of the ministerial reforms that 'every of these enterprises was great, and the least of them to our commonwealth much expedient.'[40] Too many of them were dropped once the political pressure was over, but the scheme for the Privy Chamber account was carried out to the letter: the quarterly block payments were handed over on time and the account books, though they do not survive, were certainly kept.[41]

But in a sense Wolsey's victory in 1519 had the opposite effect from what he intended. The measures limiting the groom's account also conferred official recognition on it. The result was that when Compton resigned in Wolsey's second purge of the Privy Chamber in 1526, he handed over to his successor, Henry Norris, not only the groomship but also the quasi-office of 'our purse bearer [and] keeper of our everyday moneys.'[42] The actual name of Privy Purse had not quite appeared (and seems not to have done so until the later sixteenth century); otherwise all the essentials of the post of keeper of the king's Privy Purse were present and fully formed.

Norris's keepership of the Privy Purse (as we can call it by anticipation) began uneventfully, with the Privy Purse remaining pretty much within the guidelines laid down in 1519. Norris's own early account books have disappeared, but two of the running accounts kept by the clerk who actually did the work survive and show that in the last nine months of 1528 Norris handled £3,000. This was £4,500 less than Wolsey had allowed for such a period; on the other hand, the groom was once more picking up building bills and even starting to make wage payments.[43] Then in 1529 came dramatic change, followed by the most important three years in the history

39 BL Cott. MS Titus B. I, fo. 188 ff.
40 *LP* IV. iii. 5750.
41 Starkey, 'Privy Chamber', 373 ff.
42 C 66/646, mm. 41–2.
43 Starkey, 'Privy Chamber', 377 ff.

of the Privy Purse. These years coincide with the only surviving Privy Purse account book for Henry VIII's reign.[44] As it happens, the title-page of the book—and hence the name of the accountant—is missing. But fortunately payments noted in the book appear as receipts in other accounts, where they are unambiguously identified as being 'paid and delivered by the hands of Mr. Henry Norris Esquire.'[45]

Norris's book covers three years and two months. During this period £53,488 was spent. Three main classes of expenditure can be distinguished: £33,000 went on the king's personal needs (including £5,000 on building, £3,000 on gambling, and no less than £11,000 on jewels); £5,000 on wages for the private household of falconers, fools and the like; and £16,000 on expenditure of state. The incompleteness of the treasurer of the Chamber's accounts and the method of calendaring them in *Letters and Papers* makes an exact comparison with the Privy Purse almost impossible and certainly impossibly difficult. But we can produce a useful approximation. In the eighteen months between 1 October 1529 and 30 April 1531 the treasurer accounted for an expenditure of £83,500.[46] So in terms of volume the Chamber was still three times the size of the Privy Purse. But its expenditure was made up very differently. Much the largest sum, £35,000 or no less than 42 per cent of the whole, went on wages. The running costs of defence—for the Marches, Calais, and the navy—took up another £11,000. Other items, however,—ambassadors (£11,000), goldsmiths (£2,900), and transfer payments (£13,000)—seem only to duplicate the Privy Purse. But the appearance is deceptive. The Chamber met all usual ambassadorial expenses; the Privy Purse paid for Benet's embassy to Rome, which was Henry's last-ditch attempt at a papal solution for the divorce.[47] The Chamber paid goldsmiths for ambassadorial plate, cramprings, and the king's stereotyped New Year gifts of plate; but the Privy Purse bore the cost of choice silver for Henry's own table. And nothing in the Chamber parallels the Privy Purse's

---

[44] BL Add. MS 20,030, printed *in extenso* by N. H. Nicolas, ed., *The Privy Purse Expenses of King Henry VIII* (London, 1827).

[45] E 101/465/20 (*LP* VII. 250).

[46] This and the following figures are based on my analysis of the calendared abstracts in *LP* V. 315–25. It is reassuring to note that my figure for wage payments tallies very closely with the treasurer's own estimate of 'almost £40,000' in 1537 (see Elton, *Tudor Revolution*, 152).

[47] Nicolas, *Privy Purse*, 186.

expenditure on secret matters of state, such as the cost of Wolsey's arrest.[48]

Clearly the old Chamber account of Henry VII's reign had been split into two between the Chamber and the Privy Purse. The Chamber was still larger, but its expenditure was overwhelmingly routine. The Privy Purse, in contrast, dealt with the king's wildly fluctuating private expenses, as well as the cost of high policy. Something of this division had long been apparent. But it seems clear that the date when the Privy Purse book begins, November 1529, is of more than accidental significance. In the year 1528–9 the treasurer had disbursed £3,600 on building works; in the eighteen months after November 1529 he spent only £900. In the year before November 1529 he advanced £23,500 to the cofferer of the household; in the eighteen months after, only £13,000.[49] The axis date—autumn 1529—is of course the time of Wolsey's fall. The king, we know, resolved to take the reins of government into his own hands. It now seems as though he took over finance as well, turning for a brief moment the Privy Purse accounts into a pale imitation of his father's Chamber books. (He even managed to bring himself to sign them, if not like his father on every page, at least by the main monthly totals.) So the 'marked and persistent decline in the scope and competence' of the Chamber, which Elton identified, began in 1529 and not 'with Cromwell's ministry'.[50] Moreover, the decline owed everything to long-term developments within the household on the one hand, and short-term political considerations on the other. It owed nothing to any structural changes in the theory or practice of government.

Nevertheless, Cromwell has an important part to play in the story. From January 1531 he started to act as an informal royal treasurer, and from 1532 to 1536 he effectively paid for the expenses of his government of England from the funds under his control.[51] Professor Elton saw the minister carving out his position at the expense of the Chamber. In fact the real victim was the Privy Purse. The minister had taken over the funding of high policy—one of the key elements of expenditure in the expanded Privy Purse between 1529 and 1532—and to pay for it he made deep inroads into

[48] Ibid. 115.
[49] *LP* V. 303 ff (my calculations again).
[50] Elton, *Tudor Revolution*, 170.
[51] Ibid. 139 ff.

the groom's revenues as well. These, like the Privy Purse itself, underwent major change in 1529. Ever since the temporary emancipation of the first years of Henry VIII's reign, the Privy Purse had been funded by large block payments from the Chamber. These payments cease in June 1529; thereafter the relationship reversed and the Privy Purse replenished the Chamber to the tune of £6,143.[52] Thus, into the place of the Chamber steps another royal treasury, the Privy Coffers.

The Privy Coffers was the collective name for a series of jealously-guarded palace treasuries in which cash reserves were kept. The whole subject of the reserves and their administration is deeply obscure. But there are occasional shafts of light. In 1523, for example, the Privy Coffers at Greenwich could pay out £49,000; while the Coffers at Windsor contained at least £3,000 when they appear to have been cleared out in 1530.[53] At first there is no sign of any relationship between these treasuries and the Privy Purse. But, once again with the fall of Wolsey, a new pattern emerged. At the 'fall of the late lord Cardinal', Thomas Alvard, keeper of his palace of Whitehall, was reappointed by the king. As such, he was in charge both of the reconstruction of the palace as Henry's principal residence and, also, of a new deposit treasury. The Whitehall treasury soon eclipsed the rest. Between November 1529 and April 1531 Alvard accounted for £34,000, of which £8,000 was spent on the rebuilding, and £18,000 paid out 'as well to our said sovereign lord's own hands and to others by his Grace's assignment.'[54] Norris received at least £1,000 (and probably much more) of this, as well as the contents of the defunct treasury at Windsor. At the same time, however, Norris paid Alvard £2,000. This sequence of payments and repayments will be familiar to anyone with a bank account. When the current account (Norris) was flush with cash, money was transferred to the deposit account (Alvard); conversely, when Norris was short, he was topped up by Alvard.[55]

So 1529 saw the appearance of an integrated system of direct royal finance, fashioned from two hitherto disparate household agencies, the Privy Purse and the Privy Coffers. Clearly the Privy Coffers must have contained very substantial reserves (between

52 Starkey, 'Privy Chamber', 388; *LP* V. 312; Nicholas, *Privy Purse*, 19, 22, 24.
53 Starkey, 'Privy Chamber', 397, 400; E 36/221, fo. 9ᵛ; Nicolas, *Privy Purse*, 22.
54 Starkey, 'Privy Chamber', 399; SP1/69, fos. 265–6.
55 Starkey, 'Privy Chamber', 400.

1527 and 1529, for example, Henry VIII was able to pay Francis I of France £50,000 cash from the King's Coffers).[56] But the Coffers were no widow's cruse of oil. Luckily they were topped up by two sources. Wolsey had contributed to both. Alvard's original funds were no doubt the Cardinal's own confiscated treasures (like the mountains of gold and silver plate catalogued by Cavendish).[57] And thereafter both Alvard and Norris benefited from what the Cardinal, in the last uncertain throw of his diplomacy, had been able to rescue from the wreck of Cambrai. By the Treaty signed in August 1529 Francis I undertook to pay both the arrears of the pension originally granted to Edward IV at Picquigny, as well as to redeem Charles V's huge debts to Henry VIII.[58] The need for French support at Rome in the divorce negotiations led Henry to remit large sums; nevertheless, between 1530 and 1532 he was receiving between £20,000 and £50,000 per year clear from France, paid on the nail every six months at Calais in golden crowns of the sun.[59] Much of this certainly circulated through the private financial machine of the Coffers and the Privy Purse: Norris gave orders for the bringing over of the money from Calais in 1531 and actually received it in 1530;[60] while both he and Alvard frequently dealt in the actual French coins rather than sterling.[61]

The pension was the foundation of royal finance in these years. But it was a foundation built on the shifting sands of chaotic international politics. Here at last Cromwell comes in. The original purpose of his treasurership was, I suspect, to find a more reliable source of revenue by exploiting the king's prerogatives over the church.[62] And like the first surveyor of the king's (secular) prerogative, Belknap under Henry VII, Cromwell paid much of the early fruits of his labours to the Privy Purse.[63] But Cromwell soon began to spend what he raised, and more, on his own ministerial expenses. The shortfall was made up from the only available source: the Privy Coffers. On 5 October 1532 £20,000 was transferred from the Privy Coffers at Greenwich to a great chest in the Tower, in the charge

[56] *LP* IV. iii. 5515.

[57] R. S. Sylvester and D. P. Harding, eds., *Two Early Tudor Lives* (New Haven and London), 102–3.

[58] J. D. Mackie, *The Earlier Tudors* (Oxford, 1952), 319.

[59] *LP* IV. iii. 5515, 6040, 6710; V. 222, 1065, 1504–5.

[60] SP 1/68, fo. 28 (*LP* V. 487); Nicolas, *Privy Purse*, 34.

[61] SP 1/53, fo. 273.

[62] See particularly the list of his receipts in SP 2 N, fos. 114–17 (*LP* VI. 228).

[63] Especially *LP* V. 1285/ix.

(principally) of Thomas Audley, the new keeper of the great seal.[64] In the course of the following year Audley paid out all but £1,000 to Cromwell. The minister also received £3,000 from Alvard and, rather circuitously, £2,000 from Norris. That made up £24,000 of the minister's total receipts of £33,000 for the year 1532–3.[65]

In other words the interlocking system of deposit and current accounts established in 1529 survived, but with a change of personnel. Cromwell substituted his own account for Norris and the Privy Purse, while Audley and the Tower treasury largely replaced the king as dispenser from the Privy Coffers. At first sight this looks like the 'Tudor Revolution' with a vengeance, as minister and bureaucrat displace courtier and king. But there is a more straightforward politico-fiscal explanation. In 1532–3 money was tight, and Cromwell could only run government effectively if his own hand controlled the flow of cash. But the success of his ministry (which can be seen as a dramatic fulfilment of his first brief as what we might call surveyor of the ecclesiastical prerogative) transformed the financial situation from penny-pinching to affluence. With affluence Cromwell's hostility to the household evaporated. The Privy Purse never resumed its role in national finance (it was in any case only the crisis of 1529 which had propelled it onto the public stage). But the Privy Coffers grew ever larger. From 1536 the Coffers took £178,000 from Augmentations, £96,000 from parliamentary taxation, £28,000 from the jewel house, and £60,000 from First Fruits and Tenths. This totals £362,000 and is by no means exhaustive. The proportions are as impressive as the gross figures: between 1536 and 1539 half the yield of Augmentations; in 1540–1 half of the subsidy, and in 1542–3 no less than 80 per cent of it.[66] Most of these sums finished up in the charge of Sir Anthony Denny, chief gentleman of the Privy Chamber and Alvard's successor as the keeper of Whitehall and its deposit treasury. Denny's book of receipts has survived.[67] It shows that between 1542 and 1547 the Whitehall treasury received £240,000 and became (to judge from our imperfect knowledge of its disbursements)[68] the largest warchest hitherto accumulated by an English king. The treasury was

---

[64] BL Royal MS 7 C. xvi, fo. 75. Professor Elton did not turn up this document, which plays a crucial part in unravelling Cromwell's treasurership.

[65] Starkey, 'Privy Chamber', 402–3.

[66] The calculations are set out in detail in Starkey, 'Privy Chamber', 406 ff.

[67] E 315/160, fo. 264 ff.

[68] Starkey, 'Privy Chamber', 409.

also, since Henry handled much of the money himself and kept it, if not under the bed, at least at the back of his bedchamber in the secret jewel house, a dramatic reassertation of the vitality of household administration.

From Signet to Sign Manual

The rise of the secretary is normally presented as a smooth ascent from fifteenth-century obscurity to sixteenth-century eminence. The record speaks differently. The foundation of the secretary's office was his custody of the smallest royal seal, the signet. By the later fifteenth century the signet had become the *primum mobile* of government. It validated the king's letters to foreign powers and his own subjects; gave orders to other household departments; and set in motion the formal machine of the privy and great seals which alone could authorize the payment of money from the Exchequer or make grants of patronage. In short, by the reign of Richard III royal action meant an act under the signet: Richard's secretary, John Kendal, was one of his principal agents and Kendal's register or docket-book is the prime record of Richard's government.[69] But this marked the high noon of the signet and its keeper. Then there is a gap of sixty-five years before the next surviving docket-book, which was kept by Ralph Sadler, secretary to Henry VIII.[70] In the interval lie archival chaos and obscurity from which a new secretaryship arises. The new secretaryship was based, not on the signet like the old (though it still retained control of the seal), but on the sign manual. The story is untold in essentials and badly needs telling.[71] But it is too big to be tackled here in full. So I shall deal with only a part of it: the rise of the sign manual and its relationship with the Privy Chamber.

The sign manual, as the royal signature was formally known, had developed concurrently with the signet.[72] It could be used in three ways. It could serve as a warrant or instruction to the signet; it could be used in conjunction with the signet, as a reinforcement of

[69] *British Library Harleian Manuscript 433* (Harl. MS 433), eds. Rosemary Horrox and P. W. Hammond (4 vols., Upminster and London, 1979–83).

[70] BL Add. MS 33,818 and A. J. Slavin, *Politics and Profit: A Study of Sir Ralph Sadler, 1507–1547* (Cambridge, 1966), 55 ff.

[71] Cf. Elton's account in *Tudor Revolution*, 261 ff. Only Tout seems to have understood the way things were going: see T. F. Tout, *Chapters in the Administrative History of Medieval England* (6 vols., Manchester, 1920–33) v. 226–30.

[72] J. Otway-Ruthven, *The King's Secretary and the Signet Office in the Fifteenth Century* (Cambridge, 1939), 24–5.

the seal; or it could be employed on its own, bypassing the seal altogether.[73] Under Henry VI there were still doubts about the validity of the sign manual (reinforced quite clearly by doubts about the signer).[74] But as the century wore on these doubts disappeared and the sign manual was used ever more frequently and confidently. For instance, under Henry VI it was exceptional for the sign manual to appear on a signet warrant; under Edward IV, however, 'perhaps half or rather more' signet warrants carry the sign manual;[75] and by Henry VII's reign the practice had become universal.[76] The ever-increasing demand for the royal signature even produced a change in Henry VII's sign manual itself. On 28 August 1492 he replaced the spiky gridiron monogram, awkwardly made with several strokes, which he had used since the beginning of the reign, with a cursive 'HR', formed with one long, flowing movement of the pen.[77]

But despite its close connection with the signet, the sign manual was an 'altogether different method of authentication'[78]—and, it might be added, a rival one. Only the secretary could apply the signet; anybody could and did get the sign manual. The more important, then, that the sign manual became, the less was left of the secretary's original position. Personal and other considerations, of course, could override this logic. That is what happened under Richard III. He had the highest regard for Secretary Kendal; he also found the signet office useful as a general co-ordinator of the governmental machine.[79] But under Henry VII these considerations ceased to apply. He co-ordinated government himself; and though his first secretary Fox was one of the king's closest advisers, he quickly moved on to better things, leaving the post to the obscure and often absentee.[80] The difference quickly showed in the number of direct warrants to the Chancery. These warrants—usually in fact suitors' petitions or 'bills' signed by the king—were the most sensitive use of the sign manual. Under Henry VI they had been the instruments of the king's prodigal patronage, and in 1444 the Council had tried

[73] Ibid. 25–6, 39; *Harl. MS 433*, vol. i, pp. xvii ff.
[74] Otway-Ruthven, *King's Secretary*, 25.
[75] Ibid. 26.
[76] See, for example, the files of warrants to the Great Wardrobe, E 101/413/11, 414/8, 415/7, 416/7, etc.
[77] R. L. Storey, *The Reign of Henry VII* (London, 1968), 102 and plate 9.
[78] Otway-Ruthven, *King's Secretary*, 24.
[79] *Harl. MS 433*, vol. i. pp. xiii, xviii–xix.
[80] Chrimes, *Henry VII*, 116–18.

to get rid of them. No longer were 'signed bills' to go direct to the chancellor; instead they were to be passed to the secretary. He would then issue a signet warrant to the lord privy seal, who in turn would draw up a privy seal warrant to the chancellor.[81] Richard III largely kept to this arrangement. Not, of course, because of pressure from his Council, but because he found that records of the signet office kept a valuable tally on his use of patronage.[82] Bound by this self-denying ordinance he issued very few direct warrants, of which even fewer survive (only forty-eight for the whole reign).[83] At first Henry VII followed his predecessor's practice, and in his first patent roll only twenty-seven grants are warranted 'By the King' (which in practice means by a signed bill)[84] as against 299 'By privy seal' (which means that the full course of the seals had been gone through).[85] But in the early 1490s, coinciding roughly with the adoption of the new sign manual, the number of signed bills rises rapidly until in the two last patent rolls of the reign the two kinds of warranty are almost evenly balanced: in 23 Henry VII (1507–8) 103 patents are warranted 'By the king' as against 100 'By privy seal'; while in 24 Henry VII the respective figures (perhaps reflecting the king's failing powers) are sixty and ninety-five.[86] 'The sign manual [was] coming into the administrative stream above the signet.'[87]

The change emerged fully into the light of day under Henry VIII. 'The next time that his Grace sign'[88] was the moment on which hung the plans of councillors and the hopes of suitors; while the sign manual, now manifestly the prime motor of government, was given the protection long afforded to the great seal. An Act of 1536 declared anyone who should 'falsely forge and counterfeit the king's sign manual' a traitor,[89] and on 23 December that year a priest was duly hanged drawn and quartered for infringing the statute.[90] But there were more dangers than forgery in the new

---

[81] Otway-Ruthven, *King's Secretary*, 35 ff.

[82] *Harl. MS 433*, vol. i. p. xiii.

[83] Ibid. xliii n. 52.

[84] Ibid. xvii–xviii.

[85] *CPR* (1485–94), 1–40.

[86] *CPR* (1494–1509), 548–93, 594–626.

[87] K. W. M. Pickthorn, *Early Tudor Government* (2 vols., Cambridge, 1934), i. 141 n. 1.

[88] See n. 118 below.

[89] G. R. Elton, *The Tudor Constitution: Documents and Commentary* (1st edn., Cambridge, 1960), 63.

[90] W. D. Hamilton, ed., *A Chronicle of England*, by Charles Wriothesley (Camden Society, new series, xi, 2 vols., London, 1875–7), i. 60.

dispensation. The informality of the sign manual made no odds under a king as organized and disciplined as Henry VII. Under Henry VIII, who was spasmodically generous and frequently inattentive, it was a different story. At first the problem was headed off. The young king's Council, conservative and deeply wedded to proper form as we have seen in finance, moved quickly to reintroduce the full course of the seals. There followed a striking change in the Chancery's files of warrants. In April 1509, the first month of the reign, nine signed bills and no privy seals survive;[91] in May the respective figures are twenty-three and sixty-two;[92] and in June, fourteen and ninety-four.[93] Moreover, most of the June signed bills are easily explained: two deal with the marriage settlement for Katherine of Aragon;[94] two concern the master of the rolls;[95] and four made arrangements for the coronation.[96] So only three were the usual sort of signed petition,[97] and one of these testifies to the new hurdles which such grants had now to leap. For accompanying a signed bill granting a sinecure to Anthony Leigh, the chief clerk of the kitchen, is a further warrant, also under the sign manual, specifically instructing the chancellor to pass Leigh's grant.[98] These formalized procedures broke down in the first French war;[99] and thereafter the floodgates were opened. Signing more or less whatever was put in front of him, the king found himself granting office or lands twice over to different suitors. An attempt to tackle the resulting problems was made by an Act of Parliament of 1515.[100] Whether it achieved much may be doubted.

But a longer-term solution was in the offing. Underlying this confusion, and at first abetting it, then later taming it, was the development of a new secretarial routine in the hands of the Privy Chamber. Some such development (on the lines of the displacement of the Chamber by the Privy Purse in finance) was predictable. But the Privy Chamber's role was made more pronounced by a well-known trait in Henry VIII's character: his detestation of the actual business of writing—even of writing his signature. Any excuse was good enough to put off the signing of documents: a cold, a

[91] *LP* I. i. 11.
[92] Ibid. 54.
[93] Ibid. 94.
[94] Ibid. 94/36, 41.
[95] Ibid. 94/44, 99.
[96] Ibid. 94/43, 87–9.
[97] Ibid. 94/60, 71, 110.
[98] Ibid. 94/60.
[99] *LP* I. ii. 1948.
[100] *Stat. Realm*, iii. 134.

headache, or the lateness of the hour.[101] He would sign only when the mood took him—and who better to spot the time than the Privy Chamber, perpetually in attendance and deeply versed in the royal foibles?[102]

Quite soon we see state papers accumulating in the hands of the groom of the stool, Compton or Norris, who submitted them for signature at a propitious moment after supper or during mass.[103] These were papers prepared by Wolsey's own secretariat. But the Privy Chamber also took a less passive role. There survives a twelve-page letter book for the latter part of 1517.[104] Its contents are very mixed. Some letters are on state business, like the workings of the enclosure commission, but most deal with the personal interests of Henry's intimate attendants. Similarly letters from the king are blended indiscriminately with letters from his servants. The book, written in a clear secretary's hand, ends 'fynys quod Sygyr'.[105] If 'Sygyr' is the name of the clerk who compiled the book, he is unidentifiable; but the prominence of 'our well-beloved servant . . . and in our singular favour', Nicholas Carew, in the matters dealt with suggests that 'Sygyr' may well have been his clerk.[106] Since Carew was the dominant figure in the Privy Chamber in 1517, 'Sygyr' was effectively the clerk of the Privy Chamber, and the book the record of his activities. As such it is a vivid insight into the informality and casualness of a government, in which decisions were taken and implemented in the Privy Chamber. What happened, it seems, was this. The king agreed to make a grant. 'Sygyr' was then summoned into the Privy Chamber and took down in hasty dictation a letter from the king. Standing around were probably the interested parties and their backers, and when the king had completed his business they came in with letters of their own: explaining the royal decision, rounding up support, or heading off opposition.[107]

But all this is very fragmentary. The 'Sygyr' book itself contains only fourteen letters, while there are only a couple of references for the whole of the Wolsey's ministry to the groom's procuring the

---

101 *LP* III. ii. 1399, 1429.
102 See the sequence of events in *LP* XIV. ii. 149, 153, 163.
103 *LP* I. ii. 1960; IV. ii. 4409.
104 Bod. Lib., Ashmole MS 1148, section xi.
105 Ibid. p. 12.
106 Ibid. p. 8.   107 See n. 108 below.

king's signature. At first sight, it is hard to explain why the Privy Chamber's secretarial role should have been so slow to take off. Certainly there was no good administrative reason, but there was, as the 'Sygyr' book shows, a compelling political one. Four of the letters deal with the suit of William Coffin of the Privy Chamber to marry the wealthy widow, Mrs Vernon of Haddon Hall in Derbyshire.[108] Opposing Coffin was Wolsey himself who wanted the widow for one of his own servants.[109] But Coffin, backed to the hilt by Carew, was able to procure the king's own letters, and so inflicted public defeat on the minister, 'whereat', as Compton smugly reported, 'my lord cardinal is not content with all.'[110] So the Privy Chamber's access to the sign manual was a valuable weapon in the armoury that turned the newly appointed Gentlemen into some of Wolsey's most feared rivals. He could never allow the sign manual to be formalized in their hands.

Ironically, similar political considerations limited the effectiveness of Wolsey's own counter-measures. Periodically he would single out someone at Court to handle the mass of his secretarial business conducted with Henry: that is, to cope with the stream of letters between king and minister and to get documents signed. At various times the quasi-secretary was Richard Pace (the *real* secretary), Thomas More, a councillor attendant, or William Fitzwilliam, the treasurer of the Household.[111] Always the result was the same. Wolsey became jealous of the chosen intermediary, fearing that he would exploit his favourable position to undermine the minister's own, and the arrangement was abandoned. Only at the end of his ministry was Wolsey forced to take his Court agents more seriously. In response to the rise of the Boleyn faction at Court, the cardinal had put a powerful group of his own supporters in the Privy Chamber. These included Thomas Heneage, who had been head of Wolsey's own Privy Chamber, and Sir John Russell, whom Wolsey had written into the new Privy Chamber list of January 1526 with his own hand.[112] In the summer of 1528 Heneage

---

[108] Bod. Lib., Ashmole MS 1148, section xi. pp. 7, 9, 11.
[109] Edmund Lodge, *Illustrations of British History* (3 vols., London, 1791), i. 28 ff.
[110] Loc. cit.
[111] Elton, *Tudor Revolution*, 56–9.
[112] SP 1/37, fo. 65 (*LP* IV. i. 1939/4); *LP* IV. ii. 3964; *LP* III. ii. 2132; *LP* IV. i. 338/3, etc.

handled most of the ministerial correspondence at Court;[113] then, as the old problem of distrust reappeared, Russell and Dr Bell, the royal almoner and another creature of the cardinal's, took over. By autumn their role was sufficiently well established for Robert Crawley, the Court agent of an Irish faction, to recommend to Wolsey that he 'send to Sir John Russell, Dr. Bell, and such others as promote bills or letters to the King's sign, that they pass no matters of Ireland till your Grace be made privy to the same.'[114]

So, under threat politically, Wolsey had at last done the obvious and made the poachers of the Privy Chamber into ministerial gamekeepers. But the arrangement was only rudimentary, and it was swept away by the new minister, Cromwell. He excluded the Privy Chamber absolutely from the 'promotion' of documents to the sign manual, and instead entrusted all ministerial business at Court to servants of his own, in particular to Ralph Sadler.[115] All this was on the most informal footing. Sadler held no official post, while the Privy Chamber were kept out merely by the threat of Cromwell's displeasure. But more radical measures were taken. The first was to restore the ancient course of the seals established in 1444. This did not of course touch the sign manual directly; but at least it meant that signed bills would normally have to pass through the hands of the secretary (that is, Cromwell) rather than, as so frequently happened, going straight to Chancery. As we have seen, both Richard III and the Council of the young Henry VIII had already revived the course of the seals for their own purposes; now Cromwell would do the same, but on the basis of statute.

The Act was passed in 1536.[116] For Elton it was a major advance in the bureaucratic revolution. In fact it was an old and increasingly old-fashioned solution to the perennial problem of the vagaries of royal patronage. More important still, it was a solution that was not put into effect. For almost before it received the royal assent, it was overtaken by the great political crisis of the early summer of 1536. The outcome of this crisis proved to be Cromwell's double triumph over both his old allies, the Boleyns, and his recent partners, the Aragonese. He now had absolute control over the Privy Chamber, of which the first fruit was the appointment of Thomas Heneage,

113 *LP* IV. ii. 4005, 4144, 4299, etc.
114 *St. Pap.* ii. 140–2.
115 Starkey, 'Privy Chamber', 321–2.
116 Elton, *Tudor Revolution*, 270 ff.

once Wolsey's client and now his, as groom of the stool.[117] With the groom in his pocket, Cromwell's attitude to the Privy Chamber and the sign manual reversed. Instead of deflecting business from the groom, the promotion of papers to the sign manual was now concentrated in his hands. And instead of relying on the remote and inefficient long-stop of the signet, Cromwell now regulated the application of the sign manual directly.

Quickly a recognizable procedure developed. The minister's office sent a batch of papers to the chief gentleman at Court, who in turn got them signed and returned them to the minister, usually at Austin Friars. As well as ministerial papers, documents from other government departments, in particular Augmentations, and the bills of private suitors, were sent to the groom for signing. When Heneage went off duty any unsigned papers were handed over to his colleague, Sir Francis Bryan; and by the end of the 1530's there even seem to have been semi-formal sessions, known in advance to well-informed suitors, when 'next . . . his Grace [shall] sign.'[118] Nevertheless, and this is the important thing, every stage of the process was controlled by Cromwell. The chief gentleman reported to him on the progress of state papers across the royal desk; Rich, the chancellor of Augmentations, told Cromwell when he had sent in papers, and once begged him to 'be a suitor . . . for the expedition of the signature'.[119] Private clients would solicit a ministerial letter to the chief gentleman to convey Cromwell's formal consent that 'he shall proceed and get my bill signed';[120] and—the ultimate sanction—it looks as though Cromwell himself was present at Court for the later mass-signing sessions.[121] The minister even took back his control a stage further, to the negotiations that preceded the signing of a bill. This was done by 'Mr. Heneage's Book of Remembrance for the king.'[122] Cromwell had projected the setting up of the King's Book (as it was usually known) in his own memoranda for May 1537.[123] The note fully describes its purpose: 'a book [to] be made of the names of such persons to whom

[117] G. R. Elton, *Reform and Reformation* (London, 1977), 253–4; Starkey, 'Privy Chamber', 239 ff.

[118] Ibid., 324–30; SP 3/4, art. 76 (*LP* XV. 291).

[119] SP 1/158, fos. 54–5 (*LP* XV. 347).

[120] SP 1/125, fo. 19 (*LP* XII. ii. 739).

[121] Starkey, 'Privy Chamber', 330.

[122] *LP* XI. 227.

[123] BL Cott. MS Titus B. I, fo. 457 (*LP* XII. i. 1315).

the King's Majesty will give any lands, fees or offices.' The Book played, and no doubt was intended to play, an important part in policing the scramble for preferment that followed the Dissolution, since an entry in it took precedence over any other commitment (even a promise from the chancellor of Augmentations).[124] But Cromwell also had less altruistic motives. For once again, despite the Book's name and its custodian, Cromwell seems to have been the true recording angel: if one wanted to put a name in the Book, ensure that an entry materialized into a grant, or overturn an entry, one wrote to Cromwell.[125] Cromwell, in short, had done what Wolsey never fully could or would and controlled the sign manual. No longer could suitors 'run in at the window the next way, making immediate pursuits to the King's Highness'. The window was barred and locked.[126]

Here then is a Cromwell both familiar and strange. The familiar Cromwell fulfils what Wolsey promised and shows an unstoppable urge to translate power into regular procedures and record keeping. The unfamiliar Cromwell puts both the procedures and the records in the hands of the royal household. Once again, there is no principled distinction between different types of administration; only a sensible political discrimination between men you can trust and command and those you cannot.

Principal among those whom Cromwell could trust was Ralph Sadler, his general Court agent in the first part of his ministry. Sadler was put into the Privy Chamber as a groom in July 1536, a month or so after Cromwell's other client Heneage had been made groom of the stool. Thereafter the two largely divided any ministerial business about the king between themselves. While the signing of documents was handled by Heneage, Sadler was the main channel of communication between king and minister: expounding Cromwell's minutes to the king and writing the royal replies. Sadler's role was institutionalized in April 1540 when Cromwell divested himself of the secretaryship and divided it between his two clients, Thomas Wriothesley and Ralph Sadler. Wriothesley continued as head of Cromwell's private office; Sadler as go-between in the Privy Chamber.[127]

[124] SP 1/153, fos. 30–1 (*LP* XIV. ii. 47).
[125] SP 1/124, fos. 159–60 (*LP* XII. ii. 629); SP 1/125, fo. 101 (*LP* XII. ii. 810); SP 1/105, fos. 240–1 (*LP* XI. 227 misdated).
[126] See n. 114 above.
[127] Starkey, 'Privy Chamber', 333.

So the result of the second half of Cromwell's ministry was to recreate the fifteenth-century secretaryship, but in the Privy Chamber and corporately, between Heneage and Sadler. Their fate, and that of their several tasks, varied widely. Sadler was dismissed from the secretaryship in 1543 and none of his successors was a member of the Privy Chamber. So the department lost the role of go-between. The revived secretaryship (no longer held by men who were too small—like the pre-Cromwellian secretaries— nor too big—like Cromwell himself) also began to reclaim a large part of the business of signing documents from the groom. But then chance dealt the groom a trump-all. Inflamed by illness and old age, Henry's reluctance to sign became an aversion. Eventually he freed himself by setting up the machinery of the 'dry stamp'.[128]

This was done in September 1545, although it was only formally authorized nearly a year later in August 1546.[129] There had long been a 'wet stamp', used to rubber (or rather, wooden) stamp circulars. The dry stamp was quite different. It left an uninked impression on the paper which was gone over in pen-and-ink by an expert clerk. The result was a near perfect facsimile, that was used henceforward to authenticate all documents to which the sign manual would ordinarily have been applied. And the dry stamp was firmly in the hands of the Privy Chamber. In overall control was Sir Anthony Denny, the second chief gentleman; while the office routine was dealt with by William Clerk, the 'king's clerk'. He both applied the stamp and kept the monthly registers of documents stamped, which were then submitted to the king for clearance by his real signature. Even the stamp itself, originally held by the king, was entrusted in February 1546 to John Gates, gentleman of the Privy Chamber and Denny's brother-in-law and factotum.[130] Henry had thus alienated the sign manual to Denny as completely as a seal to its keeper.

CONCLUSIONS

In the last years of the reign, then, the Privy Chamber's governmental activities flourished. They were unpruned by any ministerial hand; and they were fertilized by war (which always brought the

[128] Ibid. 342 ff.
[129] *LP* XX. ii. 706; Rymer, *Foedera*, xv. 100.
[130] E 315/160, fos. 266^v, 267.

king to the forefront of government) and Henry's final physical
decline (which put unwonted power in the hands of his immediate
attendants). The key figure in this was Sir Anthony Denny, second
chief gentleman from the beginning of 1539, and groom of the
stool from October 1546. He controlled the dry stamp; he was also
custodian of the hugely expanded Privy Coffers. He had a general
personal secretariat run by his brother-in-law, Gates; Clerk handled
the secretarial duties of the dry stamp; whilst Nicholas Bristowe,
clerk of the Wardrobe of the Robes, was chief bookkeeper and
accountant of the Privy Coffers (and the Privy Purse as well,
though that did not come within Denny's province till he had taken
over from Heneage as groom of the stool). Round Denny, therefore, was a true inner household administration—answerable to
Denny as first acting and finally formal head of the Privy Chamber—
which was actually based in the multitude of strong rooms and
closets honeycombing off the privy lodging at Whitehall.[131]

There is a certain rhythm in all this, as the Privy Chamber usurps
one by one the functions of the Chamber. First it takes over the
task of intimate personal attendance on the monarch; then it dis-
places the administrators of the Chamber, the treasurer and the
secretary, from their original household tasks (the keeping of the
Privy Purse and the authentication of documents); finally it tres-
passes on their national responsibilities as well. But the rhythm was
not new or progressive. We are not seeing, as Professor Elton
thought, a linear movement from medieval to modern. Rather
government was dancing to an ancient roundelay: the cycle of
'going out of Court'. A household department is given national
responsibilities; it abandons the Court and settles down in Westminster. In the mean time its neglected tasks about the king are
taken over by another household department, which then begins to
encroach on the national activities of its predecessor. And so on.
The cycle begins under the Anglo-Normans; it is still turning, we
now know, under the Tudors. At last! There is a Tudor revolution
after all. But it is in their sense of the word, not ours. And the
Tudor cycle of 'going out of Court' is never completed. The Privy
Purse, well on the way to displacing the Chamber as the principal
national treasury in the early 1530s, was, with Cromwell and an
altered politics, cut short. The dry stamp became a fully-fledged
fourth 'seal' between 1545 and 1547, wholly depriving the signet of

---

[131] Cf. Starkey, 'Privy Chamber', 417.

original force, but it did so only as a result of the circumstances of the king's failing health and its dominance died with Henry. Thereafter the sign manual was recaptured by the secretary, while the Privy Chamber were reduced (as under Elizabeth) to mere barometers of the royal mood to be tapped by the secretary before he submitted documents for signature.[132] Thus not only is the cycle of going out of court incomplete; it is not autonomous either. It is subject to pressures of circumstance. But, as subsequent essays will show, so were the most formal parts of the governmental machine, including the Council. And, like everything else, the cycle is subject to ministerial pressures.

We have already sampled these in our brief account of the rise of the Privy Chamber as a household department. Wolsey was its inveterate enemy; Cromwell its eventual friend. Much the same, it is now clear, would go for their response to 'household'—in effect, Privy Chamber—government as a whole. This is not to try to stand *The Tudor Revolution in Government* on its head and show Cromwell as a back-slider from Wolsey's advanced position. (Though it is worth remembering that the original thesis of the withdrawal of the household from national administration was formulated by A. P. Newton, not Elton, and had Wolsey, not Cromwell, as the prime architect of change.)[133] Rather than invert *The Tudor Revolution* (or even perhaps stand it the right way up), I would wish to deny the relevance of its categories altogether. Neither Wolsey nor Cromwell had any theoretical conception of separate models of government, the 'household' or the national/ bureaucratic. Both instead were practical politicians, concerned with the realities of power. And power alone shaped their attitudes to the Privy Chamber. Wolsey's power base lay outside the Court; so he viewed the rise of a new constellation within the Court—the Privy Chamber and its agencies—always with unease and usually with outright hostility. Cromwell, on the other hand, began his career where Wolsey finished his, as a leader of a Court faction. And it was as a jealous faction leader that he reacted. Until he controlled the Privy Chamber his opposition to its activities in government (or anything else) was implacable—as Norris and the Privy Purse discovered. Once the coup of May 1536 gave him that control,

[132] Conyers Read, *Mr Secretary Walsingham and the Policy of Queen Elizabeth* (3 vols., Oxford, 1925), i. 437.
[133] Newton, 'Tudor Reforms'.

however, all was sweetness and light: he did not merely tolerate the Privy Chamber, but as Heneage and the sign manual show, he vigorously developed its activities as agents of his own power.

None of this of course is intended to suggest that the ministers' only concern was the household. They had many other things to think of (though in 1525 Wolsey put the ordinary business of government on the back burner for several months whilst he purged the Privy Chamber). Nor am I suggesting that the household was the government. It was not, and its governmental activities usually took a back seat to other agencies, above all the Council. Yet it was always important, and in the right circumstances, decisive—as the last weeks of the reign bore out. Then it was the dry stamp alone which authenticated both the attainder of the duke of Norfolk and the king's will. The former removed the only possible challenge to Edward Seymour's take-over of power under the future Edward VI; the latter provided the constitutional machinery to set up the Seymour regime. In 1529, before Cromwell, 'household' government had unmade a minister; in 1547, after Cromwell, 'household' government made both a Protector and a Reformation.[134]

[134] Elton, *Reform and Reformation*, 331 ff.

CHAPTER 3

THE PRIVY COUNCIL: REVOLUTION OR EVOLUTION?

J. A. GUY

A central feature of *The Tudor Revolution in Government* was the argument that the Privy Council was created by Thomas Cromwell, between 1534 and 1536, as a conscious act of administrative reform designed to modernize the existing King's Council as inherited from Wolsey's regime.[1] The medieval King's Council, according to Professor Elton, was large, cumbersome and inefficient; by contrast that created by Cromwell was small, flexible and effective. Furthermore, Cromwell divorced the Privy Council from Star Chamber and other aspects of the former Council's judicial function, so that each body could independently concentrate on the work which was its principal *raison d'être*. Conciliar justice was to be provided in institutionally separate courts, though the Privy Council retained quasi-judicial powers in the manner of a board of arbitration. Star Chamber and Requests thus became settled courts of the realm as an integral aspect of Cromwell's work.

Much of this account remains valid. The characteristic government of the later Tudors was the Privy Council, an élite board of (normally) fewer than twenty members, most of them leading officers of state and household, who met nearly every day at the

[1] G. R. Elton, *The Tudor Revolution in Government* (Cambridge, 1953), 60–5, 316–69. The following works are also essential: Elton, *The Tudor Constitution* (2nd edn., Cambridge, 1982), 88–116, 163–99; his papers, 'Henry VII's Council', and 'Why the History of the Early Tudor Council remains unwritten', and 'Tudor Government: the points of contact, the Council', in his *Studies in Tudor and Stuart Politics and Government* (3 vols., Cambridge, 1974, 1983), i. 294–9, 308–38, iii. 21–38; J. A. Guy, *The Cardinal's Court* (Hassocks, 1977); A. F. Pollard, 'Council, Star Chamber, and Privy Council under the Tudors', EHR xxxvii (1922), 337–60, 516–39, xxxviii (1923), 42–60; C. G. Bayne and W. H. Dunham, eds., *Select Cases in the Council of Henry VII* (London, Selden Society, 1958); L. M. Hill, ed., *The Ancient State, Authoritie, and Proceedings of the Court of Requests by Sir Julius Caesar* (Cambridge, 1975); D. E. Hoak, *The King's Council in the Reign of Edward VI* (Cambridge, 1976).

itinerant Court of the sovereign. This new-style Privy Council existed by 10 August 1540, when nineteen councillors resolved that a clerk should attend upon them, to record minutes of their deliberations in a new series of Council registers.[2] The separation of the clerkship and registers of the Privy Council from those of Star Chamber confirms that institutional bifurcation had occurred. However, the split was much more than a functional division between executive work and justice. The Privy Council met at Court without reference to the law terms and vacations. It was thus closer to the small, but active, Council attendant of Henry VII than to the large King's Council under Wolsey, which had assembled in the Star Chamber at Westminster in term time only. Henry VII's Council had included 227 members in the course of his reign, of whom some twenty trusted administrators formed the 'inner ring'.[3] Wolsey's board comprised around seventy persons at any one time, some thirty-two of whom regularly attended meetings in Star Chamber.[4] All sworn councillors prior to Wolsey's fall in 1529 were in theory of equal status. However, the 'privy' or 'close' councillors of the Tudors were elevated ten years later above their former colleagues in the Council, who now enjoyed strictly subordinate duties as 'ordinary councillors' or councillors 'at large' during their lifetimes.[5] Since nothing fairly to be described as the Privy Council had existed before the 1530s, it is clear that structural change had taken place. The question is, was this change the result of an act of fundamental reform by Thomas Cromwell, or was it impelled to some degree by Wolsey's planning or Henry VIII's immediate needs?

The changing structure of the King's Council in the years from 1485 to 1540 is summarized in Figure 1. In Henry VII's reign, the Council attendant flourished apart from that at Westminster in Star Chamber, though the respective memberships of the two parts were interchangeable and their functions, too, were undifferentiated. Administration and justice were intermingled in the late-medieval Council. We must emphasize that the Council which

[2] Privy Council Register, PC 2/1, p. 1; printed in N. H. Nicolas, ed., *Proceedings and Ordinances of the Privy Council of England, 1368–1542* (7 vols., London, 1834–7), vii. 3.

[3] S. B. Chrimes, *Henry VII* (London, 1972), 102–14; Bayne and Dunham, pp. xxix–xli.

[4] Guy, *Cardinal's Court*, 26–30.

[5] Elton, *Tudor Revolution*, 336.

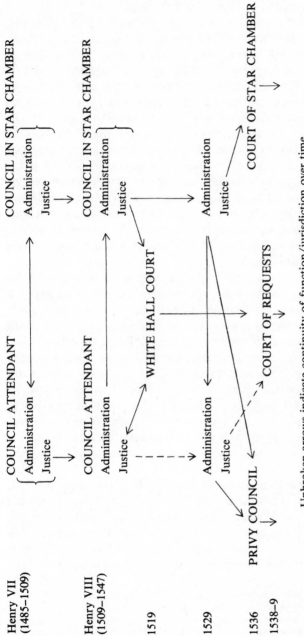

Fig. 1. The Structure of the King's Council, 1485–1540

Henry VII
(1485–1509)

Henry VIII
(1509–1547)

1519

1529

1536

1538–9

COUNCIL ATTENDANT
Administration
Justice

COUNCIL ATTENDANT
Administration
Justice

WHITE HALL COURT

COURT OF REQUESTS

PRIVY COUNCIL

COUNCIL IN STAR CHAMBER
Administration
Justice

COUNCIL IN STAR CHAMBER
Administration
Justice

Administration
Justice

COURT OF STAR CHAMBER

Unbroken arrows indicate continuity of function/jurisdiction over time.
Broken arrows indicate linked but fluid relationships.
Unbroken arrows with heads at both ends indicate shared functions at the
time stated.

attended the king while he travelled about the country on progress, and that which met in Star Chamber during the four law terms, were still protean forms of the same institution. The Council's twin parts reunited each time the king was in residence at his palace of Westminster during term, which happened frequently in Henry VII's reign. The one guiding principle was that councillors were chosen at the king's will, and the nature of a man's service depended solely on royal requirements at the time.[6] Councillors might thus be employed on the king's affairs at formal meetings at Westminster in Star Chamber, in attendance at Court during a royal progress, within the royal household, or even in Chancery without in any way changing their status as members of the whole body. There were no 'committees' of the Council, senior or junior. There was no delegation or relegation of business, except when representatives treated with foreign ambassadors. The contrast with the executive Privy Council and mature Courts of Star Chamber and Requests could not be more striking.

Henry VII's councillors included forty-three peers, forty-five courtiers, sixty-one clerics, twenty-seven lawyers, and forty-nine lay administrators.[7] However, more than thirty members could rarely be assembled at any one place or time, and a list of the Council attendant in 1494 mentioned sixteen names.[8] Between 1493 and 1508, forty-seven councillors sat both with the king on progress and in Star Chamber, while eight other persons sat only in the attendant Council. Other councillors sat only in Star Chamber. The maximum recorded attendance at a meeting of the Council attendant in this period was eleven, whereas in Star Chamber it rose as high as sixty-five. The king, though, was the magnet when he sat in state at Westminster: an average attendance when he was away on progress was fifteen.[9]

This pattern changed after Henry VIII's accession in 1509, though change at first came slowly. The initial context was the need to counsel a young and inexperienced monarch, and the persons best fitted for this task were the survivors of the 'inner ring' of Henry VII's Council, most of whom were also executors of his will. From 1509 to the moment of Wolsey's appointment as lord

6 Elton, *Studies*, iii. 23–4.
7 Bayne and Dunham, p. xxix.
8 Hill, *Ancient State*, 39–40.
9 Bayne and Dunham, pp. xxiv–xxv, xlvii–xlviii, 25–47.

chancellor in December 1515, the discernible identities of the Council attendant and that in Star Chamber were maintained, but the institutional niceties were eclipsed by the dominant presence in both parts of the Council of some twelve members. The leaders were Richard Fox, bishop of Winchester, Thomas Howard, then earl of Surrey, Thomas Ruthal, bishop of Durham, Charles Somerset, the lord Herbert, George Talbot, earl of Shrewsbury, Sir Henry Marney, Sir Thomas Englefield, Sir Thomas Lovell, and William Warham, archbishop of Canterbury.[10] These men now comprised the close advisers of Henry VIII, taking decisions and countersigning warrants for the great seal almost after the fashion of councillors during a royal minority.[11] Yet the same men were most active in Star Chamber, too, though attendances there at plenary sessions of the Council were in no sense restricted to their group and continued much as under Henry VII.[12] However, the effect of the primacy of the 'inner ring' was to pave the way for Wolsey's monopoly of the Council after 1515, and to undermine the structure of the attendant Council of Henry VIII. For Bishop Fox and the rest could hardly follow the Court satisfactorily if they were obliged to commute almost daily to Westminster during the law terms. Lesser men were thus deputed to stand in as required, but the overall effect was to downgrade the Council attendant, which even ceased, apparently, to provide justice for suitors at Court between April 1512 and May 1514.[13]

Wolsey's advent signalled wider changes. First, the minister reorganized the Council about himself in Star Chamber, where he presided at meetings held almost every day in term time. He reabsorbed into Star Chamber the chief conciliar functions exercised there and elsewhere during the previous thirty years. He maintained the size of the working Council at the levels of Henry VII's reign, but dispersed the 'inner ring' of the early years of Henry VIII. The result was to magnify Wolsey's personal power, and to give 'his' Star Chamber the capacity almost to rival Henry VIII's Court as a centre of political attention.[14] Next, Wolsey gave unprecedented emphasis to the Council's judicial function. Rarely do judges advertise their willingness to

---

[10] Guy, *Cardinal's Court*, 23–4.

[11] Chancery, Warrants for the Great Seal, Series ii, C 82/335, 338, 341, 355, 364, 365, 374.

[12] Henry E. Huntington Library, San Marino, California, Ellesmere MS 2655, fos. 7–9ᵛ.

[13] Hill, *Ancient State*, 88.

[14] Guy, *Cardinal's Court*, 26–35.

provide better justice, but Wolsey did and the impact on Star Chamber was instant. In Henry VII's reign, a mere 300 or so suits had been initiated before the Council in Star Chamber (12.5 per annum). During Wolsey's ascendancy, 1,685 suits (120 per annum) were filed, a workload which was the clear consequence of ministerial encouragement.[15] For Wolsey was not shy to bring water to the mill in defiance of conventional wisdom. No doubt aware of the drawbacks and anomalies of certain aspects of contemporary common law, while confident of his own ability to supply the impartial justice he so desired as lord chancellor and keeper of the king's conscience, Wolsey boasted the renewed availability of the conciliar courts, at the same time allowing in Star Chamber the relaxation of ancient procedural checks designed to facilitate the prompt elimination of frivolous suits. The result was, as Edward Hall observed and the records confirm, that the people complained without number and brought many an honest man to trouble and vexation.[16] In short, Wolsey's idealism swamped the Council with a deluge of complex litigation on real property, work for which it was structurally unprepared and with which it could not cope.

Wolsey was thus soon obliged to modify his scheme for the Council. Specialization, both of business and personnel, increasingly became the touchstone of his policy, since more sophisticated arrangements—notably differentiation and timetabling of business —had become the key to control of a system under siege from litigants.

Although an archival disaster has limited our knowledge of the Henrician Council, evidence of 580 Council meetings in Star Chamber can be discovered for Wolsey's chancellorship. In respect of 200 meetings we have some form of *acta* or minutes, and in seventy cases we have both *acta* and presence lists.[17] We find that 120 councillors served Henry VIII under Wolsey, thirty-two of whom attended formal meetings in Star Chamber at least once a week during term. The smallest reported attendance in this period was two, the highest fifty-four persons. The typical daily presence varied from between eleven (frequent) to twenty-five (less usual) councillors.[18] This format generally conforms to habits established

---

[15] Ibid. 15, 51.
[16] Ibid. 34–5.
[17] Ibid. 27. I have here updated my figures in line with my latest research.
[18] Ibid. 26–30.

by Henry VII's Star Chamber. Yet there is one important difference. For Wolsey began to appoint specific councillors as deputies
to perform the Council's judicial function, both inside and outside
Star Chamber. He did so in order to free himself and the leading
officers of state and household from the relentless pressure of
suitors. While, then, there was no split of the component parts of
the King's Council before 1529 institutionally speaking, Wolsey
began to make an essential distinction between the Council's executive work and justice.

The initial step was taken in 1517–20, when Wolsey hived off three
committees from Star Chamber 'for the expedition of poor men's
causes'. Staffed by lesser councillors, these tribunals were always
intended to be distinct from Star Chamber, and they did not sit in
the *Camera Stellata* but elsewhere in the palace of Westminster
(mainly in the White Hall and in the treasurer's chamber).[19] Strictly
speaking they do not demonstrate differentiation in the Council
between administration and justice. In and after 1520, however,
Wolsey referred the growing backlog of judicial business in Star
Chamber expressly to junior councillors who met separately from
the plenary Council in Star Chamber, yet whose decisions were
given in the name of 'the king's most honourable Council in the
Star Chamber', and were recorded as its *acta* by the Council's clerk
in the official Star Chamber register.[20] Eight councillors served in
this capacity in 1521 and 1522, and six others joined them later. In
other words, Council committees exclusively devoted to matters of
justice had been provided by Wolsey. The arrangements remained
informal. Wolsey's committees were actually the tangible expression of the Council's need for a separate Court of Star Chamber in
the light of the minister's encouragement of suitors. Yet they were
also a tentative move towards structural change, because they
represented organized distinction between the duties of senior and
junior councillors, and illustrated the validity of special sittings of
Star Chamber which dealt with matters of justice only.

These elementary principles were supplemented by advance timetabling of Council business. At the beginning of Wolsey's chancellorship, justice and administration were freely intermingled at meetings
in Star Chamber. Litigants were normally heard at the bar before
the board (newly erected for the purpose), after the completion

[19] Ibid. 40–2.
[20] Ibid. 38–40.

of the day's executive agenda. Furthermore, both substantive and procedural aspects of legal business were still discharged before the whole Council.[21] Faced with a vastly expanded workload in the wake of his arrival, Wolsey was persuaded of the need to organize efficiently his own and the Council's time. It was resolved in Star Chamber in June 1517 that 'the Lordes have appointed to sitt here on the Mondaie, Tewesdaye, Thursedaye, and Satersdaie; and in the Chauncery on Wensdaye and Fridaie everye weeke.'[22] This order was superseded the following October: 'For reformacion of misorders and other enormityes in the kinges severall Courtes, the Lords have appointed to assemble here everye weeke twoe dayes, that is to saye Wensdaye and Fridaie.'[23] The second order more plainly implied Wolsey's decision to differentiate between the executive and judicial work of the Council in Star Chamber. Better timetabling of the conciliar agenda was preferable to the Council's previous practices: it had become necessary to reserve two sitting days a week for hearing suits, of both alleged 'enormities' and more traditional complaints. The days chosen, moreover, were those adopted by the mature Court of Star Chamber for its weekly sittings. Until abolished by the Long Parliament in 1641, Star Chamber met on Wednesdays and Fridays in term time.

Yet Wolsey's popularization of conciliar justice was not limited to Star Chamber, and the impact of his advent was quickly felt by the councillors attendant on Henry VIII, too. In 1519 Wolsey transferred most of the attendant Council's judicial function to a new sedentary court at the White Hall at Westminster. This court was given appropriate personnel, being staffed by the specialists in conciliar justice from among the former attendant councillors. The first judges were Dr John Clerk, Richard Rawlyns, John Vesey, John Gylberd, Dr Roger Lupton, Dr John Longland, and Dr John Stokesley.[24] The court's sessions, too, were confined to the law terms, and its members only moved away to rejoin the royal progress on those very few occasions when the presence of all available councillors was required at Henry VIII's Court. Styled 'the king's most honourable Council in his Court of Requests', the White Hall Court simultaneously relieved attendant councillors of their

21 Ibid. 36–8, 79–94.
22 BL Lansd. MS 1, fo. 108.
23 Ibid. fo. 108ᵛ.
24 Guy, *Cardinal's Court*, 42–3.

backlog of cases at Court, while sparing suitors the inconvenience and expense of following the itinerant royal entourage.[25] And since Wolsey was soon also delegating Star Chamber business to the White Hall judges as required, the court quickly became recognized as a separate conciliar court of justice, hearing lawsuits only, with a professional, if fluid bench, and developing its own rules of procedure. In fact, the White Hall Court under Wolsey was a clear example of innovation in the Council before 1529. A new conciliar court outside the traditional structure of the late-medieval King's Council had been created. Furthermore, this court was the immediate ancestor of the mature Court of Requests, which was firmly institutionalized after reconstructions of its personnel in 1529 and 1538.[26] Yet in respect of its name, its jurisdiction and venue, the Court of Requests evolved directly out of Wolsey's earlier tribunal.

Wolsey's aspirations for the Council were consummated in his Eltham Ordinance, published in January 1526, and in a supplementary blueprint of uncertain date.[27] In the wake of wider household reforms, Wolsey proposed the creation of a reduced King's Council from within the larger body which was to attend upon the king and perform the administrative and remaining judicial work of the old Council attendant. The twenty 'honourable, virtuous, sadd, wise, experte, and discreete persons' who were to compose this Council were the principal officers of state and household, the bishops of Bath and Lincoln, and the dean of the chapel royal and Dr Richard Wolman—the last pair indicating Wolsey's continued resolve to maintain a Council attendant in which administration was intermingled with justice. However, by allowing the necessary absence in London of the important office-holders, Wolsey reduced this Council for practical purposes to a committee of ten and then to a subcommittee of four, it being finally provided that two councillors at least from among those resident in the household should always be present to advise the king and to supervise matters of justice: 'which direction well observed, the King's highnesse shall

[25] Court of Requests, Miscellaneous Books, REQ 1/104, fos. 68ᵛ, 88ᵛ; Guy, *Cardinal's Court*, 43.

[26] See below, pp. 71, 82–4.

[27] Wolsey's parchment 'original' of the Eltham document is Bod. Lib., MS Laud. Misc. 597. The Council proposals appear there on fos. 30–1. The best printed text is in *A Collection of Ordinances and Regulations for the Government of the Royal Household* (London, 1790), 159–60. Two copies of the supplementary document exist: State Papers, Henry VIII, SP 1/59, fo. 77; SP 1/235, fo. 37. These are calendared in LP IV. App. 67, *Add.* 481.

alwayes be well furnished of an honourable presence of councellors about his Grace, as to his high honour doth apperteyne.'[28] This phraseology was tainted with irony, because Wolsey's obvious motive in removing the leading councillors from Court and concentrating them in Star Chamber was the political one of fortifying his own ministerial power at the expense of Henry's daily counsel. Nevertheless, the Eltham Ordinance commanded the attendant councillors to meet each day in the king's dining chamber at 10 a.m. and 2 p.m.—evidence that Wolsey recognized in token form Henry VIII's enduring wish for a working Council in attendance at Court.

The Eltham Ordinance was supplemented by a scheme for 'the devision of suche maters as shalbe treated by the kinges Councell'. It seems that Wolsey had further refined his thoughts, for he now planned to reform the Council at Westminster by applying the principle of differentiation of function to the full operations of Star Chamber. Twenty-eight named lesser councillors, together with 'the residue of the judges', 'the remnaunt of the barons of theschequyer', the attorney-general and serjeants-at-law were appointed to deal with 'mater in lawe'.[29] Whether the twenty-eight were to constitute an organized Court of Star Chamber or simply a standing committee of councillors working at Wolsey's future direction is not stated. Nor is it apparent whether they were to become 'ordinary councillors' or councillors 'at large' as a result, being excluded from the executive 'inner' (Privy?) Council and retained only for justice, or to remain full members in theory of an undivided King's Council but to specialize exclusively in the judicial component of conciliar work. However, Wolsey's object was probably to streamline the system in Star Chamber in such a way as to permit the principal officers of state and household to undertake future judicial work on a voluntary basis only, thus enabling them to concentrate wholly on the Council's executive function if they wished, while reserving their rights to sit in the 'Court' of Star Chamber should they so desire.

Wolsey's fall transformed this position. Although Sir Thomas More was appointed lord chancellor, his dislike of the king's proposed divorce limited his freedom to participate in the consultative process by which Henry's will was translated into official policy. Henry VIII told More that he would never 'put any man in ruffle or trouble of his conscience', and Edward Foxe, Thomas Cranmer,

---

[28] *Household Ordinances*, 160.
[29] SP 1/59, fo. 77.

and Thomas Cromwell (none of whom was initially in the Council proper) became instead the king's men of business working from Court.[30] Furthermore, without Wolsey's drive and ambition to guide it, the Council ceased to orbit around Westminster rather than Henry's Court, and attendances in Star Chamber under More steadily declined. Seven councillors turned up to meet representatives of the City of London in February 1530.[31] Three plus the lawyers dealt with justice in that month.[32] Six members heard cases in July 1530, and one fewer the following October.[33] Ten councillors mustered themselves for justice in February and May 1531, a larger number because Henry's Court was resident at Westminster and Greenwich respectively on these occasions.[34] The general exodus seems proven, however. Wolsey's departure had left a power vacuum in Star Chamber. We should make no mistake, either, about who was in command after Wolsey's fall. It was Henry VIII himself who directed government strategy after 1529. His influence was never again eclipsed by that of a ministerial *alter rex*. The divorce crisis witnessed the king's first prolonged attention to public affairs, further reinforcing the process by which political gravity shifted away from Star Chamber towards the itinerant Court. In these ways, then, Wolsey's structure was eroded.

Since Henry VIII visited Westminster no more than twenty times between 1529 and 1532, his one extended stay there being from January to early April 1531, the Council attendant again came into prominence.[35] A new 'inner ring' of close councillors advised the king on the divorce and made formal contact with the relevant ambassadors, notably Chapuys (Charles V's envoy) and the papal nuncio. This 'inner ring' comprised the dukes of Norfolk and Suffolk, the earl of Wiltshire (Anne Boleyn's father), Stephen Gardiner, William lord Sandys, Robert Ratcliffe, earl of Sussex, Henry Courtenay, marquess of Exeter, and Sir William Fitzwilliam.[36] Thomas Cromwell joined their ranks towards the end of 1530.

---

[30] J. A. Guy, *The Public Career of Sir Thomas More* (Brighton, 1980), 98–112, 127–36.

[31] Star Chamber Proceedings, Henry VIII, STAC 2/17/405.

[32] STAC 2/2/160.

[33] Ellesmere MS 2659; Star Chamber Proceedings, Miscellaneous, STAC 10/4, Pt. 2 (11 Oct. 1530).

[34] STAC 2/17/399; STAC 10/4, Pt. 2 (5 May 1531).

[35] Henry VIII's itinerary, OBS 1419.

[36] *LP* V. 45, 216, 564, 1013, 1633; Guy, *Public Career,* 127–30.

When need required, the 'inner ring' commuted to Star Chamber and to Parliament, but it remained informal and unorganized—it was not a Privy Council. It marked, rather, the configuration of 'political' or 'secret' councillors within the larger body to whom Henry turned for guidance on his 'great matter'. Yet executive affairs were vested firmly in its hands and not in More's in Star Chamber. An intermediate stage had been reached between Wolsey's system and that which prevailed on 10 August 1540. One aspect of this new situation was that executive policy and decisions had become concentrated in the hands of a chosen few at Court several years before the creation of the Privy Council. This development was a pragmatic response to political reality, not a planned exercise in statecraft.

When Sir Thomas More resigned the chancellorship in May 1532, he was succeeded by Sir Thomas Audley. It was Cromwell, however, who became Henry VIII's second minister. As the king's parliamentary manager since the end of 1531, Cromwell helped prepare the Act of Annates and the Supplication against the Ordinaries, and took part in drafting an abortive treason bill in readiness for the session of 1532.[37] But Cromwell knew better than to burden himself with the chancellorship and full judicial duties of Star Chamber and Chancery, as Wolsey had done. When the time came for him to assume major offices, Cromwell initially ensured that key Court posts were among his choices: the mastership of the jewels was acquired on 14 April 1532, the principal secretaryship obtained about 15 April 1534.[38] As Professor Elton observed, 'Cromwell was never more powerful, more ubiquitous in the administration, more completely in control of the day-to-day government of the country, than he was through the office of principal secretary.'[39] Although there had been no historic connection between the King's Council and the king's secretary, Cromwell had changed this as early as May 1533, when he was still no more than a substitute secretary in the absence of Stephen Gardiner, the king's official secretary. Cromwell had then jotted down on the back of a letter a list of matters under the heading 'Remembrancys to be put into my boke for thinges done in the Cownsayle', which already suggests his responsibility for executing Council decisions.[40] The

37 Guy, *Public Career*, 176–89.
38 Elton, *Tudor Revolution*, 99, 123–5, 298–303.
39 Ibid. 127.   40 *LP* VI. 551; Elton, *Tudor Revolution*, 360.

business included Irish affairs, wrongful imprisonment of the
king's servants, replies to letters, the recovery of lead embezzled
from the crown, and the decay of husbandry—perennial Council
matters. A cache of more important policy documents dated
December 1533 concerning the Reformation and its defence reveals
that by then Cromwell had achieved control of the Council's agenda
and minutes after the fashion of any attentive (or aspiring) minister
for internal affairs.[41]

Yet Cromwell's context was circumscribed. First, Wolsey had
already introduced specialization and timetabling of business into
the operations of the Council. Star Chamber sat as a superior court
of the realm on Wednesdays and Fridays, and its bureaucratic
machinery had been improved shortly after More's resignation. The
office of clerk of the writs and processes before the King's Council in
the Star Chamber at Westminster (a cumbersome but exact title) was
created by letters patent on 5 October 1532: Thomas Pope was named
its first incumbent.[42] He was to organize the writing, issue and return
of writs of *subpoena*, attachments, commissions or any other legal
process ordered by the Council, and no one was henceforward to
engage in such work save at the new clerk's direction. Whereas Star
Chamber had hitherto been reliant on Chancery clerks for its legal
process, a situation which had caused delays and confusion, now it
had its own professional secretariat—recognition of the extent to
which the mature court's effective emergence was perceived before
the advent of the Privy Council.

Second, Wolsey's White Hall Court continued to function, and it,
too, was becoming institutionalized, since its personnel had been
reconstituted by Wolsey in January 1529. Fifteen councillors or legal
specialists were appointed 'for the heryng of power Mennes causes in
the kynges Courte of Requestes', and thereafter these judges worked
regularly together, sometimes in groups and sometimes alone, sitting
three or four times a week during the law terms, and functioning independently of the Council attendant or Star Chamber.[43]

Third, the Council's executive activities, as already said, were
necessarily concentrated in the hands of Henry VIII's 'political'
councillors at Court during the divorce crisis and break with Rome.

---

[41] Elton, *Tudor Revolution*, 361–7.
[42] *LP* V. 1499 (8); *LP* VII. 1601 (33); Chancery, Patent Rolls, C 66/664, m. 33
(ultra-violet photograph).
[43] REQ 1/5, fo. 43ᵛ; Guy, *Cardinal's Court*, 49–50.

In this respect, it was no accident that Cromwell kept his own 'boke for thinges done in the Cownsayle', because the official Council record, prior to the creation of the new series of Privy Council registers in August 1540, remained the Westminster register of Wolsey's Star Chamber.[44] Manifestly, the lack of convenient access to its official registers must have caused the executive Council immense inconvenience after 1529—hence Cromwell's private record. This problem was compounded by the fact that the White Hall Court had already appropriated the old registers of the Council attendant for use as court books of orders and decrees, and those records, too, were kept permanently at Westminster.

We should explore here a little further the Council's clerical arrangements, since these highlight its formal structure on the eve of the Privy Council's birth. Richard Eden, archdeacon of Middlesex, had been appointed principal clerk of the Council in 1512.[45] He was previously employed as junior clerk during the tenure of John Meautis in the principal clerkship. As the senior officer after 1512, Eden received a fixed annual stipend of 40 marks. The junior clerkship carried a stipend of £20. Two assistant clerks worked under Eden during Wolsey's ascendancy: Richard Lee had succeeded Eden in the junior clerkship by May 1516;[46] Thomas Elyot was appointed by Wolsey to an extraordinary clerkship in the last months of 1523.[47] These three remained in office until 20 April 1530, when a new patent was issued. This granted the senior clerkship to Richard and Thomas Eden in survivorship on the surrender of Richard's patent of 1512.[48] Lee resigned his post early in Sir Thomas More's chancellorship, and Elyot was dismissed.[49] In May 1530 Thomas Eden was sworn in as principal clerk by More: his uncle, having secured the succession, withdrew from active service.[50] Yet the junior clerkship of the Council was left vacant in 1530, only to be filled in January 1533 by Thomas Derby. But when Derby was appointed, he was named 'Clarke of our Counsaill *at-*

---

[44] J. A. Guy, 'Wolsey's Star Chamber: a study in archival reconstruction', *Journal of the Society of Archivists*, v (1975), 169–80.

[45] *LP* I. i. 1462 (26).

[46] *LP* II. i. 1857.

[47] S. E. Lehmberg, *Sir Thomas Elyot* (Austin, 1964), 28–9.

[48] *LP* IV. iii. 6490.

[49] Lee's hand disappears from the Star Chamber records in More's chancellorship; Elyot's does not (e.g. STAC 2/3/219, 2/10/263–4, 2/13/64–8, 2/15/93), but his dismissal is on his own admission (Lehmberg, 28).

[50] BL Harg. MS 216, fo. 127ᵛ.

tending uppon our person'.[51] In other words, the informal 'inner ring' of executive councillors attendant on Henry VIII at Court had now been provided with a salaried clerk—the first test of institutional veracity. This junior clerkship had long been attached to Wolsey's Star Chamber, but was now linked to the king's 'political' councillors. Derby's warrant, too, authorized him to receive back-pay from midsummer 1532, which suggests that he had served the Council at Court from the moment More resigned. Above all it was Derby who, five years later, in March 1538, first appeared in the accounts of the treasurer of the chamber as 'clerk of the Privy Council', again at the junior clerk's salary of £20.[52] We cannot read too much into terminology alone. Yet it appears from the records of Star Chamber that Derby never served the Council there as junior clerk. Thomas Eden's hand alone is found in the Westminster archive after 1530, and it seems that Eden became sole law clerk to what was becoming a sole law court. However, other clerks besides Derby handled the paperwork of the executive Council under Cromwell, and it was William Paget, not Derby, who was named clerk of the Privy Council on 10 August 1540.[53] Yet Paget's place was descended from Derby's. In March 1539 Derby received his full year's salary of £20, and in June following was paid £10 in advance from his next year's pay despite already having been appointed secretary of the Council in the West.[54] When Paget was named the Privy Council's clerk in August 1540, his salary was maintained at the effective £30 of Derby's last year.[55] In this way the junior clerkship was silently abolished, and Eden and Paget became equals, serving separate institutions at comparable salaries.

It is clear that a new stage in the Council's development had begun when Henry VIII's 'political' councillors gathered at Court after Wolsey's fall. The executive Council was closer again to the small, but vibrant, Council attendant of Henry VII than to the large King's Council under Wolsey. It was not the Privy Council. However, our view that the reshaped Council attendant of More's time may justly be regarded as a precursor of the Privy Council is reinforced by its need for a clerk in mid-1532. In complementary vein, Eden's sole

51 Elton, *Tudor Revolution*, 335, 441–2.
52 *LP* XIII. ii. 528; Elton, *Tudor Revolution*, 335.
53 PC 2/1, p. 1; Nicolas, vii. 4.
54 *LP* XIV. ii. 306, 311.
55 *LP* XVI. 107 (3).

clerkship in Star Chamber after 1530 and Pope's new process office there suggest that the mature court's effective arrival preceded the reforms of Thomas Cromwell. This is not to deny that Cromwell's work had major repercussions for the bench in Star Chamber. It is simply to doubt whether the Court of Star Chamber sprang substantially from his conscious innovation.

What, then, was Cromwell's contribution? When the Privy Council of nineteen members met on 10 August 1540, twelve days after his execution, it resolved:

That there shuld be a clerk attendaunt upon the sayde Counsaill to writte, entre and registre all such decrees, determinacions, lettres and other such thinges as he shuld be appoynted to entre in a booke to remayne alwayes as a leger aswell for the discardge of the sayde Counsaillors touching such thinges as they shuld passe from tyme to tyme, as alsoo for a memoriall unto them of their owne procedinges, unto the whiche office William Paget, late the Quenes Secretary, was appointed by the kinges highnes, and sworne in the presence of the sayde Counsaill the daye and yere abovesayde.[56]

Had Cromwell provided the executive arm of the Council with a professional secretariat and its own registers, this order would be redundant and inexplicable. It is plain that Cromwell did not give the Privy Council organized bureaucracy beyond that furnished by Derby's haphazard junior clerkship of the Council and his own 'boke for things done in the Cownsayle'. However, the King's Council of 1540 was a Privy Council, whereas that of 1532 was not. Cromwell's work was thus to reduce the size of the Council to the level first mooted in Wolsey's Eltham Ordinance, and to exclude from the Privy Council and Court of Star Chamber those persons not chosen as members of the streamlined body. Second-rank former members of the unreformed Council now became 'ordinary councillors' or councillors 'at large', enjoying honorific status during their lifetimes, while being employed at Court to sift through suits and petitions and to pass them on to the Privy Council, Star Chamber or Court of Requests for appropriate action.[57] In this way, the post-1529 'political' Council attained definite institutional embodiment: the 'close', 'secret' or privy councillors of Henry VIII became the sole King's Council, though it will be shown that the

---

[56] PC 2/1, p. 1; Nicolas, vii. 4.
[57] Elton, *Tudor Revolution*, 323, 335–6; see below, p. 78.

consequential reorganization of the Courts of Star Chamber and Requests was not completed during Cromwell's lifetime.[58]

To some extent conciliar reform must have been impelled by the break with Rome and Henry VIII's promulgation of royal supremacy. For at no time since 1485 had the need for radical decisions and confidentiality in the Council been so pronounced. We cannot doubt that Cromwell's influence was dynamic. In June 1534 he noted on the back of a letter, 'To remembre the Kyng for the establyshment of the Counsayle', and we readily concur with Professor Elton that Cromwell was thinking of the changes which were manifest by 1540.[59] However, the Council had already started to contract in practice. When Chapuys met it at Westminster in May 1534, in order to be told of the obstinacy of Queen Katherine and Princess Mary in refusing the oath of succession, fourteen councillors were present plus 'all the principal judges'.[60] When it tackled executive business in October, November and December the same year, it again comprised fourteen members, including two judges.[61] Henry's 'political' councillors predominated, but the transitional nature of the Council's membership in 1534 is highlighted, too, by the October list. Out of the fourteen names included, we find ten former leaders of Wolsey's Council, nine members of the Council in 1536–7, and seven members of the Privy Council of 1540.[62] There was a certain underlying continuity in the Council's membership during the 1530s. Yet the retention of the judges as Council members in 1534 proves that the Privy Council did not exist then. As finally reformed, the Privy Council excluded the judges, king's serjeants, and lord mayors of London, who had traditionally taken the councillor's title.[63]

---

[58] See below, pp. 80–4.

[59] *LP Add.* 944; Elton, *Tudor Revolution*, 342.

[60] *LP* VII. 690; Elton, *Tudor Revolution*, 337.

[61] STAC 10/4, Pt. 2(? Oct., 4 Nov., 25 Nov., 2 Dec. 1534).

[62] Of the fourteen, the dukes of Norfolk and Suffolk, the earls of Wiltshire, Oxford, and Sussex, William Kingston, Richard Weston, John Dauncy, Robert Norwich CJCP, and Anthony Fitzherbert JCP were prominent in Wolsey's Council; Sir Thomas Audley, the dukes of Norfolk and Suffolk, the earls of Oxford and Sussex, Thomas Cromwell, Stephen Gardiner, Edward Foxe, and William Kingston were members of the Council in 1536–7; and Audley, Norfolk and Suffolk, Sussex, Cromwell, Gardiner, and Kingston were privy councillors in 1540. This unpublished document is badly damaged but still legible. It was discovered among unsorted miscellanea in 1982, but it was added to STAC 10/4.

[63] Elton, *Studies*, iii. 27 and n. 55.

The exact moment when the Privy Council was created is elusive. A Privy Council may indeed have existed informally before it was fully organized as a new institution. Professor Elton dated Cromwell's 'fundamental reform' of the Council to the middle of 1536.[64] Yet the evidence of Council structure in the late summer of that year is somewhat equivocal. Henry VIII was then concerned about an outbreak of plague at Westminster and its effect on his plans for Jane Seymour's coronation. Should the event be postponed? Henry was at Windsor on 27 September 1536, musing on the problem. He needed advice from Cromwell and the Council, and dictated his wishes to Ralph Sadler, his acting secretary and Cromwell's agent at Court.[65]

'Wherefore . . . it were good, that all my Counsaile were assembled here, that we might consulte, and determyn uppon every thing, touching the same accordinglye. And so', quod he, 'wryte to my Lorde Pryvey Seale, and sende him worde that my Lorde Admyrall[66] is here, Mr. Comptroller,[67] and the Bisshop of Hereford[68] be here, and pray him, also,' quod he, 'to come hither indelayedlie; and then,' quod he, 'we shall sone be at a poynte. And,' quod he, 'in case my Lorde Chauncelour be nere London, and all that be there of the Prevye Counsaile, pray my Lorde Prevy Seale to bryng them with him.'

Sadler urged Cromwell to make haste, and he repeated Henry's instructions: 'It may please your Lordeship to bryng with you suche, as be there, of the Prevy Counsaile, and my Lorde Chauncelour, also, if he be nere London, for so is the Kinges pleasure.'[69]

Was Audley, then, not one of the Privy Council in September 1536? Was the Privy Council less than 'all my Counsaile' at that date? The organized Privy Council should unquestionably have included the lord chancellor of the day. On 10 August 1540 he was second on the official list of nineteen privy councillors; in 1541 he was described as 'head' of the Privy Council in London.[70] Henry VIII, too, had personally to summon this meeting of the Privy Council some months after that body's presumed arrival at Court as a fixed institution emancipated from the whim of the moment

---

[64] Ibid. 28.
[65] *St. Pap.* i. 459–61. The calendared version at *LP* XI. 501 is inadequate.
[66] Sir William Fitzwilliam.
[67] Sir William Paulet.
[68] Edward Foxe.
[69] *St. Pap.* i. 461.
[70] PC 2/1, p. 1; *St. Pap.* i. 683.

and its former dependence on the royal household. A meeting of the whole Privy Council would have been unremarkable, save for the fact that Henry had to use his own secretary to convene it. The procedure adopted by the mature Privy Council in the 1540s, when the board was often split between the Court and London, was that members themselves summoned absent colleagues by letters composed in the name of the Council.[71] Henry's instructions to Sadler belie any easy assumptions that regular meetings of a permanent board of government were already an established feature of the Privy Council's existence.[72]

In fact, the permanent Privy Council was probably structured during the crisis surrounding the Pilgrimage of Grace in the autumn of 1536. Cromwell, who with Audley and others was singled out in the Pontefract Articles for 'condyne punyshment', made a tactical withdrawal from the scene of action, and the Council as a body came into prominence.[73] Its membership, simultaneously, was more precisely defined. Henry VIII listed twelve members in his reply to the rebels' demands:

In our Pryvey Counsell We have the Duke of Norfolke, the Duke of Suffolke, the Marques of Excester, the Lorde Stewarde (when he may com),[74] the Erle of Oxforde, the Erle of Sussex, the Lorde Sandes our Chamberleyn, the Lorde Admyrall Tresourer of our House,[75] Sir Willyam Poulet Comptroller of our House: and of the Spiritualtee, the Bisshop of Hereford, the Bisshop of Chichester, and the Bishop of Wynchester.[76]

We should add Cromwell, Audley, and Cranmer to the list—the overseers of the Reformation whose existence it was prudent to forget during the Pilgrimage.[77] This yields an executive Council of fifteen, the term 'Privy Council' being manifestly significant in this context. Yet even more important is the concrete evidence of Council membership obtained from Professor Elton's study of instructions to captains in the field between 14 October 1536 and 8 April 1537.[78]

---

[71] Nicolas, vii. 49, 70, 72, 215; *St. Pap.* i. 655–6; Elton, *Tudor Revolution*, 323–4.

[72] Although Henry VIII had personally to summon the Privy Council to Westminster in the winter of 1540, this was because members had temporarily been allowed to disperse 'to their owne howses'. Nicolas, vii. 89.

[73] This paragraph summarizes Elton, *Tudor Revolution*, 337–40.

[74] George Talbot, earl of Shrewsbury.

[75] Sir William Fitzwilliam, created earl of Southampton in Oct. 1537.

[76] *St. Pap.* i. 508.

[77] Elton, *Tudor Revolution*, 338.   [78] Ibid.

Linking Elton's findings with Henry's own list of 'privy councillors', we may finalize the membership of the 'emergency' Council of 1536–7:[79]

> Thomas Lord Cromwell, vicegerent in spirituals, lord privy seal, etc.
>
> Thomas Cranmer, archbishop of Canterbury
>
> Sir Thomas Audley, lord chancellor
>
> Thomas Howard, duke of Norfolk, lord treasurer
>
> Charles Brandon, duke of Suffolk
>
> Henry Courtenay, marquess of Exeter
>
> George Talbot, earl of Shrewsbury, lord steward of the household
>
> John de Vere, earl of Oxford, lord great chamberlain
>
> Robert Ratcliffe, earl of Sussex
>
> Cuthbert Tunstall, bishop of Durham
>
> Edwarde Foxe, bishop of Hereford
>
> Richard Sampson, bishop of Chichester
>
> Stephen Gardiner, bishop of Winchester
>
> William Lord Sandys, lord chamberlain of the household
>
> Sir William Fitzwilliam, lord admiral, treasurer of the household, chancellor of the duchy of Lancaster
>
> Sir William Paulet, controller of the household, master of the wards
>
> Sir William Kingston, vice-chamberlain of the household, captain of the guard
>
> Sir John Russell
>
> Edward Seymour, Viscount Beauchamp

The list describes a body of nineteen, the same number as that of the Privy Council established in August 1540.[80] In particular, the judges and legal professionals of the old King's Council had disappeared. We have no specific record of the means by which second-rank councillors and the judges and lawyers were excluded. However, their undoubted absence after the outbreak of the Pilgrimage is confirmed by a list of 'The Conseill' prepared in October 1537, which mentions none of them.[81]

---

[79] I have reproduced Elton's list with the addition of the earl of Shrewsbury and Bishop Gardiner, as he suggested (*Tudor Revolution*, 339–40).

[80] Ibid. 340.

[81] *LP* XIII. i. 1. The document lists fourteen names, and excludes the judges and lawyers, and the clergy.

It is clear that the 'emergency' Council of 1536–7 and the Privy Council of August 1540 were directly related. Seven members of the 1536–7 body dropped out: Cromwell and the marquess of Exeter by execution, the earls of Shrewsbury and Oxford and Bishop Foxe by natural death, and Sir William Paulet and Bishop Sampson by exclusion. To fill their places, seven men holding key appointments in state and household were promoted: Sir Richard Rich, chancellor of the Court of Augmentations, Sir John Baker, chancellor of First Fruits and Tenths, Sir Thomas Cheyney, treasurer of the household, Sir Anthony Browne, master of the horse, Sir Anthony Wingfield, vice-chamberlain of the household, and Thomas Wriothesley and Ralph Sadler, who jointly acted as principal secretary after Cromwell.[82] The twelve other members of the Council of 1536–7 carried on as members of the organized Privy Council. There was no return to the relative informality of the Council attendant's proceedings since 1529. A new institution had been born, the élite board of politicians and departmental ministers that governed England under the crown until the breakdown of 1641–2. Yet the 'emergency' Council had been Henry's and Cromwell's pragmatic response to crisis, rather than a conscious exercise in statecraft.

The case for Cromwell's pragmatism—by which I mean his willingness to act within the confines of political reality and Henry VIII's immediate needs—is developed by a closer look at the events of 1536–7. The 'emergency' Council at work during the crisis of the Pilgrimage included six obvious religious conservatives: Thomas Howard, Henry Courtenay, George Talbot, Cuthbert Tunstall, Stephen Gardiner, Sir William Fitzwilliam, and Sir William Paulet. It is really quite striking how difficult Cromwell's task of managing such men must have been, given his radicalism as vicegerent in spirituals and his doctrinal affinity to Cranmer. It is true that Cromwell's radicalism was more apparent after July 1537 than before.[83] Yet Cromwell's task of Council reform in 1536 was hardly a bed of roses. Not only was he under immense pressure from Catholic opponents during and after the Pilgrimage—it was his conservative enemies, after all, who destroyed him in 1540—but the

---

[82] This was first deduced (with minor errors) by Pollard, see *EHR* xxxviii (1923), 43–4.

[83] J. A. Guy, *Christopher St German on Chancery and Statute* (London, Selden Society, 1985), 46.

king himself was also challenged head on by the Pilgrims to expel Cromwell and Cranmer from positions of influence as 'subverters of the good laws of this realm and maynteners of the false sect of those heretiques.'[84] The Pilgrims next exhumed a fifteenth-century debate about Council membership that focused on the supposed duty of the monarch to share political power with the old aristocracy and others born to traditional conciliar status (*consiliarii nati*) —this debate was itself an extension of medieval haggling. Thus when debating their grievances at Pontefract Castle, the rebels received one contribution in the form of a paper by Sir Thomas Tempest, who was ill and unable to attend in person, that expressly demanded a 'Council for the Commonwealth' and made ominous remarks about the depositions of Edward II and Richard II.[85]

In other words, the politics of 1536–7 were turbulent, volatile, and tense: this was not a period conducive to tidy administrative planning. This chapter accepts that Cromwell had a vision of conciliar reform which he had inherited from Wolsey. It is, however, too much to suppose that the context of his work permitted administrative reform as a matter of fundamental principle. Whether or not Cromwell espoused coherent principles as a human being (the evidence does not permit us to debate this question), he lacked the political pre-eminence in 1536–7 to implement his wishes save by the back door. The magnates were on the alert; Council membership was a political issue. If the reformed Privy Council was Cromwell's achievement it was always a Trojan horse.

Our impression of Cromwell's pragmatism is reinforced by the evidence of his work in Star Chamber. For the usual assumption

[84] *LP* XI. 1246; Anthony Fletcher, *Tudor Rebellions* (London, 2nd edn., 1979), 128.

[85] *LP* XI. 1244. Fletcher's version of this document is truncated and misleading. Evidence of the political debate on Council membership in the 1530s may be found *inter alia* in the writings of Christopher St German, Sir Thomas Elyot, and Thomas Starkey. See Guy, *St German*, 26, 127–8; Elyot, *Pasquil the Playne* (London, 1533); K. M. Burton, ed., *A Dialogue between Reginald Pole and Thomas Lupset* (London, 1948), 155–6, 166–7. Forthcoming articles by Professor T. F. Mayer will illuminate Starkey's thought and its historical context, see especially his 'Faction and Ideology: Thomas Starkey's *Dialogue*', *HJ* xxviii (1985), 1–25. Elyot's writings will be treated by Mr Frederick Conrad in a Johns Hopkins University dissertation. For a window into late fifteenth-century debate on the Council see the writings of Sir John Fortescue: *The Governance of England*, ed. C. Plummer (Oxford, 1885); *De Laudibus Legum Angliae*, ed. S. B. Chrimes (Cambridge, 1942); *The Works of Sir John Fortescue, Knight, Chief Justice of England and Lord Chancellor to King Henry the Sixth*, ed. T. Fortescue (Lord Clermont), privately printed (London, 1869), 475–6.

that the Privy Council's advent automatically gave the Court of Star Chamber its settled constitution needs revision. The Court of Star Chamber was the King's Council sitting as a court. If Cromwell's reform of 1536–7 had defined the membership of the new executive Council as a matter of constitutional principle, then logic dictates that those not of the Privy Council should not be found sitting in Star Chamber thereafter. But such men sat in Star Chamber for several years. From February 1540 to May 1544 former councillors or puisne justices who were not privy councillors sat as full judges in the Court of Star Chamber.[86] They included Lord Mordaunt, Lord St John (formerly Sir William Paulet), Sir Thomas Denys, Sir William Essex, and Sir John Gage. Two of these were soon to become privy councillors, Gage in October 1540, and St John in December 1542. However, the other three persons had no claim to sit in Star Chamber—unless of course Cromwell's reform was progressive, rather than fundamental. By October 1544 the bench of Star Chamber was normally restricted to privy councillors plus the chief justices, the composition that was to remain unaltered until the court's abolition in 1641, and it is plain that the unquestioned existence of the Privy Council for four years was responsible.[87] In fact, we need not doubt that Cromwell originally initiated this change in Star Chamber, for the creation of an organized Privy Council was the perfect opportunity for providing the court with the small professional bench that completed its development. Yet the process was pragmatic—Cromwell did his best within the limitations of the moment. As in the case of the Privy Council established and given a permanent clerk and records in August 1540, his work had to be completed by others after his execution. Even then the theory of Star Chamber's restricted membership was not always accepted. The issue was contested in 1563 in the earl of Hertford's case, when non-conciliar barons who claimed a right to sit in the court had to be ousted by Nicholas Bacon, lord keeper of the great seal.[88] Sir Thomas Smith, too, was unsure of the rules: he thought that Star Chamber's bench comprised

---

[86] Corpus Christi College, Oxford, MS 196, pp. 116–56; Bod. Lib., MS Eng. hist. c. 304, fos. 317–46ᵛ; BL Add. MS 4521, fos. 120–51ᵛ; Guildhall Library, London, MS 1751, pp. 199–250. Two extracts are printed (with minor slips in references to MSS) in J. H. Baker, ed., *The Reports of Sir John Spelman* (2 vols., London, Selden Society, 1977–8), ii. 351–2.

[87] Elton, *Tudor Revolution*, 344.

[88] Elton, *Tudor Constitution*, 165.

'the Lorde Chauncellor, and the Lordes and other of the privie
Counsell, so many as will, and other Lordes and Barons which be
not of the privie Counsell' plus the chief justices.[89] Insiders knew
better. William Mill, an Elizabethan clerk of Star Chamber, was
'often told' by his father, an attorney in the Henrician court, that
'noe man should sitt in ye Courte but if hee were sworne of the
Councell, and that the Clerke of the Councell should goe unto him
and declare unto him that hee ought not to sitt there but if hee were
sworne.'[90] Yet this definition remains imprecise when applied to
Henry VIII's last years. Councillors 'at large', excluded from the
Privy Council but sworn councillors none the less, were still within
its terms, and the probability is that membership of Star Chamber
was settled in the last resort not by constitutional principle (always
presumed), but by practical politics. What counted was the crown's
ability to advise those whom it preferred not to attend Parliament,
Privy Council, or Star Chamber to stay away.[91]

Outside Star Chamber the impact of the new situation was most
forcibly felt in the White Hall Court at Westminster. The Privy
Council's creation severed the direct link between Wolsey's
tribunal and the King's Council, which raised the issue of the
authority by which the former might best continue its work.[92]
Under Sir Thomas More the White Hall Court was still served by
the councillors Wolsey had appointed in 1529. After May 1531
these judges described themselves in decrees as Henry VIII's
'Courte of Requestes'.[93] However, by 1536–7 Richard Sampson,
bishop of Chichester, was the only member of the White Hall
bench who remained in the Council proper. On 23 January 1538
Cromwell thus commissioned Sampson, Nicholas Hare, Thomas
Thirlby, Edmund Bonner, and Edward Carne as judges in the
court.[94] Sampson had been left over from Wolsey's bench of 1529,
and Hare and his fellows were active in the court under Cromwell.[95]

[89] *De Republica Anglorum* (STC 22857), cited from Scolar Press reprint
(London, 1970), 94.   [90] BL Harg. MS 216, fo. 103ᵛ.
[91] For instances of this method of management, see S. E. Lehmberg, *The Reformation Parliament* (Cambridge, 1970), 183, 218. Yet it is curious that direct
evidence of the means by which former councillors were excluded from the Privy
Council is absent. This has to be seen as a victory for consensus politics.
[92] D. A. Knox, 'The Court of Requests in the Reign of Edward VI' (Cambridge
Ph.D. thesis, 1974), 99–117; Elton, *Tudor Constitution*, 187–8.
[93] REQ 1/5, fos. 127ᵛ, 129, 138ᵛ, 140 ff.
[94] Hill, *Ancient State*, 132.
[95] Court of Requests, Proceedings, REQ 2/3/112, 2/12/184.

The five judges named to the bench of Requests in 1538 soon became known as masters of requests. Yet this development was not achieved during Cromwell's lifetime. The title 'master of requests' was not officially employed under the Tudors until January 1541, and then it mainly related to the sorting of petitions or 'requests' addressed to the crown which the 'masters' had undertaken on behalf of the Privy Council.[96] Thus the Privy Council resolved on 6 October 1540 that household officials should no longer trouble Henry VIII at Court with petitions or suits, but should hand them in writing 'to such of his graces ordinary Counsaill as was appoynted to attende upon his Maiestyes person for those and like other purposes; which Counsaill shuld take such order in their said sutes from tyme to tyme as shall apperteyne.'[97] The 'ordinary councillors' best qualified to hear petitions in October 1540 were the judges of Requests, and it is easy to see why they were chosen. By 1545–6 the perfected system of two masters-in-ordinary was fully operational, to be modified in 1562 when Elizabeth added two masters of requests extraordinary to the two ordinary masters.[98]

Yet one permanent feature of Requests practice was formalized under Cromwell. A rule was established that the bench should necessarily include one expert in common, as opposed to civil law—to advise the civilians on land law, deeds of title, and cases of debt. Although common lawyers had been members of Wolsey's bench of 1529, it is not obvious how many of them consistently attended in practice. Of Cromwell's nominees appointed in 1538, Hare was the common lawyer. He was succeeded by Robert Southwell in March 1540.[99]

The break with the Privy Council was a mixed blessing for Requests. On the one hand, the court gained a momentum rarely known to Wolsey. From 1541 to 1544, an average of 137 suits per annum were heard, whereas the normal ceiling before 1529 had been some 86 per annum.[100] On the other hand, the need to justify its authority as a stem of the Council frustrated its leaders under Elizabeth and the early Stuarts. Sir Edward Coke objected that in

---

[96] Nicolas, vii. 112; *LP* XVI. 427, 465; Knox, 105, 108–10. Masters of requests were active in the tasks of sorting and preferring of petitions even after the abolition of the Court of Requests. See *CSPD Charles II, 1665–6*, 575; Knox, 109 and n. 3.

[97] PC 2/1, p. 43; Nicolas, vii. 51–2.

[98] Knox, 108–10; Elton, *Tudor Constitution*, 188.

[99] *LP* XV. 436 (56); Knox, 111–13.

[100] Calculated from REQ 1/4–7, 104–5.

Henry VIII's reign the masters of requests had 'usurped power' by obtaining commissions allowing them to decide cases in equity.[101] He chose to forget the court's conciliar origins—it was a case of invincible ignorance. Yet he had a point, for the exclusive nature of the Privy Council yielded hostages to fortune. In fact, Cromwell had purposely endowed the judges of requests with symbols of Council membership. They swore a councillor's oath; they were attached to the royal household as 'the King's Council'.[102] For a while the order and decree books of Requests even reverted to obsolete terminology: 'the kinges honourable Counsell' was used instead of the 'Courte of Requestes' of More's years.[103] Such terminology was enshrined in a paper copied in 1543 by Robert Dacres. The document summarized Cromwell's measures and forms the earliest procedural conspectus of the mature Court of Requests.[104] Yet comparison of this paper with the records of the 1520s shows how little things had changed. Cromwell gave the Court of Requests its professional bench, but the procedure and rules of form he simply borrowed from Wolsey. The basic blueprint for the court's development was already in existence.

In conclusion, we should note that the organized Privy Council bore a striking resemblance to the body proposed in Wolsey's Eltham Ordinance of 1526. The Privy Council of August 1540 had nineteen members; the Eltham Ordinance had prescribed twenty.[105] The groups represented in 1526 and 1540 were the same—a mixture of church, state, new nobility, and household.[106] Some individuals were common to both lists: the dukes of Norfolk and Suffolk, Sir William Fitzwilliam, Sir William Kingston, and Bishop Tunstall. Officers present in both years included the lord chancellor, lord treasurer, lord steward, keeper of the privy seal (Fitzwilliam *vice* Cromwell), and lord great chamberlain, the treasurer, controller, and vice-chamberlain of the household, and the chancellor of the duchy, captain of the guard, and king's secretary (in 1540 the divided post of principal secretary). In *The Tudor Revolution*, Professor Elton agreed that Cromwell's reforms were 'not altogether original'. On the whole he 'simply organized the loose inner ring

101 Elton, *Tudor Constitution*, 192–3.
102 PC 2/1, pp. 41–2; Nicolas, vii. 49, 51; Hill, *Ancient State*, 24–5.
103 Hill, *Ancient State*, 133–48.
104 Ibid. 233–7.
105 Elton, *Tudor Revolution*, 347.
106 Ibid. 349.

which he found in existence on the lines of the government board which Wolsey had planned on paper.'[107]

We cannot doubt, then, that Wolsey's system of conciliar justice and the theory of his Eltham Ordinance profoundly influenced Thomas Cromwell's opinion of the optimum organization of the traditional King's Council. The divorce crisis saw the closing of ranks within the Council, and the Pilgrimage of Grace gave primacy to Henry VIII's 'political' councillors. The 'emergency' Council of 1536–7 was turned into an organized Privy Council, but Cromwell does not seem to have had the political pre-eminence needed to rule the reformed body as Wolsey had governed Star Chamber; his failure to gain an assured ascendancy was personally damaging. In the wake of these events the benches of Star Chamber and Requests needed reconstruction, since these courts had hitherto been the Council sitting judicially. Yet this task was not completed in Star Chamber until 1544. Furthermore, Cromwell failed to give the Privy Council organized bureaucracy during his lifetime. The permanent secretariat that completed the Privy Council's arrival as a 'modern' board of government was not created until 10 August 1540, when nineteen privy councillors publicly declared their hand. Cromwell's work was also limited in scope. He reduced the size of the Council and defined its membership permanently. Yet the Courts of Star Chamber and Requests continued business as usual. Venue, business, and procedure in the courts were untouched by the changes of the 1530s, save that Cromwell formalized the rule that the bench of Requests should always include a common lawyer.

In other words, reform of the King's Council in the reign of Henry VIII was progressive and pragmatic, and did not exclusively depend on any one act of fundamental change. Cromwell's role in the shaping of the Privy Council and Courts of Star Chamber and Requests was significant. Yet Wolsey's creative ideas were a genuine landmark. In addition, Cromwell was obliged to act within the limitations of prevailing conditions and Henry VIII's immediate needs. Our conclusion does not categorically deny that the changes of the 1530s were 'crowded together so thickly and so deliberately that only the term "revolution" can describe what happened.'[108] It does, however, raise questions about the authorship, periodization and causes of those changes.

[107] Ibid. 349–50.　　　　　　　　[108] Ibid. 427.

CHAPTER 4

TWO REVOLUTIONS IN TUDOR GOVERNMENT: THE FORMATION AND ORGANIZATION OF MARY I's PRIVY COUNCIL*

DALE HOAK

THE governments of Edward VI and Mary I, never much praised by historians of Tudor England, were pushed close to the edge of historiographical irrelevance in 1953 with the announcement of Thomas Cromwell's 'revolutionary' programme of governmental reform. Regimes hitherto regarded as 'bankrupt', 'sterile', or merely divisive, were rendered anachronistic as well by the new standards of institutional efficiency. It was thought that the Councils of Somerset and Northumberland, for example, because they were bigger than Henry VIII's last board, 'rapidly revived the characteristics of the fifteenth century'. Mary had only made matters worse, it was said, by entrenching an unwieldy system of committees which was thought to have been set up by Edward's ministers. Elizabeth I, allegedly, put everything right in 1558–9. 'By returning to the principle of Cromwell's reform—a small council of equivalent and equally powerful ministers—Elizabeth saved her government from that mixture of divided counsels and undue magnate influence which the creation of a large council split into committees had inevitably produced.'[1]

*I wish to express my sincere thanks to Diarmaid MacCulloch for giving me access in advance of publication to a copy of his translation and edition of BL Add. MS 48093, Robert Wingfield's 'Vita Mariae' (see n. 14). All quotations from this translation are used here by kind permission of Dr MacCulloch. My thanks also go to Dr Simon Adams, Professor G. R. Elton, Dr Robert Tittler, and the editors of the present volume; their suggestions enabled me to clarify several passages, though of course the arguments contained herein remain entirely my own. The research for this paper was supported in 1983 by a grant from the Committee on Faculty Research in the College of William and Mary.

[1] G. R. Elton, *The Tudor Revolution in Government* (Cambridge, 1953), 319, 419.

Subsequent research revised this picture in ways that both confirmed and denied the importance of the reforms which Professor
Elton had ascribed to Cromwell. It was found that the size and
composition of the Privy Council appointed by Protector Somerset
(12 March 1547–5 October 1549) closely resembled Henry VIII's
Council after 1540: the structure of the reformed board had obviously survived intact.[2] Moreover, in at least one important area
of administration—the Council's authorization of warrants for
payment—the Protector's methods appear to have been less irregular
than was once supposed; Somerset simply carried forward some
aspects of the Henrician routine.[3] None the less, the Council under
Somerset was hardly the active, omnicompetent heir of the Privy
Council described in *The Tudor Revolution in Government*; its
records reveal Somerset's autocratic assumption of many of its advisory and executive functions, if not its quasi-judicial activity.
Somerset retained the new Privy Council, but the years of his Protectorate marked the nadir of its fortunes.[4]

Somerset's overthrow paved the way for a return to more settled
methods of government. This happened during the course of 1550
and is explained not only by the Council's reaction to the failure of
Somerset's methods, but also by the capabilities, foresight, and
willpower of three men—Paget, a former council clerk and
Cromwellian protégé whose 'Advise to the Kinges Counsail' of
March 1550 re-established the procedures of the period 1540–7; Sir
William Cecil, who as a principal secretary of state after 5
September 1550 administered state business in a manner not unlike
that of Thomas Cromwell; and the duke of Northumberland, an
ambitious gangster who also happened to be an executive genius of
sorts—England's answer to Cesare Borgia. As lord president of the
Council (February 1550–July 1553), Northumberland directed
Cecil's reorganization of the king's affairs (Paget had fallen out of
favour). For political reasons the Council had grown larger (31–3
members, as against 18–22 in the period 1536–49), but increased
numbers had not reduced its relative efficiency. It was during these
years (1550–3) that Northumberland forged the administrative

---

[2] D. E. Hoak, *The King's Council in the Reign of Edward VI* (Cambridge, 1976),
51–2, 81.

[3] J. D. Alsop, 'Protector Somerset and Warrants for Payment', *BIHR* lv (May
1982), 102–8.

[4] Hoak, *King's Council*, 113–18, 221–5.

system of government-by-Council, which Cecil reinstated under Elizabeth I, as I have argued elsewhere.[5]

What happened to this tradition of efficiency and reform under Mary? In spite of what has recently been written,[6] the history of the composition, organization, and functions of Mary's Council, not to mention the question of its factions, still poses some unresolved problems and puzzles. Consider, for example, the membership of the Council at the outset of her reign. Dr Lemasters originally identified three types of Tudor careerists whom the queen appointed in 1553.[7] Mary's 'Framlingham councillors' are said to comprise a group of Catholic loyalists; these she raised to the Privy Council from among the officers of her own household and other co-religionists who flocked to her standard at Framlingham Castle during July 1553. A second group consisted of Edwardian 'professionals' whose experience was too valuable for the queen to reject or ignore; they knew how government really worked at Westminster, and were prepared to render loyal service to the legitimate sovereign. Lineage, experience, or ability similarly recommended a group of ex-Henricians, including Norfolk and Gardiner. In the case of this third group, however, one suspects that their true claim to office lay in the fact of their harassment at the hands of Edwardian reformers. Mary's high sense of Counter-Reformation justice almost certainly explains their immediate return to power.[8] (The political apotheosis of two septuagenarians, Tunstall and Gage, makes little sense in any other terms.)

[5] Cf. Hoak, 'Rehabilitating the Duke of Northumberland: Politics and Political Control, 1549–53', in Jennifer Loach and Robert Tittler, eds., *The Mid-Tudor Polity c.1540–1560* (London, 1980), 29–51. Paget's 'Advise', first printed in Hoak, *King's Council*, 273–5, has been made more accessible in Elton, *The Tudor Constitution: Documents and Commentary* (2nd edn., Cambridge, 1982), 97–8.

[6] Ann Weikel's 'Crown and Council: A Study of Mary Tudor and her Privy Council' (Yale University, unpublished Ph.D. thesis, 1966), was apparently written without reference to manuscript sources. However, in her essay, 'The Marian Council Revisited', in Loach and Tittler, eds., *Mid-Tudor Polity*, 52–73, she arrived independently at some conclusions very similar to those advanced in Glenn Lemasters's indispensable work, 'The Privy Council in the Reign of Queen Mary I' (University of Cambridge, unpublished Ph.D. thesis, 1972). See also Professor Elton's synthesis, based chiefly on Lemasters's evidence and arguments, in 'Tudor Government: the Points of Contact: the Council', *TRHS* 5th series, xxv (1975), 205–7, and *Reform and Reformation: England 1509–1558* (London, 1977), 377–8, 390–1. D. M. Loades, *The Reign of Mary Tudor: Politics, government, and religion in England, 1553–1558* (London, 1979), incorporates Lemasters's evidence in a much fuller discussion of Marian government.

[7] Lemasters, 'The Privy Council', ch. 2.

[8] Cf. Loades, *Mary Tudor*, 73.

No one has ever doubted the existence of such types in Mary's Council, though a few historians have arbitrarily redefined the composition of the groups.[9] The real problem is deciding when and in what circumstances the individuals in question made their first appearances. Until now, the best that could be said was that a Privy Council certainly existed at Framlingham during mid-July, but for lack of evidence the membership of this body has never been fixed precisely. If an 'embryonic' Council predated Framlingham,[10] its members, like its proceedings, apparently were never recorded. The Council began to keep a record of its business at Framlingham on 14 July.[11] The earliest record of a swearing-in, that of Sir Edward Hastings at New Hall (Boreham, Essex), bears a date of 28 July.[12] At the Tower on 14 August 1553 the Council recorded its first attendances: twelve names were given.[13]

Fresh evidence—an extraordinarily detailed contemporary account of goings-on in Mary's camp after 6 July[14]—shows that *before* Mary arrived at Framlingham she already possessed a Council of nineteen men and that eleven of them, including the earls of Bath and Sussex, had been drawn from the ranks of those outside her immediate (household) entourage. Of the nineteen, only one, Sir Richard Southwell, had previously sat in the Councils of Henry VIII or Edward VI.

---

[9] Weikel identified 'Catholic loyalists, personal adherents, and experienced Henrician and Edwardian Councillors': Loach and Tittler, eds., *Mid-Tudor Polity*, 71. Robert Tittler discovered two categories, 'personal followers of staunch loyalty but slight experience, and men of stout experience and skill but of suspect and recent loyalty'; *The Reign of Mary I* (New York, 1983), 13. I am grateful to Dr Tittler for allowing me to consult his work in advance of publication. Loades discussed all of these types but avoided exclusive categories: *Mary Tudor*, 70–5.

[10] The word 'embryonic' is Loades's, ibid. 100 n. 3.

[11] The 'register' in question consists of the first 32 pages of PC 2/6, known as 'Queen Mary Vol. I' in the Record Office series, and printed as Appendix I in *APC* iv. 415 ff. These pages were originally part of a collection of notes kept by Secretary Petre. Lemasters ('The Privy Council', 248) revealed this, but Loades (*Mary Tudor*, 100 n. 5) confused Lemasters's account and wrongly placed the record of the meeting of 14 July 1553 in another register which Lemasters convincingly attributed to Secretary Bourne. Bourne's register, now among the Cecil papers at Hatfield House (245/1), commenced on 16 July 1553; *APC* iv. 293.

[12] *APC* iv. 418, from a list among Petre's notes in PC 2/6 ('Queen Mary Vol. I', part 1).

[13] *APC* iv. 318, from Bourne's register at Hatfield House, Cecil Papers, 245/1.

[14] BL Add. MS 48093, the 'Vita Mariae Angliae Reginae' of Robert Wingfield of Brantham, an account of events during Mary's first regnal year, 6 July 1553 to 5 May 1554, as translated (from the Latin) and edited by Dr Diarmaid MacCulloch.

The discovery of this source throws open the whole question of the formation of Mary's government and the nature of the political base from which she moved to claim her rightful throne. In what follows, I can only suggest an introduction to this topic: the *coup d'état* that brought Mary to power—the only Tudor rebellion ever to succeed[15]—obviously demands a much fuller account than can be given here. None the less, the new evidence resolves one of the long-standing mysteries of Tudor politics—exactly when and how the Marian regime came into being.

The 'revolutions' identified in the title of this chapter comprehended two quite distinct phases in the formation of Mary's Privy Council. In the first three sections below, I discuss the emergence of Mary's 'first' Council, the pre-Framlingham Council of War appointed at Kenninghall for the purpose of directing the rebellion against Jane. Compared to its predecessors, this Kenninghall Council was truly revolutionary, but the revolution it represented was checked almost immediately by the effects of a counter-revolutionary turning within Mary's own government, an administrative coup by which a group of newly appointed officers of state, most of them former Edwardians, wrested control of the Council away from the queen and her Kenninghall men. The fourth section analyses the nature of these post-Kenninghall appointments.

The revolutionary transformation of Mary's original Council produced a governing body of almost unmanageable size, however, and Paget characteristically began to seek a means to reform a board now numbering more than forty. As it happened, his scheme to reduce the Privy Council to a 'select' six- or eight-member 'Council of state' succeeded, but only in effect, and not for the reasons advanced by Simon Renard, who tried to claim credit for acceptance of the plan. In this, as in so much else that Renard had to say about Mary's Council, the ambassador embellished a lie. (He may have been duped by Paget as to the real purpose of the 'Council of state'.[16]) In any case, discovering what principle of government the new 'Council' embodied defines yet another

---

[15] The phrase is C. S. L. Davies's, in *Peace, Print and Protestantism, 1450–1558* (St Albans, 1977), 290.

[16] See Renard's self-serving dispatch to Philip II of March or April 1555, *Span. Cal.* xiii. 150–3, which contradicts his earlier report of 6 Nov. 1553 to Charles V, ibid. xi. 343. Lemasters brilliantly exposed Renard's fictions and misrepresentations in 'The Privy Council', 109–10, 133, 147, 148, 152. On Paget's manipulation of Renard generally, see ibid. 119, 127, 137.

obscurity of Marian politics, one that I try to clarify in the fifth section, below.

In demolishing Renard's credibility as a source for the history of Mary's Council, Dr Lemasters pointed the way towards the use of hitherto unexploited materials, especially the rough-copy books of the Council's proceedings.[17] One such volume, the existence of which can be cited here for the first time,[18] provides unwitting evidence of the process by which the secretaries and clerks produced a record of the Council's business. The significance of this process will be considered in the fifth section, in the context of Paget's plan to organize a 'Council of state'.

It remains to be said, by way of introduction, that the history of the formation of Mary's government and the subsequent reorganiz-ation and reform of her Council cannot really be written without reference to the history of the queen's Court. An adequate history of the Court, i.e., of the organization, personnel, and politics of the royal household, warrants a separate study; research on this subject is presently going ahead. For the moment, perhaps it will be enough to suggest that this new history of the household, when integrated with institutionally based studies of the Council, must inevitably enlarge our understanding of the dynamics of Tudor cen-tral government. For the reigns of Edward and Mary, it has so far been the period of Northumberland's rule that has yielded the best evidence of the relationship of Court and Council.[19] Further work on the Court during the years 1547–9 and 1553–8 may well compel a re-examination of the very framework within which the political history of this period has been written. But first, the *coup d'état* of Mary Tudor.

MARY'S 'FLIGHT' TO KENNINGHALL, 4–9 JULY 1553

On 20 May 1554, Robert Wingfield of Brantham Hall, Suffolk, an otherwise obscure East Anglian gentleman, dedicated to Sir Edward Waldegrave, keeper of the queen's wardrobe, a historical treatise chronicling the circumstances of Her Majesty's recent successful

---

[17] Lemasters, 'The Privy Council', 243–52.

[18] BL Eg. MS 3723F. See n. 71.

[19] See my discussion of the organization, personnel, and functions of 'The King's Privy Chamber, 1547–1553', in D. J. Guth and J. W. McKenna, eds. *Tudor Rule and Revolution: Essays for G. R. Elton from his American friends* (Cambridge, 1982), 87–108.

rebellion against the government of the usurper Jane.[20] For some of the events described in this 'Vita Mariae Angliae Reginae'—in particular, Mary's muster of troops at Framlingham and her entertainment in Ipswich on her way to London, 24–26 July 1553—Wingfield was himself an eyewitness. For his knowledge of Mary's progress to Framlingham before 12 July he relied on someone within Mary's household, perhaps Waldegrave himself, for the nature of the remarkably precise information Wingfield acquired could only have come from one of the few persons, like Waldegrave, who had accompanied her during the tense days after King Edward's demise.

Wingfield's account confirms statements made independently by Guaras and the foreign ambassadors to the effect that during the waning days of June 1553, Court informants had primed Mary's partisans with news of Northumberland's attempt to alter the succession to the throne. Giovanni Francesco Commendone, Pope Julius III's envoy *extraordinaire* who subsequently interviewed the queen as well as members of her household, flatly stated in 1554 that Mary had been 'secretly informed by some members of the Council itself of the machinations of the Duke, of the progress of the illness of the King and finally of his death'.[21]

However, during the spring of 1553 Northumberland had kept a watchful eye on Mary and her men and had tried to cut the ground from under them by playing upon a Tudor's pride. Part of his scheme, if it can be called that as early as April 1553, was to lull Mary into the secure belief that in the event of her brother's death she 'would be Queen' with his assistance. At first, his almost daily letters 'convinced her so completely' of his steadfastness and loyalty that her written replies, had she known then the full details of his design, almost certainly would have tipped him off to the leaks within his camp. For a time, Mary's advisers reckoned that ignorance was her best shield and so kept the incoming secrets from her, but when Edward's condition began to deteriorate rapidly—this

---

[20] BL Add. MS 48093. For a description of the manuscript and the details of Wingfield's career, see Diarmaid MacCulloch's introduction to the published edition, *Vita Mar. Reg.*, 182–95.

[21] G. F. Commendone, 'Events of the Kingdom of England beginning with Edward VI until the Wedding of the most serene Prince Philip of Spain and the most serene Queen Mary', in *The Accession, Coronation, and Marriage of Mary Tudor as related in four manuscripts of the Escorial*, trans. and ed. C. V. Malfatti (Barcelona, 1956), 7.

must have been about 1 July—she was finally told the truth of 'the Duke's deceit'.[22] As Wingfield put it, 'she got wind of the aristocratic conspiracy aimed at her destruction, and being secretly informed by those most loyal to her of how near her brother was to his end, she took counsel for herself as wisely as she could.'[23] Her political education came quickly. Through those who counselled her she now learned how to 'simulate' ignorance, and tricked Northumberland 'into thinking he could get possession of her whenever he pleased'.[24] She was then residing at Hunsdon, no more than twenty miles from his grasp.

Wingfield's version of what happened next implies that by this time, in co-operation with a network of East Anglian agents, Mary's advisers had already worked out the path, if not the timing, of their mistress's flight. They needed only a signal from their spy at Court. The signal came on 3 July when 'a friend', as Scheyfve discovered the next day, suddenly warned her to beat a retreat deeper into the country, away from London; Scheyfve knew that Framlingham Castle had been selected as her ultimate destination.[25] On the night of the fourth, according to a pre-arranged plan, Mary 'set out secretly from Hunsdon' with six attendants (four manservants and two maids of honour) on the pretext, probably announced the next day, that the illness of her physician, Rowland Scurloch, had forced her to move household.[26] After 'a difficult and tiresome journey' through Hertfordshire, most of it made hurriedly under cover of darkness, Mary's party reached Sawston Hall, Cambridgeshire, the home of Sir John Huddleston, where they spent the night of 5 July. On 6 July, very early in the morning, Mary set out from Sawston towards Thetford, reportedly travelling in disguise behind one of Huddleston's men. She rode virtually non-stop for about the next twenty-eight miles to Hengrave Hall, the seat of the earl of Bath, just outside Bury St Edmunds. The next day, 7 July, she pushed on to Euston Hall, where she was entertained by Euston's mistress, Lady Burgh. It was at Euston, on either 7 or 8 July, that Robert Reyns, goldsmith and citizen of London, 'newly returned from the City', informed her of her brother's death. (Edward had

[22] *Ven. Cal.* v. 537, Soranzo's report of 18 Aug. 1554, which was obviously based on inside information revealed later.

[23] *Vita Mar. Reg.* 251.

[24] *Ven. Cal.* v. 537; Guaras, 89, said 'she dissembled with him'.

[25] Scheyfve to Charles V, 4 July 1553, *Span. Cal.* ix. 70.

[26] *Vita Mar. Reg.* 251; *Ven. Cal.* v. 537; Guaras, 89.

died between 8 and 9 p.m. on 6 July.) Because Reyns had been dispatched to Euston by Sir Nicholas Throckmorton, a gentleman of Edward VI's Privy Chamber known for his Reformed attitudes, Mary feared a trap, and discounting the goldsmith's report, would 'not let the news be spread abroad.' Nevertheless, the message made flight more urgent, and so she pressed on to her own house at Kenninghall, about twelve miles away. On 9 July a 'medical practitioner' named Thomas Hughes 'hurried there and confirmed the news of the king's death', whereupon, 'having first taken counsel with her advisers [the remainder of whom had come up from Hunsdon separately], she caused her whole household to be summoned' and announced the end of her brother's reign and the inauguration of her own. Everyone present, said Wingfield, 'cheered her to the rafters'.[27]

THE FORMATION OF THE COUNCIL AT KENNINGHALL, 9-12 JULY

It was at Kenninghall on 9 July that Mary wrote to the lords of Jane's Council in London, commanding them under her sign manual 'to cause our right and title to the Crown and government

[27] I have reconstructed from the following sources the chronology and geography of Mary's flight from Hunsdon to Kenninghall: *Vita Mar. Reg.* 251-2; *The Chronicle of Queen Jane and of Two Years of Queen Mary*, ed. J. G. Nichols (Camden Society, old series, xlviii, London, 1850), 1-2; Guaras, 89-90; Soranzo's report to the Venetian Senate of 18 August 1554, *Ven. Cal.* v. 537; Imperial envoys to Charles V, 7 July 1553, *Span. Cal.* xi. 72-3; *The Legend of Sir Nicholas Throckmorton*, ed. J. G. Nichols (London, 1874), 29. See also J. A. Froude, *History of England from the Fall of Wolsey to the Death of Elizabeth* (London, 1864), vi. 1-5. I have relied on Dr MacCulloch for the identity of the goldsmith, Reyns, and Hughes (or Huys), the physician at Kenninghall. H. M. F. Prescott, *Mary Tudor* (London, 1952), 165-6, had Mary moving slowly south from Hunsdon to Hoddesdon on 4 July, presuming that she was obeying a command from Northumberland to visit Edward VI at Greenwich. Prescott and J. M. Stone, *The History of Mary I, Queen of England* (London, 1901), 217-18, thought that an unnamed messenger told Mary of Edward's demise at Hoddesdon on 6 July and that Mary began her flight from Hoddesdon, but the evidence they cite does not support this. Wingfield explicitly states that the messenger, Reyns, informed Mary of Edward's death at Euston. Tittler, *Reign of Mary I*, apparently followed Prescott's account, the erroneous chronology of which was probably derived from Stone. Incidentally, Stone (op. cit. 217) thought that 'the rebels' set fire to Sawston moments after Mary's departure—the author said Mary 'looked back from the summit of a neighbouring hill . . . at the smoke rising from the house that had sheltered her'—but Wingfield asserted that Northumberland and his men 'caused appalling damage to the home of Huddleston' on about 13 July on their way to Cambridge; *Vita Mar. Reg.* 261-3. See also *HC 1509-58*, ii. 402 on Huddleston.

of this Realm to be proclaimed' throughout England.[28] This was the formal action of a queen regnant, and between 9 and 12 July, when she departed from Kenninghall for Framlingham, she began to put together a Queen's Council.

The men in Princess Mary's household constituted a natural pool of candidates eligible for appointment to her Privy Council. Wingfield divided them into two groups, the first including nine of her greater officers and the second, another twenty lesser, but equally trusted servants and confidants. Since on 9 July Mary began to administer oaths of fealty to newcomers—gentlemen and peers whose names subsequently appear in records officially identifying them as councillors—it is likely that at the same time she decided to narrow her pre-Kenninghall staff of advisers to those who henceforth would be her privy councillors. Eight of the nine in Wingfield's first group made the transition to the royal body: Robert Rochester (comptroller), Henry Jerningham (vice-chamberlain and captain of the guard), Edward Waldegrave (keeper of the wardrobe), John Bourne (principal secretary), Sir Thomas Wharton, Richard Freston (cofferer), Robert Strelly, and Robert Peckham.[29]

These were the men who had engineered Mary's escape from Hunsdon. Not later than 4 July they had also decided that when she could be certain of Edward's death, she should proclaim herself queen in order to encourage potential adherents to provide the kind of military support without which her declaration of war against Northumberland would be useless; a civil war in East Anglia is apparently what her advisers pessimistically envisioned from the

[28] The text is given in Tittler, *Reign of Mary I*, 84–5.

[29] Rochester, Jerningham, Waldegrave, Bourne, Freston, and Peckham were knighted on the day of Mary's coronation or the day after: *The Diary of Henry Machyn, citizen and merchant-taylor of London from A.D. 1550 to A.D. 1563*, ed. J. G. Nichols (Camden Society, old series, xlii, London, 1848), 334. Wharton was the eldest son of Thomas Lord Wharton, warden of the West Marches under Edward VI. The younger Wharton held no office of state or household under Mary, but attended between 40% and 50% of all Council meetings; Lemasters, 'The Privy Council', 295. Robert Strelly (or Strelley) died on 23 Jan. 1554. Loades (*Mary Tudor*, 102 n. 28) thought that Strelly probably owed his advancement to the Council to the influence of his wife, Frideswide. This 'Mrs Sturley' (or 'Stirleye'), a gentlewoman of the queen's Privy Chamber, was (according to the Imperial envoys) one of Mary's 'most intimate confidants'; LC 2/4(2); *Span. Cal.* xii. 144 (Egmont and Renard to Charles V, 8 Mar. 1554). On her faithfulness to the queen, see Prescott, *Mary Tudor*, 310. *HC 1509-58* contains biographical information on Rochester (iii. 204–5), Jerningham (ii. 443–4), Waldegrave (iii. 534–5), Bourne (i. 466–8), Wharton (iii. 599–601), Strelly (iii. 397–8), and Peckham (iii. 80).

outset.[30] For the conduct of this war she would need to enlarge her pre-Kenninghall Council to include military advisers, gentlemen, and peers, whose tenants and servants would form the nucleus of the army to be mustered at Framlingham. For this reason, the route of her flight was charted deliberately to take her to men from whose lands such forces could be raised, to men who themselves would serve as captains and councillors in her new government.

Huddleston's 'hospitality to Princess Mary on the night after she left Hunsdon' explains why he was the first to gain her favour, and it was through him that she began to assemble both a Council and an army. Huddleston left Sawston for Kenninghall shortly after Mary's departure, his job *en route* being to enlist the support of neighbouring gentry. Luck played into his hands when he intercepted Henry Radcliffe, one of the sons of Henry, earl of Sussex, on his way to London with letters from his father to the duke of Northumberland. Huddleston escorted the young Radcliffe to Kenninghall, which lay but a few miles south of the earl's seat at Attleborough. According to Wingfield, Mary was delighted 'just as much at the return of Huddleston, whom she greatly valued, as at the capture of the letters which revealed her enemies' plans, but especially because she hoped to be able to win over the elder Henry to her cause through his son.'[31]

In fact Mary had already 'sounded out' the earl's intentions through 'her servant', Sir Thomas Wharton, a member of her 'personal Council' who was married to the earl's sister. Wharton reported that Northumberland's son, Robert (who had been sent to apprehend Mary), had persuaded the earl that Edward VI was still alive, but 'when the earl was told of his son's capture, he made haste to come to the queen'.[32] (On his return to Kenninghall, Wharton himself barely escaped ambush at the hands of Lord Robert's servants.) At Kenninghall, Sussex 'gave his most bounden fealty to his sovereign queen in the customary form that he would uphold her course in future'. Following this, he departed with orders to rendezvous at Framlingham 'on an appointed day with a large

[30] *Vita Mar. Reg.* 251-2; *Span. Cal.* xi. 72-3, Imperial envoys to Charles V, 7 July 1553.

[31] *Vita Mar. Reg.* 254. For details of Huddleston's career, see *HC 1509–58*, ii. 401-3.

[32] *Vita Mar. Reg.* 254. Sussex may have been driven by other motives too. Dr Simon Adams has reminded me that the earl held the lord lieutenancy of Norfolk jointly with Robert Dudley in 1552, but was relieved of that office in 1553.

military force'. At Framlingham a few days later he 'brought his support as he had already promised, with a cohort of both horsemen and foot-soldiers' and assumed supreme command of Mary's growing army. Politically, as the queen's lieutenant, he also became her public mouthpiece.[33]

Although Sussex was the first peer actually to join Mary at Kenninghall, he was the second to commit himself militarily to her cause, for the earl of Bath 'had already met the queen as she was making for Norfolk from Hunsdon, and had offered his entire allegiance to her Highness.'[34] When Bath rode up to Framlingham Castle behind Sussex, on or just after 12 July, he too brought with him 'a large band of soldiers'. Presumably he was sworn in then as one of the queen's men, though one is tempted to think that at Hengrave, on 6 July, Mary had promised him a place in her Council in return for his own and his clients' arms.[35] The point is simply that before she reached Kenninghall she and her advisers had begun to recruit the members of the new Council, and Sir John Huddleston and the earl of Bath were the first to be so recruited.

Sussex came to Mary by accident, but her war against Northumberland would not be won accidentally, so while at Kenninghall 'she and her personal council decided to send out swift messengers in all directions to draw all the gentlemen of the surrounding countryside to do fealty to their sovereign.'[36] This effort immediately produced two new recruits from the ranks of the Norfolk gentry, Sir Henry Bedingfield of Oxborough Hall, who eventually replaced Jerningham as vice-chamberlain and captain of the queen's guard (1556), and Sir John Shelton, a local landowner who failed to gain any other office of importance in the state or the queen's household.[37]

---

[33] Ibid. 254, 257, 261.

[34] Ibid. 257.

[35] J. M. Stone (*Mary I*, 217 n. 2) cited 'A Sketch of Hengrave Hall, Suffolk', by Sir Henry Rookwood Gage, as the source for the assertion that Bath accompanied Mary from Hengrave to Kenninghall with 'a considerable force'.

[36] *Vita Mar. Reg.* 253.

[37] On Bedingfield and Shelton, see *HC 1509-58*, i. 408-9 and iii. 312, respectively. Shelton had served as a commissioner of the peace for co. Norfolk since 1543. He was reappointed on 18 Feb. 1554, *CPR* (1553-4), 22, and with other privy councillors, to a commission of oyer and terminer of 2 May 1554 (ibid. 27). On 29 July 1556 the Council thanked him for his report on the state of Norfolk: *APC* v. 316. He came to Court infrequently and attended fewer than one-fifth of all Council meetings during Mary's reign.

The next of the county élite to arrive at Kenninghall on or around 10 July in response to Mary's general summons was Sir Richard Southwell. Southwell possessed some thirty-odd manors stretching across central Norfolk from Swaffham to Norwich, just north of Mary's own dower lands. These and other properties yielded an income of more than £600 per annum, making him, as Wingfield knew, 'the wealthiest of his rank in all Norfolk.' As one who had signed the limitation of the crown in favour of Jane, Southwell came to Kenninghall prepared 'to make the most humble submission that he could to the queen, repeatedly recalling in his petition the many favours heaped on him by Henry VIII'. He quickly persuaded Mary of his loyalty, for 'he brought reinforcements of men, a store of provisions and moreover money, the sinews of war'. Momentarily, Southwell's money seems to have mattered most to Mary, so much so—Wingfield mentioned it three times in the course of a paragraph extolling his arrival—that the author, who conceived of Mary's cause in religious terms ('sacred Mary's righteous undertaking') might be forgiven for thinking that Southwell had bought both his office and Mary's forgiveness: 'to the end that his submission might be more welcome to the tender-hearted queen, he is said to have contributed a respectable sum of money' towards her military effort. There was also Southwell's 'skill in counsel and long experience' in a succession of royal appointments. He was the only one in Mary's camp to have held high office at Court, doubtless something of considerable importance to the provincial gentlemen around him, who talked of making war on the central government. If Mary perceived Southwell as a fellow Catholic, Wingfield does not say so. Rather, from him she reaped 'money, provisions and armed men'; under the circumstances, his membership of her Council was a matter of politico-military necessity, and she recognized it as such. Four months after her coronation she granted him a lifetime annuity of £100 'in consideration of his service' during the crisis of July.[38]

'Almost at the same time' that Bedingfield, Shelton and Southwell swore fealty to Mary at Kenninghall (between 9 and 11 July), other 'men hastened from further away to do homage to the queen'. Among the six Wingfield named in this context were four

---

[38] *Vita Mar. Reg.* 254–5; History of Parliament Trust, unpublished biography of Southwell (which contains details not in the published entry in *HC 1509–58*, iii. 352–4); *CPR* (1553–4), 63.

gentlemen of substance who, because of their local social status or personal ties to Mary, won places in the new Council: Sir John Mordaunt, Sir Richard Morgan (whom she appointed chief justice of the common pleas), Sir William Drury (then a JP for Suffolk), and Clement Heigham (also of the Suffolk gentry).[39]

THE KENNINGHALL APPOINTMENTS ANALYSED

What is the evidence that the eighteen so far identified here had actually been appointed privy councillors? The newcomers had certainly sworn oaths of fealty to the queen, but so had many others, and more were to do so during the next few days. Bound up with the papers comprising Mary's first Council register are lists of the names of 106 'Subjects sworne to the Queen's Majestie' at Framlingham on 14, 15, 16, and 17 July, and the names of the earl of Sussex, Bedingfield, Shelton, Morgan, Southwell, Drury, and Heigham appear indiscriminately among them, even though by Wingfield's account they had pledged their fealty at Kenninghall at least five or six days earlier.[40] An apparently more serious objection to the argument in favour of the appointment of councillors at Kenninghall is the existence of another, later list which has 'Mr. Henrye Jernyngham sworne of [the] Quenes Prevye Counsell' at the Tower of London on 4 August 1553.[41]

Against the evidence of these lists may be set several observations. First, the Framlingham lists of 14–17 July do not deny the probability that Mary appointed the earl of Sussex *et al.* to her Council at Kenninghall. After swearing oaths of fealty, Sussex and the others departed from Kenninghall in order to organize their clients and raise troops, and they reappeared at Framlingham to train and drill the soldiers so raised. At Framlingham a clerk (who may not

---

[39] *Vita Mar. Reg.* 255. Dr MacCulloch has pointed out to me that unlike Drury and Heigham (both Suffolk men: see their biographies in *HC 1509–58*, ii. 60–1 and 329–31, respectively), Mordaunt and Morgan (ibid. ii. 614–16 and 629–30, respectively) possessed no East Anglian connections. What explains their presence at Kenninghall in July 1553? A personal tie to Mary, reflecting Catholic sympathies, suggests the answer in both cases. Mordaunt's second wife, Joan, had served in Princess Mary's household before her death in 1545. Like his father, a Bedfordshire baron, Mordaunt opposed the religious changes of the Henrician and Edwardian Reformations. Morgan's loyalties remained clear enough in the years before 1553: for hearing mass in the private chapel of his friend, Princess Mary, he was arrested and imprisoned in the Fleet by Edward's Council (24 Mar.–4 May 1551).

[40] *APC* iv. 429–32.

[41] Ibid. 419.

have been at Kenninghall) jotted down on some loose sheets of paper the names of those who were arriving almost hourly with their tenants and servants: the names recorded were those of Mary's specially commissioned officers, sworn to bear arms as her captains. Wingfield had not confused the Kenninghall oaths with those administered at Framlingham. 'Almost simultaneously' with the arrival of the earl of Bath at Framlingham, for example, 'there hastened to aid the queen Sir William Drury, who has already been mentioned as giving his fealty to her at Kenninghall'.[42]

Although the Kenninghall oaths mentioned by Wingfield technically were not the oaths of privy councillors, some of the men who swore fealty there certainly became members of a royal Council during July. At Kenninghall Wingfield referred to Mary's Council as 'her personal council', once on 9 July when its members sent out messengers to neighbouring gentry,[43] and once on about 11 July when, on her instructions, they discussed the logistical problems of moving her headquarters to Framlingham.[44] At Framlingham, Wingfield varied the terms he used to identify this body. On 17 July 'scouts told the queen and her council that the enemy . . . had struck camp and was marching from Cambridge to Bury . . . At this news . . . she summoned her council and on their advice' ordered her field commanders to ready their men and prepare for battle.[45] On 20 July it was 'on the advice of her personal council' that the earl of Arundel, Lord Grey of Wilton and Henry Jerningham were ordered to go to Cambridge and place the duke of Northumberland and other prisoners under guard.[46] Perhaps too much can be read into Wingfield's lack of precision regarding the name of Mary's Council, for he invariably referred to Jane's London-based lords as '*the* Council' even though he was writing at a time (May 1554) when only Mary could be considered to have had a legitimate Council.

Jerningham's status on 20 July provides a clue to the real, but as yet constitutionally informal, nature of membership of Mary's

[42] *Vita Mar. Reg.* 257; *APC* iv. 432 (17 July).

[43] *Vita Mar. Reg.* 253.

[44] Ibid. 255. Wingfield said that 'the queen recognised that her house [Kenninghall] was utterly inadequate to withstand an enemy attack or fitly to accommodate her much increased forces and household.' Although more than twenty miles away, Framlingham, a Howard seat, 'was the strongest castle in Suffolk' and could absorb reinforcements in the event of open war against Northumberland.

[45] Ibid. 261.

[46] Ibid. 267.

Privy Council. When Wingfield paused to consider 'the names of those to whom their country and their most gentle sovereign owe so much', he identified 'Henry Jerningham, a vigorous, noble, and modest man', as second only to Rochester in the 'catalogue' of Mary's household heroes.[47] When the 'personal council' dispatched him to Cambridge on 20 July, he went as a royal officer, one 'whom the queen had already selected as Vice-Chamberlain and captain of the guard'.[48] (The vice-chamberlain, Wingfield explained, 'traditionally keeps watch over and protects the sovereign's person'.) Since vice-chamberlains had always been members *ex officio* of the Privy Council, it seems inconceivable that Jerningham was not also recognized then as a member of the very body that dispatched him. Perhaps his almost constant activity on horseback prevented his taking a formal oath until the Court settled in London in August. (Wingfield devoted several pages to Jerningham's exploits in the field during July.) Official evidence exists for the swearing-in of fifteen privy councillors between 28 July (when such records commence) and 17 August, and of the fifteen, Jerningham is the only one to have been with Mary before she left Framlingham Castle for London on 24 July. Moreover, the form of the evidence itself— rough notes of the swearings of both councillors and non-councillors under seven different dates (25 July–5 August 1553), all on one side of a single, loose sheet of paper, copied down while the Court was progressing from Ipswich to London, and coinciding with the record, on the same page, of the swearing-in of two clerks, one of whom probably took this note—suggests that Jerningham's swearing-in on 4 August was simply a product of the demands of record-keeping.[49] Wingfield's reference to Jerningham's appointment to the vice-chamberlainship—the earliest extant reference to the appointment of a Marian official—thus indirectly tends to confirm the existence of an appointed Privy Council, even if one to which some members had not yet been formally sworn.

Perhaps the best evidence for the existence of a Privy Council by 12 July is Wingfield's colourful description of how Sir Thomas Cornwallis, sheriff of Norfolk and Suffolk, finally came 'to do his

[47] Ibid. 252.

[48] Ibid. 267.

[49] This is p. 7 of PC 2/6, originally a loose sheet in a collection of papers kept by Secretary Petre comprising part 1 of 'Queen Mary Vol. I' in the Record Office series of registers (see note 11); *APC* iv. 418–19. The record of Petre's swearing-in on 30 July is also on this page.

homage to her Highness on the road leading from her house at Kenninghall to Framlingham'. Cornwallis and the 'chief men of Suffolk', including their 'obvious leader', Thomas Lord Wentworth, had already committed themselves to Jane at Ipswich, but when Mary's servants proclaimed their own mistress 'hereditary queen', Cornwallis 'saw clearly enough' that the sympathies of the populace 'manifestly lay with Mary'. According to Wingfield, the public outcry against Jane at Ipswich was so great that Cornwallis actually stood 'in grave peril of his life'. He had reached 'the crossroads' of his political career, 'but he had no idea which side to join for the best'. Ignoring Mary's claim to legitimacy, he calculated that against a Tudor's popularity lay Jane's superior might: 'warlike provision', the wealth of the kingdom, most of the nobility, and the artillery ('most fearsome of all'). News that 'the people of London' were prepared to use force against Jane's aristocratic Council finally persuaded Cornwallis to renounce his support for 'the false Queen' and proclaim Mary 'the true and undoubted heir to the throne'. 'It was that same day, 12 July', said Wingfield, 'that the Queen moved her headquarters to Framlingham . . . and on the way Thomas Cornwallis most humbly prostrated himself before her Highness', begging her pardon and offering 'his due fealty . . . in the traditional manner of sheriffs, by surrendering his white staff. At first the queen seemed to berate the man' for his temporizing, but seeing how 'utterly miserable he was at what he had done, she not only granted him mercy at his supplication, but even made him one of her own council, in which honourable capacity he is still engaged'.[50]

Once again, socio-political realities had forced both sovereign and subject to seek accommodation; neither faith nor principle moved Cornwallis to join Mary, and if Wingfield is to be believed, Mary's choice of councillors during the first three days of her self-proclaimed reign attests as much to her political wisdom as it does to her acceptance of the politically expedient. When Mary reached Framlingham Castle at eight o'clock on the evening of 12 July her Council numbered nineteen. The appendix at the end of this chapter identifies them in the order of their appearance or swearing-in.

---

[50] *Vita Mar. Reg.* 255–6. Wingfield said that Jerningham, who was Cornwallis's wife's uncle, 'was of no small help in making his [Cornwallis's] excuses' for Mary's pardon. On Cornwallis's later career, see *HC 1509–58*, i. 708–9.

THE TRANSFORMATION OF THE COUNCIL, 20 JULY–17 AUGUST 1553

Mary spent twelve days at Framlingham Castle, between 12 and 24 July, and while there, accepted the submission of five men who then became her privy councillors. Awaiting her in the crowd that had gathered in the deer park below the castle, 'about eight-o-clock in the evening' of the twelfth, was Sir Nicholas Hare, soon to become master of the rolls.[51] After delicate negotiations on the fourteenth, Thomas Lord Wentworth sent word from Ipswich through two of Mary's servants that 'although he had pledged his fealty to Jane by the obligation of his oath, his inner conscience' told him that 'Mary had a greater right to the throne', and so he would hasten to her with all speed. He appeared on the sixteenth 'clad in splendid armour' at the head of what Wingfield enthusiastically described as an equally 'splendid force of both heavy and light horse and of infantry'. 'There is no doubt', said our observer, 'that his arrival wonderfully strengthened the morale of the queen's army and much dispirited the enemy.[52] On the twentieth, the day Mary inspected her troops astride a 'frisky' white charger, the earl of Arundel and Lords Paget and Rich rode up with more soldiers and the news that London was hers.[53]

These five appointments—the only ones at Framlingham—were the first in a string that would permanently alter the development of Mary's government, for of the five new men, all but Hare had been Edward's councillors and two, Paget and Rich, could really be considered 'professionals'. Between 6 and 16 July the growth of the new Council had reflected the military requirements of the moment; of the thirteen men not already members of her household whom she had appointed then, twelve she accepted for the hospitality and protection they had given her or the arms and money they had contributed to the war against Northumberland (Hare was the apparent exception). When Northumberland surrendered on 20 July, her requirements changed, and Paget in particular represented the type of careerist to whom she now turned for the formation of a government in London. (Wingfield respected Paget as a true 'man

[51] *Vita Mar. Reg.* 256-7. For Hare's official career, see *HC 1509-58*, ii. 296-7.

[52] *Vita Mar. Reg.* 257, 259. This is the 2nd Lord Wentworth (d. 1584), not to be confused with his father of the same name (d. 1551); cf. *HC 1509-58*, iii. 585-6.

[53] *Vita Mar. Reg.* 265-6.

of affairs'.) In one sense, the history of Mary's reign begins on 20 July, for on that day and very soon thereafter she appointed most of the men who would really govern England in her name.

The changing pattern and nature of Mary's choices can be summarized briefly. Altogether, the queen appointed fifty privy councillors,[54] thirty of them during July 1553 before she arrived in London to claim her crown and throne. Twenty-one joined her between 6 and 16 July; twenty-four more did so by 3 January 1554, and five thereafter. With one exception (Thirlby, bishop of Norwich), the essential membership of the Marian Council became fixed during the six weeks between 20 July and 4 September 1553. At Framlingham, Ipswich, and New Hall during an eleven-day period, 20–30 July, Mary accepted nine men, seven of whom had previously been Edward's councillors. During August 1553 she added twelve more to her board in London, ten of whom were former councillors (only St Leger and West were not), five of them, Edwardians. In sum, by 4 September Mary had doubled her short-lived 'war-time' Council of twenty-one by adding twenty-two new men, seventeen of whom had served in the Privy Councils of her father and brother. A revolution in the composition of Mary's Council had taken place in little more than a month from the time she had left Kenninghall.

The significance of this rapid transformation of Mary's Council, a transformation which for the most part occurred between 20 July and 17 August, can be described in other terms by considering who among the whole number of fifty were really the most active, important members. Taking into account records of attendance, membership of commissions, influence, connections, and weight of experience, nineteen men certainly qualify.[55] Only seven of these had sat in the 'war council', between 6 and 20 July, and of the seven only one, Sussex, was a peer in 1553. To be sure, five were

---

[54] Loades (*Mary Tudor*, 475–80) lists fifty-one including Sir John Tregonwell, sheriff of Somerset and Dorset. Like Sir Thomas Pope, Tregonwell was sworn one of the queen's many councillors at large: cf. *APC*, iv. 419 (4 August 1553) for Pope's swearing-in, and ibid. v. 96, for Tregonwell's (10 Feb. 1555). That the members of the Privy Council did not consider Tregonwell a member can be inferred from the way they once addressed him as a member of a commission to enquire into a case of witchcraft; ibid. v. 143–4. Tregonwell probably was sworn a councillor at large in order to execute cases in Chancery in Gardiner's place; cf. *CPR* (1555–7), 53, a commission of 29 Nov. 1555. Neither Tregonwell nor Pope attended any meetings of the Council.

[55] Gardiner, Arundel, Paget, Winchester, Heath, Thirlby, Pembroke, Norfolk, Howard, Petre, Rochester, Sussex, Gage, Bourne, Jerningham, Wharton, Waldegrave, Hastings, and Bedingfield.

Mary's personal favourites, the five knights who had come from her household (Rochester, Waldegrave, Jerningham, Wharton, and Bourne), but none, save Rochester, really exhibited much force of personality at Westminster, while the other two, Sussex and Bedingfield, attended only about a quarter to a third of all meetings. None of the seven held a high office of state.

In any case, the queen's favourites, representing a rump of the Kenninghall Council of War, were no match for statesmen of Gardiner's mould or men of business like Winchester, Paget and Petre. Although the myth of the factions in Mary's Council was exposed in 1971,[56] too little attention has been given since then to the natural line of division among her men, the one distinguishing all those who had held office at Court before July 1553 from those who had not. By taking this distinction into account, one can, I believe, make some sense of the natural dynamics of Mary's Council, and hence of the nature of political action at her Court. Of Mary's nineteen most active councillors, twelve joined her government on or shortly after the day Northumberland's cause collapsed at Cambridge: Arundel, Paget, Hastings, Petre, Gage, Gardiner, Norfolk, Pembroke, Winchester, Heath, Thirlby, and Howard. These twelve, a numerical majority of the active, innermost 'ring', had not shared with Mary the experience of flight or resistance. Now eight of the twelve had been privy councillors before 1553; since none of the seven 'war councillors' or so-called 'Catholic' advisers had ever held such an office, the extensive governmental experience of these eight was bound to influence the conduct of the queen's business. As privy councillors these eight had survived the vicissitudes of politics at the Reformation Court. Thus Norfolk, Gardiner, and Gage, who conventionally are also labled 'conservative Catholics', functionally shared much more in common with Winchester, Arundel, Pembroke, Paget, and Petre, whom they sometimes are supposed to have opposed. Of course issues occasionally divided the Council, and none more so than the Spanish match, but this is one exception that proves the rule, that while members of the experienced group might disagree over questions of policy, all accepted the fact that they were the only ones really capable of making policy. This is why on one occasion Gardiner found himself in opposition to—of all people—Mary, for the queen's marriage happened to be the one important issue dictated

[56] Lemasters, 'The Privy Council', 110, 130–1, 200–3, 278, 291.

by the Court, and not the Council. Paget, the consummate poli-
tician, understood this and so had made the issue his own.

The discovery that Mary's Council was administratively more
'efficient' than its numbers would suggest[57] thus makes sense, not
because some members attended more meetings than others—and
so presumably constituted an 'inner ring' akin to the whole body of
Elizabeth's men—but because real power among them had passed
quite suddenly during July and August from the likes of Rochester,
Waldegrave, and Bourne to men like Arundel, Winchester, and
Paget. In effect, a Privy Council appointed after 16 July had
replaced the one appointed before 16 July. Mary's 'first' Privy
Council was composed of men who had given her England, the
second of men who had governed England.

CONSOLIDATION AND REFORM,
·NOVEMBER 1553–MAY 1555

How this transformation had occurred remains a mystery. Had
Paget and Arundel persuaded Mary of the necessity of the appointments of 20 July–17 August? If so, they had saved some of their
colleagues from the threat of almost certain extinction, thereby
probably averting a rebellion or civil war.[58] If in Council they had
effectively reinstated the remains of the post-Reformation governing élite, the result none the less was an overlarge board, and Paget
moved at once to consolidate his party's position. His aims within
the Council were two: to organize the working members into committees for the execution of business at hand ('To call in the debtes
and provide for money', 'To consyder what lawes shalbe established
in this Parliament', etc.);[59] and to settle the Council's advisory
function in the hands of five or six experienced men of government.
Administratively, the first reform essentially revived the Council's
own well-established system of standing committees (some non-
conciliar specialists were brought in too) and was in place by 23

[57] Ibid. 116, 136–8, 143, 147, 154, 279–88. D. F. Long corroborated this view in
respect of the work of Petre and Bourne: 'The Office of the Principal Secretary of
State in the Reign of Mary Tudor (1553–1558): Some Aspects of the Conduct of
State Business' (College of William and Mary, unpublished MA thesis, 1977).

[58] This is Lemasters's hypothesis, 'The Privy Council', 119–21.

[59] *APC* iv. 397–9, also printed in Elton, *Tudor Constitution* (2nd edn., 1982),
99–100. An original, briefer version is SP 11/3, fo. 78. Other examples are the so-
called 'councils' of war and finance of March 1558; see n. 78 below.

February 1554; it effectively halved the number of active councillors. The second aim, although based on considerations of
administrative efficiency, proved to be more bold and risky because
it was so obviously political. Politically, however, it succeeded, and
by early November 1553 Paget and Arundel had outmanœuvred
Renard so well, that Mary, on the imperialists' advice, had willingly
'reduced' her 'council' of advisers to six,[60] all of whom, with the
exception of Gardiner, were at one with Paget on most of the important issues of state (the others were Arundel, Thirlby, Rochester,
and Petre). Renard foolishly thought that this group within the
Council was supposed to become *the* Council. 'It had been hoped
that the reduction of the Council's numbers to six would become
permanent', he wrote to Charles V on 22 April 1554.[61] His statement which has been taken as evidence of the premature failure of
reform, really testifies to the success of Paget's political tactics.
However, if Paget hoped to institutionalize this 'inner ring' of advisers, the so-called 'select council' is not, I think, evidence of it.
What was this 'council' and what place has it in the Tudor constitution?

Since the origins, composition, and business of the 'select council' have been reviewed elsewhere,[62] I shall confine myself here to a
few summary observations. First, the name of the 'select council'
(or 'council of state') does seem to matter, but in a wholly negative
sense, for no English official ever referred to it that way in English.
For the English only one body existed, the Privy Council. It may be
true, as Dr Loades has said, that 'the omnicompetent Cromwellian
council' had disappeared by 1555,[63] but only in the sense that forty-
odd nominal privy councillors were not equally sharing the burdens
of government. There were not 'three categories of councillor after
August 1555', 'select', 'privy', and 'at large',[64] but rather, the privy
councillors and all others not *sworn* of the Privy Council—for it
was the oath that defined the institution and its exclusive membership. Only the Spanish, it seems, believed in the separate existence
of a 'select council'. King Philip certainly addressed it as such in his
letters—*selectis Consiliarijs nostris in Anglia* and, less formally,

60 *Span. Cal.* xi. 343: Renard to Charles V, 6 Nov. 1553.
61 Ibid. xii. 220.
62 Loades, *Mary Tudor*, 227, 233, 253, 255–60; Lemasters, 'The Privy Council',
219–24.
63 Loades, *Mary Tudor*, 260.
64 Ibid.

consilia escogida—but English clerks invariably endorsed all incoming correspondence as from 'The Kinges highnes to the counsaill'.[65] Similarly, all correspondence to Philip emanated not from a self-styled 'select council', but from 'the counsell'.[66] The evidence seems to me to point to one conclusion: from the English point of view, an eight-member 'select council' was meant to exist as an *ad hoc* committee of the Privy Council, with whom Philip would correspond during what the English presumed would be his temporary absence overseas. But there is no evidence that 'select' councillors met exclusively to discuss state business. If they had, they would have issued internal administrative orders to other privy councillors who are thought by this time to have been relegated to a purely administrative status. No such orders exist. Quite the contrary: extant original letters from the Council to other officers at Court ordering routine administrative matters bear the signatures of both 'select' and non-'select' councillors alike.[67]

In fact, the internal administrative history of the Privy Council probably describes the rationale for what seemed to foreigners to

[65] Philip's letter of 11 February 1556 from Antwerp: SP 11/7, fos. 13, 14ᵛ. The extant correspondence between the Council and Philip II in the PRO covers the period 31 Aug. 1555 to 27 Oct. 1558. Altogether there are twenty-four items: four in 1555, seventeen in 1556, none in 1557, and three in 1558. Eight of the twenty-four items are the king's letters to the Privy Council. Two date from 1555: SP 11/6, fo. 62, from Brussels in Oct., and ibid. fo. 86, from Brussels on c. 10 Nov. During 1556 there are six: (1) 11 Feb., Antwerp: SP 11/7, fo. 13; (2) 13 May, Brussels: SP 11/8, fo. 119; (3) 13 Sept., Ghent: SP 11/9, fo. 64; (4) 30 Sept., Ghent: SP 11/9, fos. 71-2; (5) 2 Nov., Ghent: SP 11/9, fos. 91-2; (6) 1 Dec., Brussels: SP 11/9, fos. 104-5. Two survive from 1558: SP 11/11, fos. 121-2, Brussels, 6 Apr., and SP 11/14, fo. 4, *ad arcem Flerij*, 22 Oct. Dr Simon Adams tells me that the archives at Simancas and Brussels also contain drafts of Philip's letters to his *consilia escogida* in England, drafts not to be found in the PRO.

[66] Sp 11/9, fo. 82ᵛ, from St James, 19 Oct. 1556. Drafts of fourteen of the Council's letters to Philip are on file in the PRO. For 1555 there are two: SP 11/6, fos. 25-30 (31 Aug.) and SP 11/6, fo. 128 (31 Dec.), of which SP/6, fo. 130 is Petre's English draft. Eleven date from 1556 (folios of Latin versions in parentheses): (1) SP 11/8, fo. 72 (fo. 73), 28 Apr.; (2) Sp 11/8, fos. 85-6 (fos. 83-4), 7 May; (3) SP 11/9, fo. 18 (fo. 16), 15 June, St. James; (4) SP 11/9 (fos. 25-6), 19 June; (5) SP 11/9, fos. 28-9, c.June; (6) SP 11/9, fos. 60-1 (fo. 62), 10 Sept., Croyden; (7) SP 11/9, fos. 68-9 (fos. 66-7), 16 Sept., Croyden; (8) SP 11/9 (fo. 73), c.Sept.; (9) SP 11/9, fos. 83-4 (fos. 81-2), 19 Oct., St James; (10) SP 11/9 (fos. 89-90), Oct.; (11) SP 11/9, fos. 98-9 (fos. 94-7), 22 Nov. Only one letter is dated 1558: SP 11/14, fo. 6, 27 Oct., St James.

[67] An example is Folger Shakespeare Library, MS L.b. 512, the Council to Sir Thomas Cawarden, from Richmond, 13 Aug. 1557, ordering him to deliver a canvas tent to Cuthbert Vaughan who had been dispatched northwards with 300 gunners; signed by Heath, Thirlby, Petre, Waldegrave, and Baker.

be 'a sort of privy council . . . for matters of state'.[68] This history begins with the manuscript source of the Council's own *Acts*, the printed version of which disguises the fact that for the period before 29 May 1555 the register on which it is based is a fair copy[69] of not one, but two parallel series of rough-copy books.[70] One series of registers was kept by Bourne and the other, concurrently, by Petre. At first this division could be explained politically by the genesis of the two rather different 'councils' which the two men represented, Bourne, the Kenninghall Council of War, and Petre, the professionals and others associated with Arundel and Paget. Increasingly, as Paget, Petre, and Arundel consolidated their hold on the Council's functions, the keeping of a second series of registers become superfluous and worse, confusing. Politically it was also embarrassing since Bourne, unlike Petre, was not a member of the 'inner ring' of advisers. Paget sought to remedy this situation by rationalizing the work of the secretaries and clerks: there would be one register for the working body of councillors. In order to safeguard the authenticity of letters originating in this group, the Council adopted on 20 May 1555 a seal for all correspondence 'passing this Boorde . . . the same to remayne in the custodie of the eldest Clerc of the Counsaill'.[71] At the time, the 'eldest' clerk was Bernard Hampton, first appointed during the tenures of Secretaries Petre

[68] Giovanni Michieli to the doge and Senate of Venice, from London, 9 Sept. 1555: *Ven. Cal.* vi (1), 183.

[69] PC 2/7, called 'Queen Mary Vol. II'.

[70] Lemasters ('The Privy Council', 243-60) discovered this. However, in his discussion of the Council registers for Mary's reign, Lemasters chose to describe the volumes in question not chronologically, according to the date of their production, but by place of archival deposit. Moreover, neither he nor anyone else who has written on the subject of the Tudor Council seems to have noticed the existence of BL Eg. MS 3723F, which came to light sometime after 1924 when an unknown copyist produced a typed transcription of it together with notes describing its provenance and appearance and its relation to the extant fair-copy (PC 2/7) to which it is clearly superior. This twentieth-century transcription is also in the BL under the reference: Eg. MS 3723B. In another place I intend to discuss Eg. MS 3723F. In any case, it certainly substantiates Lemasters's conclusions. The six known rough-copy registers for Mary's reign, with dates of proceedings covered in each, are: (1) PC 2/6 ('Queen Mary Vol. I', pt. 1): 14 July-19 Aug. 1553; (2) Hatfield House, Cecil Papers, 245/1: 16 July-3 Nov. 1553; (3) BL Add. Ms 26748: 9 or 10 Nov. 1553-9 Mar. 1554; (4) BL Eg. MS 3723F: 13 Nov. 1554-27 May 1555; (5) PC 2/6 ('Queen Mary Vol. I', pt. 2): 29 May 1555-2 Aug. 1557. Two fair-copy registers cover the proceedings for Mary's reign: PC 2/7 (known as 'Queen Mary Vol. II') for the period 22 Aug. 1553 to 30 Dec. 1557, and PC 2/8 ('Mary-Elizabeth Vol. I-A') for the period 1 Jan. 1558 to 12 May 1559.

[71] *APC* v. 130. See L. W. Labaree and R. E. Moody, 'The Seal of the Privy Council', *EHR* xliii (1928), 190-202.

and Cecil on 24 September 1551.[72] Since the senior, or 'eldest', clerk was also charged with the production of the Council book (in this case, under Petre's supervision), it cannot be coincidental that at almost the same time, on 29 May 1555, there begin the first entries in what was now one master, rough-copy register.[73]

The seal and the inauguration of a new register in May 1555 represented the administrative side of Paget's attempt to reorganize the Council. It has been thought that his promotion of the idea of a 'select council' was part of this plan, the seal especially becoming the instrument ensuring the secrecy of the 'select Council's' communications with Philip,[74] but this cannot be the case since the seal was applied to domestic letters from a Council on occasion numbering fifteen corresponding members,[75] while the register, which was clearly the product of the reforms of May 1555, never became the exclusive book of record of a 'council of state'. Was the 'council of state' a diplomatic deception designed to make Philip think that he was dealing formally with a 'select' few who governed in his and the queen's name, and at his command? The Council's own extant records seem to suggest as much. If Paget had created an institution in the mind of the future king of Spain, the deception served his purposes doubly well; it gave him the appearance of the king's full support, and preserved the integrity of the queen's Privy Council whose 'household' members, because of their connections with the ladies of the queen's Privy Chamber,[76] would have been able to overpower any formal attempt to replace them with eight councillors 'of state'.

CONCLUSION

In conclusion, the history of the formation of Mary's Privy Council in 1553 is really the story of two Councils that become one. To her 'personal' Council, appointed between 9 and 12 July, Mary in effect added another body of advisers of a very different complexion

---

[72] Hoak, *King's Council*, 271.

[73] This is the second part of 'Mary Vol. I' covering the period 29 May 1555 to 2 Aug. 1557: PC 2/6. See n. 71.

[74] Lemasters, 'The Privy Council', 274–6.

[75] *APC* vi. 261, the order for a letter to Lord Eure at Berwick, 6 Feb. 1558.

[76] Six of the ladies of the queen's Privy Chamber were wives of privy councillors: the Ladies Waldegrave, Jerningham, Cornwallis, Wharton, Strelly, and Petre; LC 2/4/(2).

on and shortly after 20 July. Rapidly changing military and political circumstances forced this pattern of appointments on her. However, the resulting Privy Council, although large and of diverse composition, functioned much in the manner of the ones appointed by Henry VIII, Edward VI (during the period of Northumberland's predominance, 1550–3), and Elizabeth I.

Two unforeseen turnings in mid-Tudor politics explain how this happened. The first occurred on the road from Hunsdon when Mary decided to resist the duke of Northumberland. News of her defiance, confirmed by the success of her 'flight', generated its own dynamic, and at Kenninghall the self-proclaimed queen set up a personal Council in order to arm her rebellion against 'the false Queen Jane'. Now Jane's Council, though of questionable legality, at least represented an established authority; its members, after all, had been Edward's councillors. By contrast, Mary's Kenninghall men embodied a revolution in Tudor Court politics: in national affairs nearly all of them were novices; none save Southwell were experienced former councillors. For about ten days in July 1553 this extraordinary band of provincial gentlemen, peers, and former servants of a princess of the blood headed up a royal military government in East Anglia. No one knows what might have been the course of Tudor history after 1553 had they, as a group, translated their power to Westminister.

In fact, political expediency had driven Mary to embrace the members of this revolutionary Kenninghall Council of War; political grace required that she retain them after Northumberland's surrender. But even before she arrived in London, political wisdom, probably Paget's, recommended the appointment of additional councillors, men who had served not only her father and brother, but also the Lady Jane. The resurrection of a majority of Jane's 'London lords' signalled something more than Mary's acknowledged mercy. It marked the beginning of the second Marian revolution, one that destroyed whatever possibilities the first might have held.

Since the existence of Mary's Kenninghall Council had escaped historical detection, no modern observer could have noticed the appearance of a 'second' Privy Council in 1553, that is, the one appointed between 20 July and 4 September. At Westminster the members of this 'second' Council assumed the direction of all of the most important matters of state; by the end of 1553 they had effectively replaced the Kenninghall men in the prime seats of power. Because this 'second' body of councillors consisted mostly of 'professionals' who had been active under Northumberland, its emergence and the subsequent reorganization of the whole Council by Paget represented a counter-revolutionary turning of affairs as important as Mary's original coup. By returning to power some of the key personnel of the Reformation state—an experienced clique of the governing élite—this internal revolution of 20 July–4 September 1553 preserved the continuity of Paget's programme of governmental reform, the programme set out in his 'Advise to the Kinges Counsail' of 1550.

Somewhat ironically, three events in 1555 assured the triumph of this programme, and hence the principle of government-by-Council thereafter: Gardiner's death, Mary's false pregnancy, and Philip's departure from England. The first of these removed Paget's only real opponent; the second guaranteed Elizabeth's succession; and the third, given Mary's capacities, made the party of the professionals politically indispensable for the rest of her reign.[77]

Such occurrences give one pause to ponder received notions about the course and nature of change in Tudor central government. 'Revolutions' there were, to be sure, but in what sense? The history of the formation and organization of Mary I's Privy Council reveals two true revolutions, or turnings, in Tudor government in 1553, though only the effects of the second survived that year and only then because of a series of accidents in 1555. But of such accidents is history often made; and on them does the fate of revolutions sometimes turn.

---

[77] As lord privy seal (after 29 Jan. 1556), Paget continued to dominate the conduct of state business. The internal evidence of a recently discovered document suggests, for example, that he originated the 'councils' of war and finance of Mar. 1558. The source usually cited as evidence of the membership of these committees— an addendum to Count Feria's letter to Philip of 10 Mar. 1558 (*Span. Cal.* xiii. 369) —would not indicate this, as it is a published translation of a Spanish note whose editor failed to explain that the enclosure in Spanish is itself a Spanish clerk's translation of an original list of members' names in English in a Tudor secretary hand; the original English list immediately precedes the Spanish copy on the same side of the folio: Archivo General de Simancas, Estado 811, fo. 106. (I wish to thank Dr Simon Adams for this reference and also for graciously supplying me with a photocopy of the manuscript.) The English hand appears to me to be that of Paget's clerk. In any case, Paget was probably the architect of these committees; he alone served on both the nine-member 'council of war' and the six-member 'council of finance'; ibid. Interestingly, the lord treasurer, Winchester, was not a member of the latter which included two non-councillors, Sir Walter Mildmay and Sir John Baker. See also Loades, *Mary Tudor*, 409–10.

APPENDIX

Privy councillors of Queen Mary I in order of appearance or swearing-in
(with title at time of appointment)

Privy Councillors	Date	Place (other than London)
1. Robert Rochester	9–12 July 1533	Kenninghall
2. Henry Jerningham	"	"
3. Edward Waldegrave	"	"
4. John Bourne	"	"
5. Sir Thomas Wharton	"	"
6. Richard Freston	"	"
7. Robert Strelly	"	"
8. Robert Peckham	"	"
9. Sir John Huddleston	"	"
10. John Bourchier, earl of Bath	"	"
11. Henry Radcliffe, earl of Sussex	"	"
12. Sir Henry Bedingfield	"	"
13. Sir John Shelton	"	"
14. Sir Richard Southwell	"	"
15. Sir John Mordaunt	"	"
16. Sir Richard Morgan	"	"
17. Sir William Drury	"	"
18. Clement Heigham	"	"
19. Sir Thomas Cornwallis	12 July	on the road from Kenninghall to Framlingham
20. Sir Nicholas Hare	12 July	Framlingham
21. Thomas Lord Wentworth	16 July	"
22. Henry Fitzalan, earl of Arundel	20 July	"
23. William Lord Paget	20 July	"
24. Richard Lord Rich	20 July	"
25. Sir Francis Englefield	24 July	Ipswich
26. Sir Edward Hastings	28 July	New Hall (Boreham, Essex)
27. Sir Edmund Peckham	29 July	"
28. John Russell, earl of Bedford	29 July	"
29. Sir William Petre	30 July	"
30. Sir John Mason	30 July	"
31. Sir John Gage	4 Aug.	
32. Sir John Baker	5 Aug.	
33. Stephen Gardiner, bishop of Winchester	5 Aug.	
34. Sir Thomas Cheyney	6 Aug.	
35. Sir Anthony St Leger	7 Aug.	
36. George Talbot, earl of Shrewsbury	10 Aug.	
37. Thomas Howard, duke of Norfolk	10 Aug.	

Privy Councillors *cont'd.*   Date *cont'd.*

38. William Herbert, earl of Pembroke	13 Aug.
39. William Paulet, marquess of Winchester	13 Aug.
40. Cuthbert Tunstall, bishop of Durham	14 Aug.
41. Edward Stanley, earl of Derby	17 Aug.
42. Sir Thomas West	17 Aug.
43. Nicholas Heath, bishop of Worcester	4 Sept.
44. Thomas Thirlby, bishop of Norwich	25 Oct.
45. William Lord Howard	3 Jan. 1554
46. Dr John Boxall	21 Dec. 1556
47. Sir Anthony Browne, Viscount Montague	28 Apr. 1557
48. Edward Lord Clinton	28 Apr. 1557
49. Dr Nicholas Wotton	by 10 Aug. 1557
50. William Cordell	5 Dec. 1557

Source: *Vita Mar. Reg.* 251–71; *APC*, vols. iv and v.

CHAPTER 5

PARLIAMENT: A 'NEW AIR'?*

JENNIFER LOACH

GEOFFREY Elton was the first of the revisionists. In 1965 he was already warning against the belief that the origins of the Civil War were to be found in the Parliaments of Elizabeth's reign: 'the system of parliamentary management perfected by Henry VIII and Thomas Cromwell, and further refined in the more difficult days of Queen Elizabeth, would no doubt have required tactful and sensible adjustment as the seventeenth century developed,' he concluded, 'but there is nothing in the story of 1604 to suggest that it had already ceased to be practicable.'[1] Elton's message has been noted, and most historians would now accept that the century after 1530 was one of substantial harmony in the relationship between crown and Parliament, and that the institution itself served the needs of both ruler and ruled satisfactorily until at least the 1620s.

There is a danger, however, that we may be so dazzled by Professor Elton's successful revision of the parliamentary history of the sixteenth and early seventeenth centuries that, exaggerating the importance of his favourite decade, we too easily regard the events of the 1530s and the achievement of Thomas Cromwell as responsible for a century of consensus and co-operation. Certainly, Thomas Cromwell achieved much, in Parliament as elsewhere: by permitting and even encouraging the frequent, wide-ranging, and often outspoken discussion of all topics, social and economic as well as political and religious, he fostered the notion of building a new world through statute.[2] Thus, a peculiarly English and concrete form of 'civic humanism' was born, and the Parliaments of the

* I am most grateful to Miss B. F. Harvey and to Mr R. A. C. Parker for reading and commenting on earlier drafts of this chapter.

[1] G. R. Elton, 'A High Road to Civil War', in *Studies in Tudor and Stuart Politics and Government* (Cambridge, 1974), ii. 182: originally published in C. H. Carter, ed., *From the Renaissance to the Counter-Reformation: Essays in Honour of Garrett Mattingly* (New York, 1965).

[2] G. R. Elton, *Reform and Renewal* (Cambridge, 1973), ch. 4.

later middle ages were transformed into the institution from which would emerge, in time, men such as Wilberforce and Peel. Parliaments after Thomas Cromwell were more exciting than they had been before, as well as better organized: the events of the 1530s thus helped to ensure that the English Parliament would survive whilst other, outwardly similar, institutions decayed.

But the change, although considerable, was not total; Parliament in the sixteenth century was still recognizably the same body as its medieval predecessors. It is important that Professor Elton's insights into the development of Parliament in the century after 1530 should not obscure his own emphasis on the continuity of parliamentary history, an emphasis that has led him to investigate a number of aspects of the Parliaments of the fifteenth century and earlier.[3] Parliament, at least until the 1580s, and probably beyond, was a medieval institution. It met only when summoned by the sovereign, who could prorogue or dismiss it at will. Its sittings were infrequent and erratic.[4] Receivers and triers of petitions were still appointed at the beginning of each parliament, even if their function was becoming quite different. The House of Lords still played an important, and perhaps dominant, role in many areas of legislation: its procedure was more highly developed than that of the Commons, and its members were more skilled.[5]

Physically, it is true, the events of the 1530s had changed Parliament. The spiritual peers, once perhaps a majority of those summoned to the House of Lords, shrank after the Reformation to a bench of twenty-six bishops.[6] The lay peers, by this time an established order sitting by prescriptive right rather than as a result of royal whim,[7] thus dominated, the more so because it was from

[3] G. R. Elton, *Studies in Tudor and Stuart Politics and Government* (Cambridge, 1983), iii, ch. 34.

[4] J. S. Roskell, 'Perspectives in English Parliamentary History', in E. B. Fryde and Edward Miller, eds., *Historical Studies of the English Parliament* (Cambridge, 1970), ii. 300–5.

[5] See M. A. R. Graves, *The House of Lords in the Parliaments of Edward VI and Mary I* (Cambridge, 1981).

[6] A. L. Brown, 'Parliament, *c*.1377–1422', in R. G. Davies and J. H. Denton, eds., *The English Parliament in the Middle Ages* (Manchester, 1981), 116. Roskell noted in 1956, however, that 'in the vast majority of cases it was really exceptional for an abbot to attend parliament in person': J. S. Roskell, 'The problem of the attendance of the Lords in mediaeval parliaments', *BIHR* xxix (1956), 174.

[7] A. R. Myers, 'Parliament, 1422–1509', in *The English Parliament in the Middle Ages*, 154–9, dates this change to the fifteenth century. Cf. Helen Miller, 'Attendance in the House of Lords during the reign of Henry VIII', *HJ* x (1967), 325–51.

their ranks that the great chancellors now came. In the Commons, change was even more considerable. The reorganization and integration of outlying parts of the kingdom that was one of Cromwell's achievements resulted in the representation in Parliament of Wales and Cheshire, and, for a time, Calais.[8] Over thirty members were thus added to the House of Commons.[9] But the growth of the Commons was not restricted to this consequence of administrative reform, for the size of the House increased over the whole century from 296 members to 462.

Sir John Neale in 1949 explained this growth as a response to the needs of patronage.[10] He argued that men of influence at Court, anxious to expand the amount of patronage at their disposal, asked the monarch to create new seats into which they could put their clients. This theory is obviously correct in the case of a number of Elizabethan constituencies.[11] It is true of Newport, Isle of Wight, for instance, where the borough recorded in 1584 that 'at the special instance of Sir George Carey'—governor of the island, and cousin of the queen—'two burgesses were admitted into the High Court of Parliament'; Carey was also 'the means and procurer of the liberty' of Newtown, Isle of Wight. It is probably correct to see the duke of Norfolk's influence behind the returns from Castle Rising, the earl of Rutland as the agent of East Retford's resumption of representation, and the earl of Leicester's hand in the emergence, or, rather, re-emergence, of Andover as a parliamentary borough. However, Neale's pupils and followers became so convinced by the theory of magnate pressure that they presumed it

---

[8] The act passed in 1536 for the reform of Calais' government and administration (27 Henry VIII, c. 63) provided for the representation of the city by two members, one to be chosen by the lord deputy, the other by the mayor.

[9] Tournai, which surrendered to the English in September 1513, was told by the king in a letter dated 18 November 1513 that it should send deputies to the Parliament that was to meet the next year (*LP* I. ii. 245–50). The city may also have sent representatives to the next Parliament, that of 1515, before being handed over to the French in 1519. (See C. G. Cruickshank, 'Parliamentary Representation of Tournai', *EHR* lxxxviii (1968), 775–6.) It is of interest that the earl of Hertford, governor of the Channel Isles, directed the estates of Jersey in December 1541 to send two Members to the Parliament shortly to be summoned; the estates notified the parishes but it appears that no representatives were sent (A. J. Eaglestone, *The Channel Islands under Tudor Government, 1485–1642* (Cambridge, 1949) 34). Hertford perhaps had the example of Calais in mind when he made this request.

[10] J. E. Neale, *The Elizabethan House of Commons* (London, 1949), ch. 7.

[11] On these boroughs see the constituency reports in *HC 1558–1603*.

even in the absence of evidence: the constituency reports in the
Elizabethan volumes of the History of Parliament Trust are a
witness of this. Neale himself was sometimes led astray by his own
theory, as in the case of Aylesbury, which he believed to have been
enfranchised at the request of a local gentleman, Sir John Pakington, whom recent research has shown to have been opposed to the
town's incorporation.[12] Similarly, Sir John Mason, a local figure of
some weight, initially opposed the incorporation of Abingdon,
stating that 'nothing more continueth a daily hurt to the realm
than corporations.'[13] Once the charter had been granted and the
borough had secured the right of representation, however, Mason
was anxious to influence the elections, as Pakington was to be at
Aylesbury. Local magnates were rarely enthusiastic about towns in
their area securing their liberties, as Walter Haddon noted in 1568
when Poole was seeking a charter: 'I have stayed this matter upon
my lord Mountjoy's [lord of the manor] importune requests these
ten or twelve weeks; and in the end he saieth nothing that is
material; and the town will be bound as high as he himself can
devise that their grant shall in no ways prejudice his right.'[14] None
the less, if, in the process of incorporation, parliamentary seats
were created, magnates would seize upon them. The fact that a
magnate subsequently put his clients into new seats does not, therefore, always prove that he was the instrument by which those seats
came into being, as Neale too readily supposed.

Even where magnates were clearly responsible for the creation of
a new seat there is no evidence that they were primarily concerned
with setting up 'a parliamentary interest'. It would seem—although
here caution is necessary, since contacts between clients and
patrons in the course of a parliamentary session are likely to have
been oral and therefore to have gone unrecorded—that magnates
were more interested in responding to the demands of their clients
than in the precise form those demands took. And what clients
wanted, the argument runs, was seats in the House of Commons; if
there were not enough seats to go round, the crown would be urged
to create more. This pressure of clients on patrons, and patrons on

[12] Neale, 175; Robert Tittler, 'The Incorporation of Boroughs, 1540–1558',
History, lxii (1977), 29–30.

[13] P. F. Tytler, *England in the Reigns of Edward VI and Mary* (London, 1839), i.
361–2.

[14] BL Lansd. MSS quoted in S. Bond and N. Evans, 'The process of granting
charters to English boroughs, 1547–1649', *EHR* xci (1976), 111.

the monarch, stemmed from what has been described as a 'novel desire to enter Parliament and a subsequent competition for seats':[15] encouraged by the changes of the 1530s, men now clamoured for a place in the Commons.

The difficulty about this argument is that a growing demand for seats in the House of Commons, like the 'gentry invasion of the boroughs', is a phenomenon whose origins are lost in the mists of time. By 1422, one out of every four burgesses returned to Parliament was a non-resident.[16] By the middle of the fifteenth century this trend was 'so marked as to amount to a revolution in the personnel of parliament',[17] and in Edward IV's reign boroughs were returning more outsiders than residents.[18] Re-election was common, and contested elections not infrequent.[19] Even the creation of new seats as a response to a demand for places in Parliament cannot be regarded as a phenomenon of the sixteenth century, or a response to the events of the 1530s.

In the middle ages, as in the sixteenth century, the size of the House of Commons had varied. Three hundred and two men had been summoned to the Parliament of 1295,[20] for example, but the numbers fell back in the early fifteenth century to about 250.[21] However, growth began again well before the reign of Henry VIII. May McKisack noted in 1932 that 'of the three parliaments of Edward IV for which returns are preserved, that of 1476 has returns from at least ninety-six boroughs, that of 1472 from at least ninety-seven, and that of 1478 from at least 101.'[22] The historian explaining why the House of Commons increased in size therefore needs to begin not with 'the latter part of Henry VIII's reign', nor even with the parliament of 1510—usually taken as the base from which calculations about, for instance, 'a fifty-six per cent increase' in size are estimated[23]—but with Henry VI's summons to Wootton Bassett, Hindon, Westbury, Heytesbury, and Gatton.

[15] G. R. Elton, *The Tudor Constitution* (2nd edn., Cambridge, 1982), 249.

[16] J. S. Roskell, *The Commons in the Parliament of 1422* (Manchester, 1954), 48–9.

[17] May McKisack, *The Parliamentary Representation of the English Boroughs during the Middle Ages* (Oxford, 1932), 113.

[18] Roskell, 133.

[19] K. N. Houghton, 'Theory and practice in borough elections during the later fifteenth century', *BIHR* xxxix (1966), 130–40.

[20] A. F. Pollard, *The Evolution of Parliament* (London, 1926), 398.

[21] Brown, 117–18.

[22] McKisack, 45.   [23] Elton, *The Tudor Constitution*, 248.

Even then, the pattern of representation was not fixed, however, for the concept of a 'parliamentary borough' was not yet clear,[24] nor did it become so for at least another century. In the middle ages, as we have seen, the number of boroughs returning men to Westminster fluctuated considerably; the highest number of boroughs returning representatives under Henry IV was 81, the lowest 71, and under Henry V, for example, the number varied from 87 to 74.[25] A borough that had once sent men did not necessarily do so again, nor do so consistently. This was because the instructions sent to sheriffs ordered them to secure the return of the knights of the shire and 'de quale civitate comitatus illius duos ciues et de quodlicet burgo duos burgenses'. In the late thirteenth and fourteenth centuries sheriffs had interpreted the meaning of their writs in very different ways. In 1295, for instance, the sheriff of Worcestershire had asked for returns from Worcester and six other boroughs, but his successors in 1307, 1314, and 1319 asked only the city. In 1298 the sheriff of Buckinghamshire returned no boroughs as fit for or liable to representation, whereas his successors in 1300 and 1308 asked for representatives from Amersham, Wendover, and Wycombe, as well as from, in 1308, Marlow; in 1302 and 1311 the sheriffs returned Wycombe alone.[26] The list of boroughs returning to Westminster solidified somewhat later on, as a tradition grew up 'as to which towns should be summoned and which should be exempt', and in 1382 a statute was passed requiring sheriffs to send only to 'ancient' boroughs.[27] None the less, considerable fluidity remained, and remained well into the sixteenth century. Thetford, for example, sent representatives in 1529, when they are named at the end of a list of knights and burgesses, together with those from two other Duchy boroughs, Lancaster and Preston,[28] but it did not send men again until 1547. Cirencester, which had returned at least once in the fourteenth century, sent burgesses in 1547, when the borough appears on a list

---

[24] J. F. Willard, 'Taxation boroughs and parliamentary boroughs, 1294–1336', in J. G. Edwards, V. H. Galbraith, E. F. Jacob, eds., *Historical Essays in Honour of James Tait* (Manchester, 1933), 417–35; T. F. T. Plucknett, 'Parliament, 1327–36', in *Historical Studies of the English Parliament*, i. 218. I am most grateful to Miss S. Reynolds and Mr P. A. Slack for discussing with me this problem of definition.

[25] McKisack, 44–5.

[26] Pollard, 396.

[27] McKisack, 28.

[28] SP 1/82, fo. 59.

almost at the end of the independent towns.[29] Its name also appears in October 1553 on one of the first extant crown office lists—that is, a list of returning constituencies drawn up by the clerk of the crown in Chancery—but was left blank.[30] On the next list, for the Parliament of April 1554, it was crossed out.[31] In 1571 it returned again, and despite having its case referred to a Commons committee, it continued to send thereafter.

Neither the clerk of the crown nor the House of Commons itself seems at this time to have had a clear notion of which boroughs were entitled to send representatives. The drawing up of a crown office list obviously went some way towards fixing the list of parliamentary boroughs, but it was in essence a record of returns, and not one that dictated the sending out of writs. The 'parliamentary pawn', the master list of summonses, whether of right, attendance or election, continued throughout this period to list only the sheriffs, leaving to them the question of which boroughs they should select for election writs.[32] That shadowy figure, the sixteenth-century sheriff, thus almost certainly retained in the choice of boroughs to which he sent writs some of the freedom of action of his predecessors. Neale believed that no sheriff would have dared to send to a 'new' borough without a special writ from Chancery, and that Chancery would not have issued such a writ without a warrant from the crown,[33] but there is no evidence in the records of any such procedure: his argument failed to take account of the fact that for centuries sheriffs had been deciding for themselves what was and what was not a suitable borough. Moreover, the surprise of the clerk of the crown at the first appearance of St Ives in 1558, when he had to squeeze it in at the end of his list of Cornish boroughs, suggests that he had received no prior warning of this addition to the list.[34]

---

[29] Hatfield MS 207.

[30] Bodley MS e museo 17, fo. 8. On crown office lists, see N. Fuidge, 'Some sixteenth century crown office lists at the Public Record Office', *BIHR* xlii (1969), 200–11.

[31] C 193/32/1. Cirencester does not appear at all on the next list, for November 1554 (Huntingdon Library, Hastings MSS Parliamentary Papers).

[32] C 218/1.

[33] Neale, 135.

[34] C 193/32/2. By the time that the William Salt list (Stafford County Record Office, William Salt Library 264) was drawn up, however, after the fall of Calais, the addition had been assimilated.

Of course, the sheriff, when deciding to which boroughs he should send his writs, may sometimes have been acting at the direction of the crown. More often, however, local circumstances would dictate his choice. Thus, as Neale noted, many boroughs with powerful patrons, men such as Cecil, Leicester, or the duke of Norfolk, acquired the right of representation during this period. Perhaps, as Neale envisaged, these magnates approached the queen directly and sought the right to return for boroughs under their care: Thomas Wilson's report to the earl of Rutland in 1579 that 'all the articles' had been allowed for the town of Newark 'save the nomination of two burgesses' perhaps implies some direct intervention by the earl.[35] But the patron may simply have approached the sheriff, or the sheriff himself have considered it tactful to send a precept to a borough protected by an influential figure. Certainly the fact that Andover resumed its returns two years after the earl of Leicester, the high steward, had been informed that he was mistaken in his belief that the borough normally returned men to Westminster, suggests that someone had told the sheriff to add it to his list.[36]

There is also some correlation between the grant of a charter and the sending of a writ to elect, despite the fact that few charters made mention of parliamentary representation, as if, when deciding on the suitability of a borough for the receipt of a writ, the sheriff was impressed by the recent grant of a charter. This explains, for instance, the returns from Grantham that followed the grant of a charter in 1463,[37] those of Boston, which sent men to Westminster from 1547 despite the absence of any mention of representation in its charter of 1545,[38] and those from St Albans, Minehead, Tamworth, and other places. It was, in fact, unusual for parliamentary representation to be granted for the first time in a charter. In the mid-fifteenth century Ludlow and Much Wenlock had secured the right to representation via their charters,[39] but the practice remained rare until the later sixteenth century. Thus, of the forty-two boroughs receiving grants of incorporation between

---

[35] *HMC Rutland*, i. 117.

[36] *HC 1558–1603*, i, constituency report.

[37] *CCR* vi. 199.

[38] *LP* XX. i. 846 (38): M. Weinbaum, *British Borough Charters, 1307–1660* (Cambridge, 1943), 69–70.

[39] *CCR* vi. 155–61, 229–32.

1540 and 1558,[40] only five—Abingdon,[41] Aylesbury,[42] Banbury,[43] Higham Ferrers,[44] and St Albans[45]—appear to have included a grant of the right to representation amongst their clauses. (The charters for Buckingham, Chippenham, Droitwich, High Wycombe, and Maldon recognized an already existing right.) The infrequency with which parliamentary boroughs were created by charter is, however, hardly surprising since, as Sandys acknowledged in 1621 and Prynne noted later, parliamentary representation was in essence 'no franchise, but a service', and not, therefore, something to be granted in a charter of 'liberties':[46] a charter was, indeed, not infrequently a means by which parliamentary representation might be avoided, as in the case of Woodstock, where the charter granted in 1453 promised that 'the mayor and commonalty shall not be compelled to chose any burgesses for the borough to come to the king's parliaments'.[47]

The only sanction of their presence that most members could produce was, therefore, the precept sent them by the sheriff. The first return for Knaresborough rests its validity entirely, as far as is known, on the warrant sent by the sheriff 'by veryue of the quenes majesties writt vnto him directed':[48] the first election at Morpeth, in October 1553, rests only on the precept of the sheriff of Northumberland.[49] Not enough first returns survive for us to be certain, but it is possible that boroughs returning for the first time, or for the first time after a long gap, took care to mention their precept; thus, the first return for Stockbridge, Hampshire, in 1563, declares that 'the sayd bayliffe and burgesses by authoryte of a precept lately to vs directed by the said sheriff' have proceeded to an election.[50] The first return from Boston in 1547 mentions the sheriff,[51] as does that from Aldeborough in 1571.[52]

[40] Robert Tittler, 'The Emergence of Urban Policy', in Jennifer Loach and Robert Tittler, eds., *The Mid-Tudor Polity* (London, 1980), 93.

[41] *CCR* (1555–7), 380–6.

[42] Ibid. (1553–4), 45–7.

[43] Ibid., 246–7.

[44] Ibid. (1555–7), 200–3, does not mention representation at Westminster, for which see C 66/904/27.

[45] *CPR* (1553), 33–4.

[46] W. Prynne, *The First Part of a Brief Register* (London, 1659–64), iv. 1182.

[47] *CCR* vi. 125–7.

[48] C 219/21/20.

[49] C 219/21/115.

[50] C 219/27/5.

[51] C 219/18c/58v.

[52] C 219/29/136.

Parliamentary boroughs were thus 'created' by the receipt of a writ from the sheriff more often than they were created by a charter. In the reign of Charles II some members were to argue that the right of representation could not be created by means of a charter;[53] in the sixteenth century members seem to have been very unclear as to how such rights were conveyed. In 1563 the returns of St Mawes and St Germans were challenged, as were those of Minehead, Tamworth, and Stockbridge.[54] All these boroughs were returning for the first time, or for the first time for at least a century. Their cases were considered by a committee of the House, as was that of Tregony, which had, in fact, returned in 1559 for the first time since the fourteenth century. (However, the committee was not instructed to consider the claims of Clitheroe, Sudbury, and Newton, all of which had returned in 1559 for the first time, nor that of Beverley, which sent representatives for the first time in 1563.) The members for the boroughs under consideration were asked by the speaker to show 'letters patents, why they be returned in this Parliament.' Presumably, none could do so. Minehead's charter of 1559 makes no mention of Parliament, nor does that of Tamworth, incorporated in 1560.[55] None of the other boroughs had recently received charters or grants of letters patent. Despite this, all continued to send representatives to Westminster. When the right of East Looe, Fowey, Cirencester, Queenborough, East Retford, Christchurch, Aldeborough, and Eye was challenged in 1571, a committee ordered 'by Mr. Attorney's Assent, that the Burgesses shall remain according to the returns; for that the Validity of the Charters of their Towns is elsewhere to be examined, if Cause be.'[56] Burgesses were always returned for these boroughs thereafter. However, the majority had no charter at all; Eye had none granting the right of representation until 1575, and East Looe none before 1587:[57] the question of which court had the right to scrutinize charters was therefore irrelevant. Thus the House seems to have been uncertain, even when it began to look

[53] E. de Villiers, 'The parliamentary boroughs restored by the House of Commons, 1621–1641', *EHR* lxvii (1952), 202.

[54] For what follows, see *CJ* 19, 22 Jan. 1562/3, and *HC 1558–1603,* vol. i, constituency reports. (That on Clitheroe fails to point out that the 1559 return was the first of the sixteenth century.)

[55] For Minehead, see *CPR* (1558–60), 2–3; for Tamworth, ibid. (1560–3), 7–8.

[56] *CJ* 6, 7 and 9 Apr. 1571.

[57] For Eye, see *CPR* (1572–5), 384–5; for East Looe, *HC 1558–1603,* vol. i, constituency report.

more systematically at returns, about what constituted a valid claim to representation.

Moreover, it is probable that, at least until the reign of Elizabeth, any borough that wished to send representatives could do so without having its right questioned by the House. Thus, boroughs such as Bossiney, Mitchell, and Petersfield returned from 1547 onwards unchallenged. The only recorded instance of the House intervening is the case of Maidstone, which returned men for the first time in March 1553, perhaps on the strength of a charter granted in 1549, although the charter made no mention of Parliament.[58] More than halfway through the session, two lawyer members were ordered to scrutinize the charter and see whether the burgesses had a right to sit.[59] There is no record of what they reported, nor, indeed, whether they did so. However, the borough did not return again until 1563, when it acted on a specific clause in its new charter of 1559.[60] Whether the gap was the result of the lawyers' report, or whether it stemmed from the revocation of the Edwardian charter claimed by Lambarde as Mary's punishment of the town for its part in Wyatt's Rebellion is not known, although the revocation of the charter, if it happened, should not *per se* have prohibited the borough from returning members. However, with this possible exception, it was not until the second of Elizabeth's Parliaments that the House appears to have taken any sustained interest in its own composition, and even then the setting up of the committee to consider the case of the boroughs returning for the first time was the result of a chance call of the House taken because the Chamber appeared too full. Moreover, boroughs continued, as one disgruntled burgess noted, to send representatives 'rather by usurpation than of any lawful right or authority'.[61] During this period the notion of parliamentary representation as a duty rather than a privilege seems to have prevailed with most members of the Lower House, who would not therefore challenge any borough taking the obligation upon itself.

It is, of course, significant that boroughs did claim or claimed afresh, the duty of representation, whereas in the late fourteenth century towns such as Colchester, Maldon, Hull, and Torrington

[58] *CPR* (1548-9), 174-6.

[59] *CJ* 21 Mar. 1552/3.

[60] *CPR* (1558-60), 413-14. See also the constituency reports in *HC 1509-1558*, vol. i, and *HC 1558-1603*, vol. i.

[61] Ibid. 130 (East Looe), citing E 112/6/9, fo. 42, and E 134, 28 Eliz Hilary 8.

had been anxious to secure exemption.[62] However, boroughs remained very conscious of the financial burden of representation, as the example of Newborough shows. Newborough, the newly created shire town of Anglesey, returned members to the Parliaments of the 1540s until a statute of 1549 demoted it and restored Beaumaris to its former primacy.[63] A clause in the Act freed the inhabitants of Newborough from 'any of the charges or expenses of any the Burgesses which hereafter shall be returned to any Parliament for the town of Beaumaris and village of Newborough or either of them'. Newborough was thus deprived of any representation at Westminster, but seems to have regarded that as a fair price to pay for its release from a financial burden: not until the eighteenth century were the Newborough authorities to claim that freedom from payment 'was only compensation for their loss of status and did not represent a loss of voting rights'. Indeed, the shift from reluctance to readiness was not yet complete, as the history of Woodstock indicates. Although protected by its charter of 1453 from the burden of representation, Woodstock sent members to the Parliament of October 1553, and again to the Parliaments of April and November 1554.[64] This looks like a complete reversal of earlier policy, but after the departure for Guernsey of the local grandee, Sir Leonard Chamberlain, Woodstock reverted and did not return men again until 1571. Chamberlain had presumably been responsible for the sheriff's dispatch of a writ in 1553 and 1554; without him it did not arrive, and was not actively sought by the town itself.

Moreover, some boroughs that might be thought to have had an excellent case for representation, either because of their economic importance or because they had returned members in the past, made no attempt to send men to Westminster in the sixteenth century. Thus, for example, Warwick, Coventry, Nuneaton, Birmingham, Tamworth, Coleshill, Alcester, and Stratford had all been represented in the Parliament of 1275, whereas only Warwick, Coventry, and Tamworth returned in the sixteenth century, Tamworth being the only borough of these to secure its right afresh after a long gap. This reluctance by boroughs to claim a right that

[62] On 25 May 1413, Colchester was given permission not to send representatives for 12 years. *CPR* (1413–16), 23. For Maldon, Hull, and Torrington, see Pollard, 394.

[63] P. S. Edwards, *Welsh History Review* x (1980), 64. I am grateful for this reference to Mr C. S. L. Davies.

[64] *CCR* vi. 125–7; *HC 1509–1558*, vol. i, constituency report.

had once been theirs contrasts very markedly with the situation in the 1620s, when Pontefract, Ilchester, Hertford, Amersham, Wendover, Marlow, Weobley, and Milborne Port were all to argue, successfully, that they were entitled to elect because they had done so in the remote past; Ashburton, Cockermouth, Honiton, Okehampton, New Malton, Northallerton, and Seaford were to make the same claims in 1641.[65] In the sixteenth century, however, these boroughs were content without representation.

The seventeenth-century restorations were often encouraged by local magnates wishing to extend their electoral influence, as Sir Thomas Wentworth did at Pontefract and Sir Robert Phelips at Ilchester:[66] the restorations of the 1620s in particular 'served to strengthen the county representation by increasing the number of seats available for the neighbouring gentry'.[67] Even the restorations of the Long Parliament were the result of 'local and haphazard' initiative.[68] The fact that jockeying for seats in this manner did not occur until nearly a century after the fall of Thomas Cromwell must throw some doubt on the argument that what happened in the 1530s made gentlemen anxious to have a voice in Parliament. Boroughs and potential members of the Commons alike seem to have been able to restrain their enthusiasm for seats at least until the end of the 1570s, and probably until the turn of the century. Pollard's nebulous observation that the increase in the size of the Commons was a reflection of 'the general growth of national sentiment and of the popular desire for a voice in its own affairs' has some truth in it, provided that 'popular' is interpreted in a narrow and essentially propertied sense.[69] So has Professor Elton's view that the 1530s increased 'the real involvement in parliamentary affairs of both gentry and free holders',[70] but the development was a patchy and partial one.

Pollard was, of course, writing as he did in an attempt to counter the nineteenth-century view that the growth in the size of the Commons was a result of Tudor 'packing'. He was correct in wishing to demolish the concept of packing—the creation of single-member

[65] E. de Villiers, 175.

[66] A. J. Fletcher, 'Sir Thomas Wentworth and the Restoration of Pontefract as a Parliamentary Borough', *Northern History* vi (1971), 88–97.

[67] E. de Villiers, 185.

[68] Ibid. 199.

[69] Pollard, 164.

[70] Elton, *The Tudor Constitution*, 248.

constituencies is, of course, in itself a substantial argument against it, since any monarch interested in packing would not have thrown away the opportunity to create two seats—but he, and historians after him, have perhaps gone too far in their dismissal of the monarch as an interested party in the growth of the Commons: Elton, for example, declares that 'it used to be supposed that the Crown wished to pack Parliament; but it is now established beyond doubt that this expansion arose from entirely different causes', and goes on to discuss pressure from boroughs and the gentry's growing desire for a seat in the Commons.[71] Yet, as he himself has so clearly shown, the crown's requirement of 'useful' men in the Commons was acute.[72] More and more privy councillors found seats in the Lower House, but they were not the only agents of the crown whose presence was needed: lawyers, civil servants, and men of discretion and proven worth were crucially important if this amateur and often aimless body were to be pushed to the completion of necessary business. In order to find seats for such men, the crown was sometimes required to intervene in elections, as Thomas Cromwell did with such success, and as the duke of Northumberland attempted to do in 1552 and 1553. The creation of new boroughs was an obvious complement to this policy.

The crown, therefore, very substantially increased the number of boroughs returning men to Westminster in areas under royal control. Duchy of Cornwall boroughs such as Newport, Camelford, Grampound, Bossiney, Saltash, West Looe, and East Looe were given representation, as were some boroughs in which the crown had direct influence, such as Banbury, Taunton, and Bishop's Castle. The bulk of the new constituencies lay, however, in the Duchy of Lancaster. Lancaster, Liverpool, Thetford, Wigan, and Preston began to return in the reign of Henry VIII, and Aldborough, Ripon, Knaresborough, Boroughbridge, and Higham Ferrers in the 1550s. Elizabeth added Clitheroe, Stockbridge, Sudbury, and Newton, Lancashire. Writs of election for constituences within the Duchy were issued directly by the Duchy office, and the records show that very considerable influence was exerted in the elections. At Ripon and Knaresborough, for example, the names of members

---

[71] Ibid. 248–9.

[72] 'Tudor Government: The Points of Contact. I. Parliament', in *Studies in Tudor and Stuart Politics and Government*, iii. 18–19: originally published in *TRHS*, 5th series xxiv (1974).

are often in a different ink from the remainder of the return, suggesting that blank spaces were left for the names to be inserted. A letter written in 1555 to the earl of Shrewsbury, president of the Council in the North, noted that the members for Ripon had been 'appointed by Mr. Controller', that is, by Sir Robert Rochester, chancellor of the Duchy and comptroller of the Household.[73] Another letter to Shrewsbury, in the same year, from Sir William Petre, reveals the interest taken by the Privy Council in these elections. Petre declared, 'for the matter you wrote me to haue one of the counsayle ther in Mr. Chaloners place, my lords haue not yet resolued, nor moued the Queens Majestie';[74] quite what was at issue here is not clear, but Sir Thomas Chaloner, whose name was on the return, appears to have been replaced as one of the burgesses for Knaresborough by George Eden.

The pattern of representation in such boroughs is clear. Preston, for example, was represented in 1545 by a privy councillor, Sir Ralph Sadler, and by a servant of the chancellor of the Duchy, John Bourne, himself to be a councillor a decade later. In 1547 the borough was represented by John Hales, a close associate of Protector Somerset, and in March 1553 by a lawyer shortly to be elevated to the peerage as Viscount Montagu, and by a courtier and civil servant, Thomas Fleetwood. Mary's equerry, John Herle, sat for the borough in 1555, and the distinguished lawyer, Sir Robert Southwell, a brother of the privy councillor, represented it in 1558. In 1559 Cecil's servant, Roger Alford, sat for Preston, together with one of Cecil's brothers-in-law; thereafter Sadler's sons-in-law, attornies of the Duchy, and, in 1601, the clerk of the Privy Council, filled the seat. Buckingham, a manor in the hands of the crown, provides another example of the way in which such boroughs were used. It was represented in 1529 by a teller of the Exchequer, John Hasilwood, in 1536 by an Augmentations official, Thomas Pope, and by George Gifford, a close adherent of Thomas Cromwell; the pattern remained in Elizabeth's reign, with John Fortescue, the future privy councillor and chancellor of the exchequer sitting in 1586, and his son taking over when he moved to one of the seats for Buckinghamshire—which he also represented, of course, in 1604.

[73] College of Arms, Talbot MS P 268, printed also in Edmund Lodge, *Illustrations of English History* (London, 1838).
[74] Talbot MS C 139, also printed in Lodge. I am grateful to George Bernard for the College of Arms references.

Bishop's Castle, a Shropshire borough in the hands of the crown, returned from 1584 onwards; Exchequer officials and Cheshire lawyers filled the seat.

The fact that the crown used the boroughs at its disposal in order to find seats for useful men is well known: what needs to be recognized is that a significant number of the boroughs thus at its disposal were new creations. Moreover, the scale of those creations is very large. Until the middle of Elizabeth's reign there can be little doubt that the needs of the crown were a far more important reason for the creation of new boroughs than was any pressure from magnates seeking seats for their clients, or from gentlemen anxious to join in 'the political government of the nation'.

Around the middle of Elizabeth's reign things changed.[75] The first claim to representation in the sixteenth century known to have been refused by the crown is that of Newark in 1579, which Thomas Wilson explained as because 'it is thought that there are over many [burgesses] already and that there will be a device hereafter to lessen the number for divers decayed towns'.[76] Before 1579 there appears to have been no anxiety about decayed boroughs seeking the right of representation. The boroughs summoned for the first time by Henry VI were all small. A statute of 1542 dealing with decayed towns had covered Buckingham,[77] which returned from 1529, while another statute, two years later,[78] included in its scope Lancaster, which had returned men to Westminster in 1529 and was to do so from 1545 onwards, Preston, of which the same is true, Liverpool and Wigan, both of which began to send representatives in 1545. Indeed, in a debate in 1571 on the residential qualifications of members of the Commons, an unknown speaker argued at some length, and to the obvious approval of the anonymous diarist who recorded his speech, that it was particularly important that decayed boroughs should be represented in Parliament, since their representatives 'feeling their smart can best make

[75] In an attempt to explain why new creations came to an end in 1586, the editor of the Elizabethan volumes of *The House of Commons* makes an uncharacteristic error when he declares that 'it may not be a coincidence that the last batch of irregular enfranchisements occurred in 1586, and that the so-called 'parliamentary pawns' survive from 1586.' It is a neat argument, but in fact parliamentary pawns, that is, the master lists of individuals and areas to which writs were to be sent, survive from 1529, 1539, 1545, and for most Parliaments thereafter (C 218/1).

[76] *HMC Rutland*, i. 117.

[77] 33 Henry VIII, c. 36.

[78] 35 Henry VIII, c. 4.

relacion of their state, and knowinge their countrey may devise of such helpes as without the hurt of other places may restore the old ruines'.[79] His words did not, apparently, pass unheeded, for the last big bunch of boroughs returning for the first time included at least two decayed boroughs, Bere Alston and Newtown, Isle of Wight.

It seems to have been the crown rather than the House itself that became worried about the representation of decayed boroughs. James I felt particularly strongly about it. His first election proclamation instructed sheriffs not to send their precepts to boroughs 'so utterly decayed and ruined that there are not sufficient residents to make such choice and of whom lawful election may be made'.[80] James was also said to have been opposed to the bill for the enfranchisement of Durham, because he felt that decayed boroughs such as Old Sarum should first lose their representatives before the House increased still further in size.[81] Amongst the boroughs 'revived' by command of the Commons during his reign, however, were a number of decayed towns; only two of them were to survive the redistribution of seats effected by the Instrument of Government, and those had only one member each.

None the less, procedure had certainly tightened up by the end of Elizabeth's reign. An attempt by Doncaster, encouraged by Robert Cecil, to secure the right of representation in 1597 failed, apparently because the clerk of the crown and the clerk of the Parliament were not prepared to accept the return.[82] In the next Parliament Harwich tried to return members and failed: the borough therefore secured a charter in 1604 explicitly granting the privilege.[83] All those boroughs returning for the first time in James's reign could claim that their right rested on a new charter, and all those 'restored' had explicitly been given permission by the House of Commons itself to send representatives again. This greater concern with legal niceties implies a change in attitudes: representation was now beginning to be seen as a right and not an obligation.

It is the business of the historian to observe change, and Tudor historians owe an enormous debt to Professor Elton for his deline-

[79] *Proceedings in the Parliaments of Elizabeth I*, ed. T. E. Hartley (Leicester, 1981), i. 226.

[80] *Stuart Royal Proclamations*, eds. P. L. Hughes and J. F. Larkin (Oxford, 1973), i.

[81] E. de Villiers, 176, citing SP 14/167/10.

[82] *HMC Hatfield MSS*, vii. 442.   [83] Weinbaum, 37.

ation of the changes of the 1530s. It is not to belittle the significance of those changes to argue that contemporaries were perhaps
less aware of them than is the historian. What happened in the
Parliaments of that decade, and the fact that it happened in Parliament, had far-reaching consequences for political as well as constitutional development, but even politically aware Englishmen
may not have been conscious of this for some decades. Gentlemen,
who had, after all, been sitting for borough seats since at least the
early fifteenth century, may have become even more anxious to do
so, and competition for borough seats, observable from at least the
later fifteenth century, may have increased, but the House of Commons of the 1540s was not generically different from that of the
1460s.[84] Elton is undoubtedly correct to see the history of Parliament in the sixteenth century as the 'transformation of the House
of Commons from a body of local representatives, charged with
communicating the locality's grievances to the king's government,
into an aspiring partner in the political government of the nation',[85]
but it may well be that the transformation was both more advanced
in the 1530s than has sometimes been suggested, and more slow and
partial thereafter.

[84] Probably the most important change in the House of Commons during this
period was the securing, at the beginning of Edward's reign, of the upper part of St
Stephen's chapel as a meeting-house. The acquisition with it of a lobby or vestibule
resulted in the development of the division, a more accurate form of counted vote.

[85] Elton, *The Tudor Constitution*, 249.

CHAPTER 6

THE STRUCTURE OF EARLY TUDOR FINANCE, c.1509–1558

J. D. ALSOP

OF all aspects of early Tudor government, the one which underwent the most profound administrative change in the half-century from the death of Henry VII to the accession of Elizabeth I was central finance. This period saw the collapse of the household 'chamber system' of Edward IV and Henry VII, the expansion of the Reformation era and multiplication of separate revenue departments, and finally the retrenchment and amalgamations which created the Exchequer supremacy of 1554.[1] The rapidity and intricacy of the alterations defy simple description; they also compound the difficulties involved in assessing the character and significance of these changes. This study is concerned with this latter topic: it is an analysis of the essential nature of fiscal administration in the light of the structural transformations of this era. Since finance, quite properly, has always been accorded a central place in the controversy over the existence of a revolution in government during Henry VIII's reign,[2] the topic possesses considerable general significance.

I

In general terms, previous historical interpretations have been characterized by two distinct approaches. Ever since serious interest in the management of early sixteenth-century crown revenue began in the first decades of this century, specialists have tended to write in

[1] For detailed exposition the reader is referred to the specialist literature cited below. The best short summaries, representing three differing viewpoints, are: G. R. Elton, *The Tudor Constitution* (2nd edn., Cambridge, 1982), 39–45, 129–34; W. C. Richardson, ed., *The Report of the Royal Commission of 1552* (Morgantown, West Virginia, 1974), pp. xvii–xxiv, xxxii–xxxiii; Penry Williams, *The Tudor Regime* (Oxford, 1979; repr. 1981), 46–54.

[2] For example: G. R. Elton, G. L. Harriss, and Penry Williams, 'A Revolution in Tudor History?', *P & P* xxv (1963), 25–30, 33, 45–8, 51–5, xxix (1964), 41, 44–7, xxxi (1965), 92, 95, xxxii (1965), 106–9; B. P. Wolffe, 'Yorkist and Early Tudor

terms of radical change and revolution. This is true of both the pioneering work of A. P. Newton and F. C. Dietz,[3] and the more elaborate administrative studies of W. C. Richardson and G. R. Elton, to which we owe most of our knowledge of this subject.[4] On the other hand, influential general writers, such as Pollard, Read, and Bindoff, have implicitly minimized the significance of innovations by devoting—at most—cursory attention to the topic.[5] Their silence has helped set the scene for the more recent emergence of a school of thought explicitly hostile to the revolutionary model. But nothing illustrates more the total lack of agreement on the essentials of government than the fact that the argument for continuity can be expressed in contrasting ways: in both the late medieval and early modern periods government was essentially bureaucratic and therefore its character remained unchanged;[6] alternatively, in both periods the household was of fundamental importance and therefore the basic nature of government was unaltered.[7] Among the advocates

Government, 1461–1509' (Historical Association pamphlet, 1966), 13–16, 19–20; M. D. Palmer, *Henry VIII* (London, 1971), 21–6; C. S. L. Davies, *Peace, Print and Protestantism 1450–1558* (London, 1976), 196, 227–8; B. W. Beckingsale, *Thomas Cromwell: Tudor Minister* (London, 1978), 50–3, 147–9; Williams, *Tudor Regime*, 52–4.

[3] A. P. Newton, 'Tudor Reforms in the Royal Household', in R. W. Seton-Watson, ed., *Tudor Studies Presented . . . to Albert Frederick Pollard* (London, 1924), 231–2; F. C. Dietz, 'Finances of Edward VI and Mary', *Smith College Studies in History*, iii (1918), 61, 72–4, and *English Government Finance, 1485–1558* (Urbana, 1921; repr. 1964), [3], 60, 77, and *passim*.

[4] The relevant works of these two writers are too numerous to list in full. The most important are: W. C. Richardson, *Tudor Chamber Administration, 1485–1547* (Baton Rouge, 1952), and *History of the Court of Augmentations, 1536–1554* (Baton Rouge, 1961); G. R. Elton, *The Tudor Revolution in Government* (Cambridge, 1953; repr. 1974).

[5] A. F. Pollard, *Henry VIII* (London, 1902; repr. 1913); A. D. Innes, *England Under the Tudors* (London, 1905); Conyers Read, *The Tudors* (New York, 1936); S. T. Bindoff, *Tudor England* (London, 1950; repr. 1955); J. A. Williamson, *The Tudor Age* (London, 1953).

[6] G. L. Harriss, 'A Revolution in Tudor History?', xxv. 24–9; Wolffe, 'Yorkist and Early Tudor Government', 4–5, and *passim*.

[7] David Starkey, 'The Age of the Household: Politics, Society and the Arts c.1350–c.1550', in Stephen Medcalf, ed., *The Context of English Literature: The Later Middle Ages* (London, 1981), 225–90. For finance see David Starkey, 'The King's Privy Chamber, 1485–1547' (University of Cambridge Ph.D. thesis, 1973), 357–413. The published views of Dr Harriss, Dr Wolffe, and Dr Starkey cannot all be placed into simple categories, and all have interpreted late medieval and early modern government as a mixture of administrative forms. But, implicitly and explicitly the first two scholars have tended to deny the presence of a revolution because of the continuity of the bureaucratic element in government, while the last has stressed the continuity of the household's significance in government.

of fundamental change, disagreement is no less in evidence. Dr Richardson, building upon Newton's tentative theories, has articulated the belief that Henry VII's Chamber was the home of an innovative, reforming approach to crown finance which largely transformed administration through the vehicle of the new revenue departments of Henry VIII's reign. In contrast, Professor Elton has argued that these new departments were not the culmination of the Chamber system, but rather, by their bureaucratic and institutionalized nature its very opposite: they were the product of a revolutionary reform movement of the 1530s, engineered by Thomas Cromwell, which succeeded in reducing personal household government to an irrevocably subsidiary role in national administration.

The battle lines have been drawn boldly across an extensive territory, taking into their compass the characteristics of medieval and modern administration, the relative importance of bureaucratic and household government, and the speed, nature, and causation of extensive structural alterations. This in itself helps account for the impasse which has been reached. Adequate definitions of what constitutes, for example, a medieval or a modern financial system are totally lacking, and in the absence of this the terms serve not as useful intellectual tools, but as irrelevant complications. Moreover, the main participants in the scholarly debate have all approached the topic from different backgrounds. It is not inevitable that scholars whose periods of specialization are up to a century or more apart, and whose primary interests are divided between finance, financial administration, and government and politics, will fail to reach agreement. But the terms of reference which each has chosen as most suitable for his own work are not fully compatible. In these circumstances it is little wonder that the experts appear to be talking at cross-purposes, and that the non-specialist has difficulty in relating the expressed positions to each other and reaching a satisfactory understanding of the subject.

What, for example, should be made of the sudden creation or formal constitution of four revenue institutions in the years between 1536 and 1542 (the Courts of Augmentations, First Fruits and Tenths, Wards—altered in 1542 to Wards and Liveries—and General Surveyors of the King's Lands and Revenues), followed by the amalgamation of the most prominent (Augmentations and General Surveyors—already merged in 1547 to form the second Court of Augmentations—and First Fruits and Tenths) with the

Exchequer in 1554? Assessments of these structural alterations contrast sharply. For Dr Harriss, who believes that the basis of late medieval government was the regular, institutionalized departments of state outside the household, the expansion of financial agencies holds little novelty and, indeed, the process can in some respects be interpreted as nothing more than the climax of personalized, ephemeral empire-building on the familiar pattern. Since the system returned to its 'medieval practice' with the 1554 revival of the Exchequer, the entire episode which began with Edward IV's expansion of the Chamber possesses no long-term significance.[8] By contrast, Professor Richardson has concentrated on the transformation in basic administrative and accounting machinery, tracing this from Henry VII's Chamber, through the new departments, into the Exchequer. Except in so far as it exemplifies the formalization and acceptance of these methods, he is relatively unconcerned about the changing overall structure. Thus Richardson can conceive of a fundamental, modern, reform in fiscal administration, in spite of the impermanence of the institutions. But it must be realized that this is limited to his own particular area of interest.[9] It is Professor Elton who has elevated the subject to its highest plane in seeking within administrative alterations the key to the essence of Tudor government itself. The new agencies play a prominent role in his coverage because the critical 'modern' development in his terms was the establishment of a dominant, institutionalized, national governmental structure. When the structural changes are placed into this visionary framework, it is clear that the life-spans of particular departments are of little general significance, so long as the ultimate arrangement consolidated bureaucratic, regularized government— as, for example, in a reformed Exchequer—and did not revert to the flexible, undifferentiated household system.[10] Dr Williams's position is more complex. Although aware of innovation and cumulative change, he too stresses the impermanence of the early Tudor edifice and the return to 'the old system of Exchequer finance'.[11] But he appears to reject the notion of a 'substantial transformation' because, as he argues, there was neither any movement towards a financial machinery which was fundamentally different in function

---

[8] Harriss, 'A Revolution in Tudor History?', xxv. 25–9.

[9] Richardson, *Chamber Administration, passim,* and *Augmentations, passim.*

[10] Elton, *Tudor Revolution,* 160–258.

[11] Williams, 'A Revolution in Tudor History?', xxv. 45–50; xxxi, 95; *Tudor Regime,* 47–8, 52–4.

or purpose (i.e. one where a single institution had control and authority over all aspects of national finance including budgets, expenditure, and revenue creation), nor was there the establishment of a strictly bureaucratic administration in which the role of the individual was regulated and of limited significance.[12] The impression from this is that Dr Williams has adopted as his yardstick contemporary British government; it is only from this perspective that Tudor finance can be described, without reservation, as far from 'modern'.

The perceived presence or absence of a revolution or transformation, therefore, has depended not only upon knowledge of the historical data, but also upon the framework in which this was placed. The point to be stressed here is that in both respects assessments have been limited. Broad concepts are not to be discouraged, but when they result in diametrically opposite views no amount of philosophizing, citation of secondary authorities, or selection of isolated facts will resolve the issue. Historians must return to the sources. This is particularly true for early Tudor finance. One might have thought that the publication of a series of specialized works covering most of the principal revenue agencies would have rendered further research redundant, or at best marginal in significance. Nothing could be further from the truth. Dietz is the only scholar to have attempted a comprehensive study of sixteenth-century finance. His pioneering work was a notable achievement of continuing value (despite the understandable presence of what are now thoroughly outdated approaches and interpretations), but he wrote very little on the subject of fiscal administration itself. All general assessments (and this extends beyond the disputes identified above), in so far as they have been founded upon original study, have been formulated from specific, and thus necessarily restricted, perspectives. In all this, the focus has remained almost universally fixed upon the very first area of inquiry—the early Tudor household. Its permutations have been explored, its 'spirit' has been sought throughout the fiscal system, and it has been used to project an antithesis—the modern bureaucratic state.

This particular attention devoted to the household—and especially to its most adaptable and nationally prominent components, first the Chamber and later the Privy Chamber—is important. Household government has been viewed by all parties as

---

[12] Williams, *Tudor Regime*, 52–4.

fundamentally personalized, irregular, and (relatively speaking) unstructured, whereas the 'regular' departments outside the household are assumed to have been inflexible, impersonal, and substantially bureaucratic. This produces a critical polarization, which leads inevitably on to controversies over the relative significance of each sector and the essential character of government in this age.

II

It is to be expected that initial historical study would focus upon the areas where change was most manifest. However, interpretations will be inadequate to the extent that they fail to investigate all aspects of central finance, particularly if they have been founded upon questionable premisses. To begin with, it is most inappropriate to view the early sixteenth-century financial system in terms of underlying polarization. This widely held view predates the debate on a revolution in government; it originated in assumptions about the relationship between the new Chamber system of Edward IV and Henry VII, and the traditional Exchequer. Despite a few brief expressions to the contrary,[13] the rise of the Chamber is customarily interpreted as a reaction against an antiquated and sterile (i.e. medieval) Exchequer.[14] This institution is believed to have been incapable of reforming itself and, in spite of some improvements imposed on it by Henry VII, to have continued to deteriorate until 1554 when the merger with the second Court of Augmentations and the Court of First Fruits and Tenths provided it with new vitality.[15] Investigations focused upon the newer Chamber finance and the developments of the Reformation era have been at pains to stress the contrast between the modern, professional and adaptable creations, and the old, rigid, medieval Exchequer.[16] This is at best a distortion, at worst a caricature.

[13] Harriss, 'A Revolution in Tudor History?', xxv. 26–7; B. P. Wolffe, 'Henry VII's Land Revenues and Chamber Finance', *EHR* lxxix (1964), 228; Williams, *Tudor Regime*, 46.

[14] M. D. George, 'Notes on the Origin of the Declared Account', *EHR* xxxi (1916), 41, 54–5; Dietz, *Government Finance*, 60–7; Richardson, *Chamber Administration*, 41–59, and *Report of 1552*, p. xvii; Elton, *Tudor Revolution*, 20–5.

[15] Richardson, *Chamber Administration*, 433–42, and *Augmentations*, 436–74; G. R. Elton, *Studies in Tudor and Stuart Politics and Government* (2 vols., Cambridge, 1974), ii. 355–88, and *Tudor Revolution*, 251–7.

[16] nn. 14 and 15 above; and Wolffe, 'Henry VII's Land Revenues', 227–9, and *The Crown Lands, 1461–1536* (London, 1970), 42–5.

The classical belief that the Chamber system evolved because the Exchequer was antiquated and decrepit will not withstand detailed analysis.[17] The Exchequer was never static; it underwent almost constant administrative change, particularly in the first half of the sixteenth century. Hence there was no need to revitalize the Exchequer in 1554. At this time the greatly increased volume of activity did bring about modifications, and in some areas—notably in the auditing of accounts and the supervision of land revenue—the Exchequer did benefit from the adoption of procedures which had originated in the Courts of General Surveyors or Augmentations.[18] Elsewhere, however, particularly (but by no means exclusively) within the Exchequer of Receipt, where the revenue was managed, the post-1554 procedures were largely a continuing mutation of extensive internal alterations which had predated the amalgamation of the departments, and were essentially unrelated to it.[19] Between 1461 and 1554, the Exchequer was not, of course, at the centre of royal finance. Nevertheless, it remained an important department with its own strengths and weaknesses and its own role to play.

In general terms, the entire perception of the main institutions—Exchequer, household, and the new departments of 1536–42—as radically different and competitive units in a fragmented fiscal structure requires thorough revision. On the whole these agencies were not rivals engaged in institutionalized competition.[20] Such disputes as did occur were more often within departments rather than between them. Occasionally individual officials, as for example in the Exchequer, complained that structural alterations had reduced their importance or their profits of office, but this hardly determined the relationships between entire departments. To some extent, the belief in rivalry follows directly from the excessive stress laid upon the intrinsic distinctiveness of each sector. It is misleading

[17] J. D. Alsop, 'The Exchequer in Late Medieval Government, c.1485–1530' (in the forthcoming Festschrift for J. R. Lander: *Late Medieval Government and Society*, ed. J. G. Rowe, Toronto University Press).

[18] George, 41–58; Richardson, *Augmentations*, 460–6 (which in some instances is untrustworthy).

[19] J. D. Alsop, 'The Exchequer of Receipt in the Reign of Edward VI' (University of Cambridge Ph.D. thesis, 1978), *passim*.

[20] Alsop, 'Exchequer in Government'. Essentially, it was not rivalry or competition which brought forth the greatest challenges to features of the Chamber system, as for example in 1509 (Wolffe, *Crown Lands*, 76–7), but rather the legalistic desire to maintain a secure judicial and authoritative basis for state finance.

to refer too often and too loosely to an 'Exchequer mentality', or 'Chamber techniques', or even to officials following in the tradition of Bray, Heron, Cromwell, or whoever. This presupposes personal connections, approaches to finance, even fiscal philosophies which are rarely known to have existed in exclusive, neat divisions. There were differences between the institutions in the methods employed to receive, store, and disburse funds, and in the auditing of accounts, but there were also underlying common approaches and techniques which deserve recognition.

Moreover, rather than view some institutions or procedures as modern and others as medieval or antiquated, it is far preferable to recognize that different departments operating in specific contexts to fulfil particular purposes did require practices tailored to their own individual needs. It is too easy to overdraw the novelty or modernism of new processes or agencies. The Exchequer may have been old-fashioned in some respects—all Tudor institutions with a past had to work within the framework of their traditions—but it too was capable of independent initiatives and modifications. All the formal accounts were kept in Latin, on parchment, and in roman numerals as was customary well past the close of the sixteenth century; but from the first decades of the century rough or semi-private accounts were not infrequently in English, on paper, and in arabic numerals; as the century progressed this tendency spread haphazardly into some of the more regular records. Conversely, in the Court of General Surveyors and other new offices, accounts were kept in English and on paper in their early years, while once they became formalized and acquired official status there was a noticeable shift to Latin and parchment. This makes the point at a mundane level, but it can be extended to technical aspects of revenue management. One of the principal advantages of the new Chamber procedures was their flexibility, but once General Surveyors and Wards became institutionalized they (and Augmentations and First Fruits and Tenths) became as 'rigid' and 'bureaucratic' as the Exchequer or Duchy of Lancaster. While in theory the Exchequer was cumbersome and slow as a revenue department, in practice it could be just as versatile as the Chamber or Privy Chamber, making payments on the basis of oral or informal written orders from the king or a minister.[21] In principle, the essence of household finance was its flexibility, yet

---

[21] Alsop, 'Exchequer in Government', and 'Protector Somerset and Warrants for Payment', *BIHR* lv (1982), 103–7.

by the 1530s the Chamber too was becoming increasingly systematic and ordered, and the same trend was beginning by 1547 to make an impression upon the freshest and most personalized revenue agency, the Privy Chamber.[22]

III

At the institutional level what stands out is the separate and distinctive nature of the departments—each autonomous, with its own role, personnel, and procedures. Nowhere is this more obvious than in the formal documents, where investigations into the administrative character of early Tudor finance must begin. The evidence is important, while it is equally valuable to discern how the system really worked in practice. This cannot be adequately covered in a short space, but some comments on personnel are clearly relevant. However convenient it is to speak impersonally in terms of the Chamber, Exchequer, and so forth, in reality everything was accomplished by individual officials who together determined the nature of the administration. This was particularly the case in an era which had not yet developed any sense of corporate responsibility or accountability for crown revenue. An examination of the personnel of early Tudor financial administration does not provide indications of neat departmental separations which might have reflected different methods or traditions. Instead, there was a complex pattern of overlapping and interrelating personal connections. Many individuals went from one revenue department to another during the course of their careers; others held posts in two or three concurrently. An illustration of this at the top of the structure is afforded by Sir John Baker. He entered the royal administration in the Duchy of Lancaster, and went on to serve concurrently as chancellor and undertreasurer of the Exchequer (from 1540 and 1543 until his death in 1558), chancellor of the Court of First Fruits and Tenths throughout its existence (1540–53), legal advisor to the Duchy (1526–58), and as an occasional consultant in the Court of Augmentations.[23] This is to list merely his

[22] A. P. Newton, 'The King's Chamber under the Early Tudors', *EHR* xxxii (1917), 368–70; Elton, *Tudor Revolution*, 177–89; Richardson, *Chamber Administration*, 236–45. For the Privy Chamber note: E 101/427/2, E 315/160; BL Lansd. Rolls 14–15.

[23] R. Somerville, *History of the Duchy of Lancaster, 1265–1603* (London, 1953), 408, 455; Elton, *Tudor Revolution*, 196; Richardson, *Augmentations*, 338, 343, 452–3.

roles within the central revenue agencies. William Paulet, first marquess of Winchester and lord treasurer from 1550 until 1572, was
consecutively controller, treasurer, lord chamberlain, and lord great
master of the household between 1532 and 1550; at the same time he
was actively involved in royal wardship administration as joint, and
subsequently as sole master of the office of Wards from 1526, and
later as master of the Court of Wards from its establishment in 1540
until 1554.[24] The longevity and diversity of his public career were
noteworthy, but far from exceptional.

Although institutions could change with bewildering swiftness,
their personnel often continued without alteration, with minimal
variation in their activities and presumably with no difference in
their attitudes. Thomas Argall began his career in government
finance in 1536 as an itinerant clerk under Thomas Cromwell,
administering ecclesiastical revenue in the aftermath of the Reformation. With the establishment of the Court of First Fruits and
Tenths in 1540 he became its keeper of the records—a humble title
which belies his important managerial role throughout the life of
this institution. When First Fruits and Tenths became a sub-
department of the Exchequer in 1554, Argall and the clerk of the
old department headed it as joint remembrancers until Argall's
death in 1563. It may also be noted that Argall was from the 1520s
employed in the archbishop of Canterbury's administration, and he
continued to exercise high office there throughout his life. He was
just one of a number of administrators with an ecclesiastical background and conservative religious views, who helped provide administrative continuity at a time of momentous changes in church
and state.[25]

The movement of officials through the central agencies of
finance undermines the belief that the system was marked by
rivalry or fundamental polarization. In 1551 Peter Osborne entered
the Privy Chamber as clerk of the royal Privy Purse. Some accounts of his activities leave the impression that he performed a
focal role in national finance during Northumberland's regime,

[24] H. E. Bell, *An Introduction to the History and Records of the Court of Wards
and Liveries* (Cambridge, 1953), 11, 16; Elton, *Tudor Revolution*, 220, and *passim*;
Richardson, *Chamber Administration*, 290–6, 433–4.

[25] J. D. Alsop, 'Thomas Argall, Administrator of Ecclesiastical Affairs in the
Tudor Church and State', *Recusant History*, xv (1980), 227–38; C. Kitching,
'Probate Jurisdiction of Cromwell as Vicegerent', *BIHR* xlvi (1973), 102–6.

embodying the versatile household approach to finance.[26] Although Osborne's work in 1551–3 possesses short-term importance, its general significance should not be exaggerated, not least in the first instance because of the relatively small sums of cash handled by Osborne, and in the second because he very quickly sought advancement to an ancient office in the Exchequer. In September 1552 he became lord treasurer's remembrancer, a mundane administrative post involved with the traditional Exchequer accounting routine. He occupied this position for the remaining forty years of his life without rising to another notable place. He did become the archetypal 'Exchequer bureaucrat', author of an authoritative treatise on Exchequer procedure, and was influential in establishing a family hold on the office which was to last until 1696.[27] A more striking example of the theory that it was the office which made the man would be hard to find, but at the same time it suggests that the distinctions between the financial 'sectors' have been overdrawn. Osborne's fiscal duties in the Exchequer were very different from those in the Privy Chamber, but these were differences in tasks not in underlying principles or mentalities, and the transition was easily made. James Joskyn was a servant of Sir Thomas Heneage, the highly important groom of the stool and keeper of the Privy Purse to Henry VIII, and was himself a clerk of the Wardrobe of Robes and Beds within the Privy Chamber in the period 1537–41 before he resigned to take up an Exchequer tellership, which he held until his death in 1549. In the Privy Chamber he had acted as a personal receiver and paymaster of the king's private funds; his duties as a teller can be viewed as the transferral of the same general type of work to a more regularized setting. Although active in office during at least his first years in the Exchequer, Joskyn's Privy Chamber background has left no impression upon his accounts, nor should one expect that it would. He was, in this respect, indistinguishable from the other active tellers, who at this time included a London mercer

[26] Richardson, *Augmentations*, 361–5; D. E. Hoak, *The King's Council in the Reign of Edward VI* (Cambridge, 1976), 210–11; G. R. Elton, *Reform and Reformation: England 1509–1558* (London, 1977), 356; D. E. Hoak, 'The King's Privy Chamber, 1547–1553', in D. J. Guth and J. W. McKenna, eds., *Tudor Rule and Revolution* (Cambridge, 1982), 106–7.

[27] W. H. Bryson, 'Exchequer Equity Bibliography', *American Journal of Legal History*, xiv (1970), 333–48; J. C. Sainty, 'The Tenure of Offices in the Exchequer', *EHR* lxxx (1965), 463; *HC 1558–1603*, iii. 158–9.

(who was also a gentleman sewer of the Chamber), and a London fishmonger cum customs collector.[28] There is no reason to believe that Joskyn was any less or any more efficient or effective in the Exchequer than he had been in his fiscal work in the Privy Chamber. Similarly, John Uvedale had the distinction to begin his career attached to Henry VII's Chamber itself, as a clerk of the signet office. Yet when he came to the Exchequer in 1517 he brought with him perhaps little more than the ability to write an elegant (but extremely formalized) receipt roll. He retained his Exchequer post up to his death in 1549, serving in person or by deputy, and advanced elsewhere to become undertreasurer for Henry VIII's and Edward VI's Scottish wars. But at no time does his Chamber background appear to have imbued in him any distinctive characteristics.[29] On the other hand, what should we make of Sir John Daunce? He first appears as an Exchequer teller in 1505, but rose spectacularly to serve as an extremely flexible treasurer of war under Wolsey in the French campaign, became customer of the port of London, receiver-general of Wards (1509–40), a principal general surveyor of lands (1514–15, 1517–42), and the first head of the Court of General Surveyors from 1542 until his death in 1545.[30] More than any other individual, he represented what Professor Richardson has termed the mature household system of Henry VIII's reign, yet he began in what was, by all accounts, the most backward and regimented of the financial institutions. The mobility present in these and other innumerable cases was occasioned by the particular office-holding and patronage structures of this period,[31] but it will be readily apparent that mobility was founded upon an essential unity, which was further augmented by these exchanges. Whatever the diversity in methods and techniques, this was not an administration profoundly divided within itself.

The distribution of individuals occupying multiple offices simultaneously also weighed against sectional divisions. Under John Heron the Chamber was at its peak, but it does nothing for

[28] Richardson, *Augmentations*, 354 n.; Alsop, 'Edwardian Receipt', 26–7, 30, 319, 323, 341–2, and *passim*.

[29] *HC 1509–58*, iii. 508–9; Alsop, 'Edwardian Receipt', 22–3, 25, 30, 61, 350–2.

[30] Richardson, *Chamber Administration*, 226, 239, 256–7, 283, 365–6; *HC 1509–58*, ii. 22–3.

[31] For which see: Sainty, 449–75; Alsop, 'Edwardian Receipt', 5–32; P. W. Lock, 'Officeholders and Officeholding in Early Tudor England *c.*1520–1540' (University of Exeter Ph.D. thesis, 1976); Williams, *Tudor Regime*, 81–108.

the customary contrasting interpretations of the Chamber and the Exchequer to reveal that at least two early sixteenth-century Exchequer tellers served concurrently as clerks to Heron. This implies a different, unified, structure, and the substantial number of royal auditors and surveyors who held places in both the Exchequer and the new agencies strengthens this conclusion.[32] The full implications of multiple office-holding become apparent when it is recognized that this was not a twentieth-century civil service occupying Whitehall offices. The treasurer of the Chamber did not (at least in Henry VIII's reign) receive and disburse the king's money in the Chamber; the master of the Jewel House did not keep the royal jewels in the Jewel House; the Exchequer tellers did not work always in the Exchequer. Very often all these functions and others were performed in their own private, London or Westminster residences.[33] An individual such as Daunce, who in the years up to 1514 was concurrently a teller, a customs collector, receiver-general of Wards, and treasurer of war, had distinct and separate responsibilities in each of his positions. But when these functions were exercised by a single individual, using the assistance of private servants, and possibly working from the same premises, the divisions necessarily became blurred. This extended so far that on occasion information relating to totally distinct offices was entered into single registers, and solitary accounts were rendered for multiple fiscal charges.[34] Regardless of theory, in practice this was a very personalized system of revenue administration.[35] Moreover, it can be argued that these unofficial relationships did as much as central control by monarch and Council to bring cohesion to what was, particularly from the 1530s onwards, a disparate structure.

[32] Alsop, 'Exchequer in Government'; Richardson, *Chamber Administration*, 257–8, *Augmentations*, 147, and 'The Surveyor of the King's Prerogative', *EHR* lvi (1941), 68; Wolffe, *Crown Lands*, 77–8.

[33] G. R. Elton, *Star Chamber Stories* (London, 1958), 114–46; Newton, 'King's Chamber', 354 n.; John Stow, *A Summarye of the Chronicles of Englande* (London, 1570), fo. 339; Alsop, 'Edwardian Receipt', 29, 81–2.

[34] R. Somerville, 'The Preparation and Issue of Instruments under Seal in the Duchy of Lancaster', in J. C. Davies, ed., *Studies Presented to Sir Hilary Jenkinson* (Oxford, 1957), 385; E 159/329, E 351/175, 2080.

[35] For Example, note in passing: J. D. Alsop, 'The Financial Enterprises of Jerome Shelton, a Mid-Tudor London Adventurer', *Guildhall Studies in London History*, iv (1979), 33–50, and 'A Manuscript Copy of John Harington's *Of the Death of Master Deuerox*', *Manuscripta* xxiv (1980), 145–54; M. L. Robertson, 'Thomas Cromwell's Servants: the Ministerial Household in Early Tudor Government and Society' (University of California Ph.D. thesis, 1975), 220–39.

IV

The preceding observations provide a necessary context for an examination of the character of financial administration in the period from 1509 to 1558. It is vital to understand how the various agencies functioned in practice. For this reason an in-depth account, such as is available for the treasurer of the Chamber's office in the 1530s,[36] is invaluable. One sees here a regular, sophisticated structure, with clearly delineated working spaces, officials with specific responsibilities and functions, and a comprehensive accounting procedure. At the same time, the intimacy and personal—even casual—nature of the entire operation is readily apparent. The staff enjoyed social relationships both among themselves and with their clients. The focal point of the enterprise was the treasurer's private residence, and on occasion transactions could be conducted in the homes of clients. It is instructive that at what is invariably viewed as the opposite end of the spectrum—the Exchequer (without a doubt the oldest, largest, and most elaborate and complex of the revenue departments)—the differences were not all that substantial. It is true that in many instances the weight of tradition hung rather heavily upon the Exchequer, making it relatively inefficient (although never ineffective). For over four centuries the institution had undergone fragmented, piecemeal alteration. This manner of change—exceedingly common in the Tudor state—necessarily produced an untidy and rather complicated structure, resplendent in the loose ends and fossilized duties and records which are repugnant to the modern progressive mentality. The Exchequer was not unique in this; it simply had a longer time-span in which to evolve. Similar processes can be traced within other fiscal units through the sixteenth and early seventeenth centuries. Nevertheless, when the documents allow the researcher to go beyond the formal Exchequer accounts, and perceive the actual management of the department, an effective, and relatively simple financial operation is readily apparent, sharing with the Chamber the intimacy and flexibility so characteristic of this period.[37] Of course the Exchequer was also a very important court of record and of law; given the importance of

[36] Elton, *Star Chamber Stories*, 114–46.

[37] Alsop, 'Protector Somerset', 102–8, and 'Edwardian Receipt', *passim*. Also relevant is J. D. Alsop, 'Government, Finance and the Community of the Exchequer', in Christopher Haigh, ed., *The Reign of Elizabeth I, 1558–1603* (London, 1985).

money and the law to English society, and the complexity of the latter, accounting and judicial proceedings were necessarily officious and deliberate. This does represent, to a degree, a contrast with the more informal agencies. But the Exchequer was far from being alone in producing red tape. As the century wore on this was increasingly a feature of the entire system, and all departments demonstrated a similar ability to cut through it when necessary and appropriate. It reflected the fine balance between the need for regulation and authority on the one side, and the necessity for flexibility and speed on the other, without which the administration could not have met the requirements imposed upon it by the crown.

Previous debates over the presence, absence, or extent of bureaucratic and household government would appear to have focused too closely upon discussions of ideal types rather than actual practices. There is a very significant difference between (for want of better expressions) national and household systems, but this did not in the period after 1509 revolve around the degree of structure, formality, or flexibility. The financial agencies were not polarized in these terms. The cofferer's department within the household had as sophisticated and regular an organization as could be found anywhere in the government.[38] Indeed, whether or not a department left the household and became an autonomous institution depended not upon its internal procedures and degree of regulation, but upon the contemporary perception of its role, its traditions, and its relationship to the monarch. It is true that once established—either by custom or statute—an institution was at least in theory more stable, restricted, and impervious to change, while on the other hand proximity to the sovereign as a component of the household increased the likelihood of royal interference and casual utilization. In practice, however, the flexibility of household offices does not appear to have been of prime importance. The Chamber's financial office possessed a distinctive organization by the 1530s, if not earlier, while even within the newer and more private Privy Chamber the financial duties and procedures had settled into a recognizable pattern before 1558. It is reasonable—as long as not too much is made of the expression—to describe all financial departments by this latter date as bureaucratic: they each had specific (occasionally overlapping) areas of responsibility, established patterns of work, trained personnel, well-defined command structures, and kept formal

[38] Newton, 'Tudor Reforms', 234; E 101/414–31, *passim*, E 351/1795.

records or accounts. The system was at the same time versatile and intimate. In particular, personal, irregular financial management was not restricted to the household agencies or personnel. Queen Mary, for example, chose to channel the receipts from the forced loans of 1556 and 1557 through two of the more traditional household officers, in the first instance the controller, and in the second the master of the Jewel House.[39] But she had already, in 1555, made Nicholas Brigham, a teller of the Exchequer who had no known direct connection with the household or the queen, a personal treasurer to manage substantial sums of money for her own use, and in 1558 he became extraordinary treasurer of all taxation and loans for the French war. Bureaucratic regimentation did not prevent a dramatic (and ephemeral) alteration in Brigham's role in the Exchequer. His own accounts reveal the intermixing of official and personal responsibilities inside and outside his tellership.[40] Hypotheses founded upon an antithesis between 'routine bureaucrats' and 'personal' government,[41] are clearly untenable. The flexible, personal approach was an essential feature of the administrative expansion and sophistication that was so evident within this period as a whole.[42]

V

An assessment of the nature and extent of reform must be placed in this context. The term 'reform' itself has been employed with extreme freedom and imprecision, so that in a number of instances it appears equivalent to nothing more than change. The present writer would prefer to abandon the expression altogether when describing administrative alterations within Tudor finance. In its present usage 'reform' possesses distinctive connotations of progress and innovation. Yet in the early sixteenth century reform was almost invariably conceived of in the sense of renewal, restoration, and regeneration. This can produce subtle—and not so subtle—discrepancies in interpretation. The amalgamation of the depart-

[39] SP 11/11, fos. 109–10, 139; SP 11/12, fos. 48–9; and SP 11/13, fo. 75.

[40] J. D. Alsop, 'Nicholas Brigham (d. 1558), Scholar, Antiquary, and Crown Servant', *Sixteenth Century Journal* xii (1981), 49–67.

[41] Palmer, 22; Harriss, 'A Revolution in Tudor History?', xxv. 27–8; Beckingsale, 49–50, 110–12.

[42] Elton, 'A Revolution in Tudor History?', xxix. 44, and *Tudor Revolution, passim.*

ments in 1554 has generally been described, with some important reservations, as a forward-looking reform;[43] in fact it was essentially a backward-looking retrenchment.[44] This is not to say that nothing new came out of the alterations; indeed there was more novelty after 1554 than the government had intended, and more than it could acknowledge. The intentions of the planners are not always a good guide to the consequences (and vice versa), but for contemporaries the reform of the early Tudor financial structure was intrinsically a less radical and less modern undertaking than might at first appear. In part this was because even the government frequently had difficulty in visualizing the 'fiscal system' as a separate entity. That was both too comprehensive and too exclusive a conception. Finance was usually thought of in terms of its component parts; this explains why totally comprehensive revenue and expenditure accounts, or literary descriptions of the system, are so rare. At the same time the financial institutions were not regarded solely, or even sometimes primarily, as simply a machinery for the raising and management of revenue. When Tudor commentators described their polity, the revenue departments were most often viewed as elements within the judicial system. The household offices could be glossed as royal service bureaux. Finance itself was customarily interpreted as possessing an importance for the monarch and his prerogative beyond monetary value, and it was necessarily a part of the patronage and political functions of the state. An even more serious impediment to radical change was the widespread (and essentially correct) belief that the financial administration was basically sound and viable. Renewal and modification were not infrequently seen as imperative in this tumultuous age, but these rarely extended beyond piecemeal attention to solitary aspects of the system.

Most of the significant alterations were instituted for short-term, pragmatic reasons to cope with specific problems or developments, rather than as the conscious working out of a protracted reform strategy. Early Tudor governments did not have the time or the resources to approach administration in these terms. Finance in particular was frequently a matter of mere existence from one day to the next. None the less, this was a half-century of momentous

[43] Richardson, *Augmentations*, 211–12, 443–4, 460, and *Report of 1552*, p. xxxiii; Elton, *Tudor Revolution*, 229–30, 237, 242, 250, 257–8.
[44] J. D. Alsop, 'The Revenue Commission of 1552', *HJ* xxii (1979), 511–33.

change in state and society, most of which (as for example the Reformation, the economic crisis, wars and social unrest) had financial implications and repercussions. Movement within the system was encouraged, and in some cases it could not be avoided. On two occasions within this era the external forces exerting pressure upon fiscal administration were of a sufficient magnitude to call for extensive, deliberate restructuring. The first was the decade of the 1530s, with the expansion of government following the Reformation and the dissolution of the monasteries. The second was the early 1550s, when the costs of successive wars, political turmoil, and inflation helped create a climate of retrenchment. In neither case were the changes total, or even completely consistent. Finance was never the crown's sole priority, and organizational alteration inevitably brought into play a number of non-fiscal factors, including the vested interests, politics, and personalities contained within the government. The distinction between these events is that the first were undeniably innovative, in keeping with the progressive temperament noticeable within Henrician government,[45] while the second were reactionary products of a distinctly conservative mentality, increasingly prevalent within crown finance by that date.

The 1530s was the only time throughout the period under review when the dominant minister (or indeed monarch) demonstrated a particular interest in and capacity for finance and financial management. The one conceivable rival to Thomas Cromwell in these terms was Wolsey, but he never revealed the same ability for sustained effort, possibly because the necessity was not so great. Cromwell, of course, was not the only individual who influenced revenue administration in the 1530s, and he did not create a completely new system (to expect that is to expect too much of him in terms of available time, resources, power, and approach). He nevertheless made an important contribution. The structure which emerged after the 1530s was dominated by six national, autonomous organizations: the Courts of Augmentations, Exchequer, Duchy of Lancaster, First Fruits and Tenths, General Surveyors, and Wards and Liveries. Additionally, for the era of the debase-

---

[45] Described in part in G. R. Elton, *Reform and Renewal* (Cambridge, 1973), and *Reform and Reformation, passim*. In respect to fiscal theory, J. D. Alsop, 'The Theory and Practice of Tudor Taxation', *EHR* xcvii (1982), 1–30, and 'Innovation in Tudor Taxation', ibid. xcix (1984), 83–93.

ment of the coinage (1542–51), the Mint in effect acted as another, extremely important, revenue agency.[46] Beyond this there existed a large number of disbursing departments, which received virtually all their funds by block transfers from the seven institutions or between themselves; the only ones of significance for national finance were the Chamber and Privy Chamber. It has been stated that government through courts was decidedly medieval and therefore hardly novel.[47] Courts were certainly traditional—although since they continued in use and indeed were instituted in England after the end (on any reasonable time-scale) of the middle ages, they should not perhaps be considered as distinctly medieval in form. More significantly, while the concept of a court was not new, what was innovatory was an arrangement of crown finance founded upon the proliferation of autonomous courts. The later middle ages knew only the Exchequer and, for unique dynastic reasons,[48] the Duchy of Lancaster. In the six years from 1536 four courts were established. More was involved than politics, personal ambition, or even the obvious presence of post-Reformation ecclesiastical revenue, and it was not the work of a single minister. The reform tendencies so apparent in this era frequently took the form of the renovation or extension of governmental activity within the framework of self-governing courts, financial or otherwise. One need look no further than the Courts of Requests and Star Chamber for illustrations of the successful institutionalization of earlier, less well-defined bodies.[49] Other attempts, for example the 1539 intention to create a conciliar court for the enforcement of proclamations,[50] were stillborn, while the novel idea of a military 'Court of Centeners' never received official endorsement.[51] The proposals were not all equally realistic or manageable, but they did reflect the widespread interest in developing the state along departmental lines.

[46] C. E. Challis, *The Tudor Coinage* (Manchester, 1978), 83–112, and 'The Debasement of the Coinage, 1542–1551', *EcHR* 2nd series, xx (1967), 441–66.

[47] Harriss, 'A Revolution in Tudor Government?', xxv. 28.

[48] Somerville, *Duchy of Lancaster*, 230, 260–1.

[49] Ch. 2, above.

[50] R. W. Heinze, 'The Enforcement of Royal Proclamations under the Provisions of the Statute of Proclamations, 1539–1547', in A. J. Slavin, ed., *Tudor Men and Institutions* (Baton Rouge, 1972), 205–31.

[51] Laurence Stone, 'The Political Programme of Thomas Cromwell', *BIHR* xxiv (1951), 1–18, as corrected by G. R. Elton, ibid. xxv (1952), 126–30. On this general subject see Elton, *Reform and Renewal*, 139–42.

It is inappropriate to describe the fiscal structure which emerged from this impulse as uncoordinated, inefficient, irrational, and predestined from the outset to fail and to be replaced within a short space of time. The topic is too extensive to be adequately covered here, but there is every indication that the administrative and ethical breakdown which allegedly occurred around the mid-century has been greatly exaggerated and essentially misunderstood.[52] The arrangements were far from perfect, but at present it is impossible to demonstrate that they were either noticeably inferior or superior to the system which superseded them. The 1554 initiative cannot be interpreted, as it sometimes has been,[53] in either intention or execution as the rejection of preceding developments. Rather, it was a particular synthesis of various features in revenue management, record-keeping, accounting procedures, and institutional forms present in early Tudor financial administration. The specific configuration—an enlarged and dominant Exchequer—was a political expediency designed to overcome an immediate fiscal crisis. The choice of the Exchequer, along with the enactment of some restrictive regulations, were influenced in part by the new conservatism within government, but the events possess little ideological import beyond this. The change manifestly cannot be portrayed as a return to a traditional medieval financial system. Not only was the Exchequer not the same institution it had been in the fifteenth century, but, as will be suggested below, the entire orientation of the fiscal system had shifted dramatically by 1558.

In addition to their emphasis on extensive structural alteration, some interpretations have stressed the procedural reform in accounting and auditing techniques or routines. It has been argued above that these were not confined to any particular department or sector. While it is true that the specific auditing methods used for crown lands did originate in the Chamber, and only came into the Exchequer in 1554 from the new departments, in a broader sense all the revenue agencies were capable of independent improvements in

[52] In terms of government in general, the following works either reverse or moderate previous beliefs: Hoak, *King's Council;* D. M. Loades, *The Reign of Mary Tudor* (London, 1979); Jennifer Loach and Robert Tittler, eds., *The Mid-Tudor Polity c.1540–1560* (London, 1980). For finance see: Alsop, 'Revenue Commission', 526–7, and 'Edwardian Receipt', ch. iv; Richardson, *Augmentations*, 214, 230, 445.

[53] Harriss and Williams, 'A Revolution in Tudor History?', xxv. 28–9, 46; Williams, *Tudor Regime*, 48.

their accounting practices. Moreover, both the modern character and the distinctiveness of the new techniques can be exaggerated. To describe the innovations as being in effect 'a new system of accountancy' is unrealistic.[54] Dr Wolffe has pointed out that 'modern' can in this sense mean no more than that the procedures were up to date; in a different context he has demonstrated that the Chamber methods were derived from late medieval private estate management.[55] The classic study of the new auditing system in effect describes the differences between the old form of account and the new as entirely stylistic: the new was clearer, perhaps more systematic, and it was processed differently, but it included precisely the same information.[56] After 1500 the use of English language and arabic numerals—especially in the less formal accounts—became one of the features of the administration. To the extent that these are still in use today, we could perhaps term this a 'modern' development, yet the relevance or utility of such a comment is dubious. Certainly contemporaries would not have viewed these as 'reforms', and it is debatable whether we should either when assessing a financial administration in which Latin and roman numerals were in accustomed and easy use. Arabic numerals are more manipulable, but the royal officials had long since developed sophisticated methods of coping with roman numerals, and the increase in neither the size nor the complexity of crown finance made a transition mandatory. The ability of the system to absorb English and arabic numerals, even to a limited degree, when it need not have done so, indeed, indicates its capacity to reflect changes within English society. Some techniques were arguably more efficient than others, and this is important. Nevertheless, it is difficult to interpret the procedural innovations, which were certainly widespread in this era, as revolutionary. Whether one worked in English or Latin, in arabic or roman numerals, accounted in the Pipe or before the auditors of the prests, or whatever, it made no difference to the basic fiscal concepts, or to the underlying mentality. Accounts, for example, remained invariably charge and discharge—not profit and loss—and there was to be no innovation at this fundamental level until after the final *quietus est* or the final declared account had been approved for the last accountant under the last of the

---

54 J. D. Mackie, *The Earlier Tudors, 1485–1558* (Oxford, 1952), 217.
55 Wolffe, 'Yorkist and Early Tudor Government', 20, and *Crown Lands*, 42–4.
56 George, 56–8.

Tudor sovereigns. Surely by this stage it is superfluous to restate that this did not make the system medieval: neither medieval nor modern is an adequate or meaningful description for the financial administration.

VI

Amidst all the structural reformations and the extensive piecemeal alteration in procedures, some cumulative in effect, others transitory, wherein lay the essential difference between financial organization at the death of Henry VII and that at the accession of Elizabeth I? It is in part to be found in the privotal issue maintained by Professor Elton: the transition from undifferentiated household administration to the management of crown revenue within departments of state.[57] This did take place, although not in the terms debated by earlier writers, and without an associated 'revolution' in administrative procedures. As has been demonstrated, it is inappropriate to distinguish between 'bureaucratic' and 'household' financial government for this era on the basis of procedure, because both could be flexible and personal or systematic and formal in their methods. Also, the location of a fiscal agency either within or outside the formal household boundaries is not in itself a reliable guide to the style of its administration. It is true that if attention is restricted to the Chamber and Privy Chamber portions of the household, a pronounced increase in regulation can be identified over this half-century. This is important, but it would not on its own appear to be the central development. The distinguishing feature of 'household' government was its undifferentiated, universal utility, regardless of the methods by which this was exercised. Henry VII's Chamber possessed a general competence in all areas of royal administration. Under Henry VIII the Privy Chamber fulfilled a similar function.[58] A revenue institution such as the Court of Augmentations, or the Exchequer, held a well-defined, restricted role.[59] An official in the Court of Wards may

[57] Professor Elton's latest restatement of this view in relation to financial administration is in *Tudor Constitution*, 132–3.

[58] Starkey, 'King's Privy Chamber'.

[59] For example, it was not until 1649 that the Exchequer's judicial responsibility for crown revenue was transformed by a legal fiction into a general common law jurisdiction: W. H. Bryson, *The Equity Side of the Exchequer* (Cambridge, 1975), 25–7.

not have been entirely bureaucratic in his conduct of business, but that business itself was specific and limited. The responsibilities of a gentleman of Henry VIII's Privy Chamber were undifferentiated in nature and extensive in scope. In terms of financial administration in general, there is an important difference between a system in which finance is administered as just one of a large number of functions by an institution and its staff, and a system where the sole function of single or multiple departments and their personnel can be defined as financial management. One might not wish to push too far the argument that the former is necessarily a 'household' form. But within the English tradition 'undifferentiated administration' was normally associated with the royal household because of the latter's close relationship with the monarch and the monarch's direct interest in the whole of national government.

Household government was not limited to the English middle ages, and it cannot be viewed as an essentially medieval form of administration. Nevertheless, it most certainly was found in that period, and from the 1460s it was the dominant aspect of central finance. In these circumstances, the almost total abandonment of this system before 1558, in exchange for one founded upon management through specifically financial departments, is of considerable importance, not least because it set the pattern for subsequent long-term developments. It is valuable first to recognize that this did indeed take place during the half-century under discussion, and second to understand the nature of the change and the processes by which the new system was created. For the origns of this alteration lay not so much in the deliberate plans and actions of a single minister, as in a vital transformation—in regard to finance —within the early Tudor state. Cromwell and the other ministers of this era contributed to the developments—with varying degrees of responsibility, planning, and insight—because they were necessarily involved in maintaining a workable fiscal structure in the face of changing circumstances. Thus, while the final administrative form was largely unintentional, and cannot be attributed to the consistent policies or actions of individuals, it was also far from being simply accidental. Rather, the system which emerged in England by the 1550s was a reasonably effective and rational reaction to the various pressures and circumstances of this period. The remainder of this study will be devoted to a general, concluding, overview of the essential development of the national financial structure during the formative half-century following the death of Henry VII.[60]

VII

The basic difference between the systems of financial administration current in 1509 and 1558 has universally been viewed as the change from a structure dominated in the first instance by the Chamber, and in the second by the Exchequer. (The disagreements which have arisen all involve the explanation of this alteration and its significance.) It will be readily apparent that this is only half of the picture, limited to the revenue agencies themselves. In Henry VII's reign it was a Chamber organization under the direct personal management of the monarch; by the late 1550s it was an Exchequer-based arrangement controlled very largely by the Privy Council. A study of fiscal administration must, necessarily, include not only the executive and managerial aspects—to be found in the departments—but also the governing or regulatory power which provided the initiative and which was located in the sovereign or his delegates. The latter extended beyond fiscal policy: more routinely it consisted of the day to day oversight of finance and the mandatory initiation and authorization of all but the most routine functions. Thus it was very much a part of the administrative structure.

For a monarch who was as intimately involved in royal finance as Henry VII, the Chamber organization had clear advantages. Nevertheless, Henry VII was the last English sovereign to devote regular attention to the details of crown finance. It is very doubtful whether even he managed to retain personal cognizance of all features of the subject. Informality stemming from royal intervention gave way in some areas to more systematic, less directly personal, procedures.[61] The personal inclinations of subsequent monarchs, and the growing complexity and scope of finance (as well as other aspects of central government), encouraged this trend after 1509. This undermined the *raison d'être* of Chamber finance at the same time that the Chamber was losing the initiative in

---

[60] As with other aspects of this survey, limitations of space restrict what follows to a summary description of important and sometimes controversial developments. This writer is presently working on a fully detailed exposition which it is believed will provide a rounded and documented analysis of the principal points.

[61] Richardson, *Chamber Administration*, chs. iii, iv, and vii; Wolffe, 'Henry VII's Land Revenues', 225–54.

general to the Privy Chamber. By 1520 this new organization was fully developed and had become the focus for the king's personal government.[62] None the less, the Privy Chamber never took over the Chamber's role as the centre of financial administration. In the first place, the Chamber kept many of its fiscal duties and, under Henry VIII, it never completely lost its connection with the crown lands through the general surveyors. As regards its role as a disbursing agency, in general the Chamber retained responsibility for a wide range of the more routine expenditure which had come to be associated with it, while the Privy Chamber took over the more intimate, directly monarchical payments.[63] More generally, the Henrician Privy Chamber—unlike the Yorkist Chamber—did not develop a national organization for finance. There was no repeat of the Yorkist structural and procedural innovations centred on land management.[64] The Privy Chamber received almost all its funds in direct transfers from other departments; hence it did not require the collecting and auditing functions associated with the rise of the Chamber. In this sense it remained very much a court, as opposed to a national institution. Finally, Privy Chamber finance was restricted in scope. Since after Henry VII English monarchs were never intimately involved in all aspects of finance, the Privy Chamber operated in a more restricted context.[65] The fiscal accounts of the officials of the Privy Chamber demonstrate that most of their expenditure lay in areas close to the monarch's personal interests. This does not mean that it was simply household or private expenditure. Beyond these categories, there is clear evidence

---

[62] David Starkey, 'Representation through Intimacy: a Study in the Symbolism of Monarchy and Court office in Early-Modern England', in Ioan Lewis, ed., *Symbols and Sentiments* (London, 1977), 197, 203–7.

[63] For example: E 101/420/11, 426/5, 6, 8, 427/17, 546/19, E 315/439, E 351/541; BL Add. MS 20, 030.

[64] Described in Wolffe, *Crown Lands*, 51–75.

[65] Readers will be aware that there is a difference of emphasis between this portrayal and that by Dr Starkey. Dr Starkey argues that the key reason for the slow development of the crucial secretarial and fiscal roles of the Privy Chamber was political rivalry, particularly in the case of Wolsey. There is insufficient space here to address this issue at length. However, my interpretation, while not wishing to deny any political influence upon events, focuses rather upon the degree and nature of the direct involvement of the monarch in early Tudor government as the essential limiting factor for the development of the Privy Chamber as a national governmental agency. A second area of dispute—the extent to which the monarch's personal involvement in government was channelled through the Privy Chamber—is relevant to the topic but is not addressed here.

of the Privy Chamber's very important financial role in subjects of national importance and direct concern to the king, especially, under Henry VIII, royal building works and the wars of the 1540s. But Henry VIII was the last king to lead an army royal out of the realm until William III, and no English sovereign has succeeded in surpassing in percentage terms the amount he spent on building. As long as the Privy Chamber's financial activities remained orientated around the monarch's personal interest—and it never developed major functions beyond this point—this feature of the institution could only decline over the long term with the degree of direct influence exerted by the sovereign.

In these circumstances, the Chamber-dominated structure—in which other organizations like the Exchequer or Duchy of Lancaster had occupied subservient, complementary positions—gave way in the early decades of the sixteenth century to an assembly of autonomous and semi-autonomous financial agencies. The development was heightened after 1536 with the creation of the Courts of Augmentations and First Fruits and Tenths and the formal establishment of Wards and Liveries and General Surveyors. An essential feature of this non-integrated system was that it was not controlled to any great extent by the monarch or by the household. Henry VIII was by no means a cipher, but central control and initiative in national finance rested primarily in Wolsey and Cromwell in turn, assisted by the Council. After 1540 this task very largely fell to the Privy Council. It is, of course, true that the Council traditionally played a role in crown finance. Under Edward IV and Henry VII, however, this appears to have been restricted to the customary conciliar functions of advice, and to the employment of individual councillors or *ad hoc* groups for specific executive tasks.[66] Regular management was limited to the new, specialized task of account auditing, assigned by Henry VII to a small conciliar committee.[67] It was only in the early 1540s that the Council emerged as an authoritative institution with a general collective competence and jurisdiction in financial administration, complete with the power to issue its own warrants for the expenditure of crown money.[68]

[66] J. R. Lander, 'The Yorkist Council and Administration, 1461 to 1485', *EHR* lxxiii (1958), 27–46, and 'Council, Administration, and Councillors, 1461 to 1485', *BIHR* xxxii (1959), 138–51, 162; Wolffe, 'Henry VII's Land Revenues', 238–9, 241–5.

[67] Wolffe, *Crown Lands*, 71–3; J. A. Guy, 'A Conciliar Court of Audit at Work in the Last Months of the Reign of Henry VII', *BIHR* xlix (1976), 289–95.

[68] *APC, passim.*

The monarch certainly retained an interest in policy and, as Dr Starkey has clearly demonstrated, Henry VIII revealed a highly developed personal involvement with the cash reserves. None the less, the administrative focus of government finance had shifted from the household to the Privy Council. The general course of events can be illustrated, for example, in terms of the relatively restricted, but noteworthy, authorization of government expenditure.[69] Under the Yorkists and Henry VII, the royal sign manual was of central importance, in terms of both the volume of business authorized by the monarch and its primacy in the administrative routine. After 1509 sign manual warrants continued to fulfil a significant function in revenue disbursement, although their role was changing. Under Wolsey and Cromwell much of the initiative passed to these ministers' own informal orders, which received official sanction—frequently retrospectively—from the sign manual or one of the seals. Significantly, it was during the 1540s that Privy Council warrants emerged as a standard, and extensively utilized authorization for crown expenditure. The sign manual and the new dry stamp, regulated in the Privy Chamber, retained a useful position, especially during Henry VIII's final active years and for much of the reign of Edward VI, when control of the monarch, the Privy Chamber, and the royal Privy Purse were part of the political processes.[70] But sign manual warrants were on the whole coming to play a more limited, directly monarchical, role. The Privy Council warrants had emerged during the 1540s as a dominant authorization under which the majority of the crown's funds were transferred and disbursed, conforming to the new executive responsibility of the Council in respect to government finance.

When more is known about the development of the early Tudor Council as an administrative body,[71] the nature of the transformation will be better understood. In general terms, the piecemeal evolution of an executive Council was clearly related to the decline in royal interest and personal control. In view of the often technical character of Tudor finance—its complexity, its mundane detail,

[69] The following is based in part on: Rosemary Horrox and P. W. Hammond, eds., *British Library Harleian Manuscript 433* (4 vols., Upminster and London, 1979–83); Wolffe, *Crown Lands, passim*; Elton, *Tudor Revolution*, 276–98; Hoak, *King's Council*, 147–9; Alsop, 'Protector Somerset', 102–8, and 'Edwardian Receipt', 281–7; Richardson, *Augmentations*, 271–370.

[70] David Starkey, 'Court and Government' (above); Hoak, 'King's Privy Chamber', 87–108.

[71] Elton, *Tudor Revolution*, 316–69, and *Studies*, ii. 308–38.

and the sustained attention which it demanded in an age of inflation, government expansion, and war—this delegation of authority to the Privy Council is understandable and not without merit. The alteration created its own problems, and arguably it was not the only conceivable outcome to the growing complexity of early Tudor finance. Nevertheless, the Privy Council came to provide a reasonably effective central focus for financial administration. Under these conditions a subsequent 'household revival' of any extent or duration was highly improbable. The Council did not share the monarch's need for undifferentiated personal assistance, nor would it necessarily look to the household when it required extraordinary administrative support. The Privy Council did, of course, on occasion utilize personnel within the household and elsewhere in central government for the performance of its financial responsibilities. With the re-establishment of Exchequer supremacy in 1554, however, the long-term tendency was for the financial affairs of the state to be controlled by the Council in conjunction with the Exchequer. Thus, for instance, the situation described by Dr Starkey in which Henry VIII retained personal control of an extensive reserve treasury within the Privy Chamber, eventually gave way to Mr Coleman's portrayal of the Elizabethan Exchequer treasury.[72] The fact that this was not a movement towards 'bureaucratization' (the Elizabethan Exchequer routine being almost as personalized and mutable as the Henrician Privy Chamber) does not detract from its significance. The monarch, the household agencies, and the surviving Court of Wards and Liveries and Duchy of Lancaster retained some importance in the financial system, but their roles and functions were complementary, restricted, and almost peripheral to the main administration.

The middle decades of the century, therefore, witnessed the consolidation of a system based upon the Privy Council and the Exchequer. Financial administration was now fundamentally different in a number of respects, not least because all the central organs of government—monarch, Council, household and revenue institutions—had significantly altered their financial roles and relationships. Although far from perfect, this structure proved capable of providing a stable and resilient framework for central finance well into the following century.

[72] See chs. 2 above and 7 below.

CHAPTER 7

ARTIFICE OR ACCIDENT?
THE REORGANIZATION OF THE
EXCHEQUER OF RECEIPT c.1554–1572*

CHRISTOPHER COLEMAN

THE reform of the 'agencies of finance' was not, for Professor
Elton, the most important of the features of the revolution he saw
taking place in the 1530s, but it was the one to which he devoted
most attention in *The Tudor Revolution in Government*. In almost
a hundred impressively researched pages, he described and explained
many of the important developments which occurred during or
shortly after Thomas Cromwell's ministry, traced their consequences
through to the reign of Elizabeth I, and located them in a historical
context extending from Richard II to Sir Robert Walpole.[1] In his
view, Cromwell transformed the nature of financial administration
by shifting responsibility for it from the uncertain hands of the
monarch and his household servants to 'national' and 'bureaucratic' institutions, capable of performing their clearly distinct
functions without the need for royal supervision or intervention.[2]
This he did by creating 'a highly developed bureaucratic structure',
principally to administer the crown's new revenues from the

* I am grateful to Dr J. D. Alsop, Professor Conrad Russell, Mrs Elizabeth Russell,
and Dr Nicholas Tyacke for commenting on the first draft of this chapter. They
made many helpful suggestions, and Dr Alsop saved me from a number of errors.
Nevertheless, the view expressed are my own, and my colleagues and friends are in
no way responsible for any error that may remain.

[1] G. R. Elton, *The Tudor Revolution in Government* (Cambridge, 1953),
160–258. It is impossible to do justice here to the full range of his ideas. For his own,
developing, summaries of his views on financial administration see *England under
the Tudors* (1st edn., London, 1955), 180–2, 209–10, 410–12 and (2nd edn., London, 1974), 479–81; *The Tudor Constitution: Documents and Commentary* (1st
edn., Cambridge, 1960), 128–33 and (2nd edn., Cambridge, 1982), 129–34; *Reform
and Reformation: England 1509–1558* (London, 1977), 214–16, 355–8. Any subsequent reference to *England under the Tudors* or *Tudor Constitution* will be to the
second edition of those works.

[2] Elton, *Tudor Revolution*, 168, 189, 211, 222, 229, 237, 251–2, 257–8.

church. It was to break down after his death, but 'men trained in
his school' survived to see that the principles of bureaucratic
government were not forgotten.[3] Foremost among them was
William Paulet, later lord treasurer and marquess of Winchester,
who put principle into practice by reorganizing the revenue courts
in 1554, re-establishing the supremacy of the Exchequer, minimizing
as far as possible the antiquated practices of that institution, and
inaugurating 'the line of the great modern lord treasurers who were
usually chief ministers'.[4] Thus the amalgamation of 1554 completed Cromwell's work, albeit imperfectly, terminated a period of
'change and experiment', and provided 'a solution of enduring
effectiveness' to the long-standing problems of financial administration.[5]

Subsequent research has demonstrated the correctness of some
of these views, though not always beneficially to the theory, and
invalidated others. Cromwell did play an important part in the
creation of a complex 'bureaucratic structure' even if, as Professor
Elton has come close to conceding, his initiatives were shaped as
much by self-interest and the needs of the hour as by ministerial
concern for bureaucratic principles, while what he did achieve had
little *immediate* effect on the governmental activity of the household.[6] It did indeed run into difficulties after Cromwell's death—
but if mainly because of the burdens imposed by Henry VIII's
wars, also because of the absence of the highly personal guiding
hand the reforms of the 1530s should have rendered redundant.[7]
Winchester did play *a* part in the reorganization of the revenue
courts in 1554, though probably not a leading one, and also an important part in the subsequent history of financial administration,

[3] Ibid. 222–3, 229, 233–4, 237, 252.

[4] Ibid. 163, 223–4, 239, 240–1, 248, 251, 255–8. See also *England under the
Tudors*, 209, 214, 410–11.

[5] Elton, *Tudor Revolution*, 163–4, 241, 251–2, 257.

[6] For Cromwell's highly personal control of the empire he was building and its
sometimes unfortunate consequences for bureaucratic development, see *Tudor
Revolution*, 185, 191–203, 211–18, 237, 251. For Professor Elton's guarded, and
sometimes highly qualified, concessions: *England under the Tudors*, 181–2, 480;
Reform and Reformation, 211–20, *passim*; *Tudor Constitution*, 132.

[7] Elton, *Tudor Revolution*, 185, 225, 234, 251. For the problems of financial
administration after Cromwell's fall see W. C. Richardson, *History of the Court of
Augmentations 1536–1554* (Baton Rouge, 1961), 111–213 and id., ed., *The Report
of the Royal Commission of 1552* (Morgantown, 1974), *passim*. It is, unfortunately,
impossible to relate Professor Richardson's work to Professor Elton's in the compass of this paper.

but there is no evidence that he was 'trained in Cromwell's school' —rather the contrary, since he was a prominent officer of the Wards from 1526 to 1554, and of the royal household from *c.*1532 to 1550 —and the part he played after 1554 was not, as we shall see, the one Professor Elton attributed to him.[8] The Exchequer was assigned a central position in financial administration: but since it was in essence a 'national' and 'bureaucratic' institution of great antiquity, there is no need to see this as a 'revolutionary' development.[9] Elizabeth I did confide the management of her finances to the great officers of the Exchequer, rather than to personal servants: but when her decision is viewed in its medieval context, it looks more like a return to an earlier style of monarchical government than a confident step towards a new.[10] However, the reorganization of 1554 did not complete Cromwell's work, or terminate a period of change and experiment (an anachronistic term), or provide an effective and enduring solution to long-standing problems. It was rather a product of the politics and problems of the early 1550s than of reforming idealism, and, as Professor Elton recognized, it was a clumsy and illogical compromise,[11] which created new problems and inaugurated a period of conflict and change in the Exchequer

[8] B. W. Beckingsale, *Thomas Cromwell* (London, 1978), 53. For Winchester see *HC 1509–58*, iii. 72–5. There is, as yet, no proper biography of this important figure, though Ms Virginia Moseley has been researching his career. I am grateful to her for providing me with both information and constructive criticism of an unpublished paper. For the amalgamations of 1554, and their effect on Winchester, see n. 11 and pp. 171 ff.

[9] Elton, *Tudor Revolution*, 169; *Tudor Constitution*, 129. For the sophisticated constitution of the 12th-century Exchequer see Charles Johnson, ed., *Dialogus De Scaccario* (London, 1950). Professor Elton has argued that the Exchequer was *transformed* by the amalgamation of 1554: *Tudor Revolution*, 250–1; *Tudor Constitution*, 133–4. It was certainly *changed*, though not as he thought, and the force of the point is much diminished by our recognition that the Exchequer was a protean and not an unchanging institution, as J. D. Alsop demonstrates in a forthcoming article, 'The Exchequer in Late Medieval Government, *c.*1485–1530' to be published in the festschrift for J. R. Lander, *Late Medieval Government and Society*, ed. J. G. Rowe, Toronto University Press. I am grateful to him for allowing me to read it before publication.

[10] G. L. Harriss, 'Medieval Government and Statecraft', *P & P* xxv (1963), 24 ff. As I shall argue below, the orientation of financial administration in Elizabeth's reign was essentially 'backward-looking'.

[11] Elton, *Tudor Revolution*, 241–2. Dr Sybil Jack is working on the political background to 1554, and I am grateful to her for allowing me to read an unpublished paper on the subject. For the first steps towards a major revision see Elton, 'Mid-Tudor Finance', *HJ* xx (1977), 737–40; J. D. Alsop, 'The Revenue Commission of 1552', ibid. xxii (1979), 511–33.

extending into the seventeenth century. There is insufficient space
to examine the whole of it here, but fortunately there is no need
to do so: even if we confine our examination to the history of the
Receipt of the Exchequer in the years between 1554 and 1572, it
will cast a new and valuable light on the 'Tudor Revolution'. It will
also complement Professor Elton's subsequent work on the Receipt
in (mainly) the later Elizabethan period, which, perhaps, weakened
his original position more than he realized.[12] Many of the details of
the story are still only dimly visible through the fragmentary and
confusing sources, and may well need to be corrected in the light of
further research, but its outlines are clear enough. In a period of
about eighteen years, the Receipt was, to use the word rather loosely,
reorganized four times, but not in accordance with 'Cromwellian
principles', or along any consistent line of development: and
although Winchester undoubtedly exerted a considerable influence
on events, it was an intensely conservative one and not ultimately
decisive. But so complex is the subject and so complicated the
developments of almost two decades, that we must preface a detailed
examination of events with a brief survey of the Exchequer's status
and internal organization on the eve of the amalgamation of the
revenue courts.

In Edward VI's reign, the Exchequer administered less than one-
third of the revenue handled centrally, and was surpassed in
volume of activity by both the Court of Augmentations and the
Mint.[13] Most of the financial transactions recorded in its accounts
were cash ones, though they were often more complex than they
now appear. The tallies of assignment which had been the stock in
trade of the Exchequer in the fifteenth century were still used to
earmark particular sums for particular purposes, but only on a very
small scale: little more than 5 per cent of each year's revenue was
dealt with in this way.[14] So the Exchequer was essentially concerned

[12] G. R. Elton, 'The Elizabethan Exchequer: War in the Receipt', in S. T. Bindoff, J. Hurstfield, C. H. Williams, eds., *Elizabethan Government and Society:
Essays presented to Sir John Neale* (London, 1961), 213–48, repr. in G. R. Elton,
Studies in Tudor and Stuart Politics and Government (3 vols., Cambridge, 1974 and
1983), i. 355–88. (Any subsequent reference will be to the more recent volume.)
In this work, Elton provided a brilliant illustration of the 'persistence of
"medievalism"' in the Lower Exchequer, and admitted that Winchester should bear
his share of the blame for it, ibid. 387.

[13] J. D. Alsop, 'The Exchequer of Receipt in the Reign of Edward VI' (University of Cambridge, unpublished Ph.D. thesis, 1978), 274–8. I am deeply grateful to
Dr Alsop for presenting me with a copy of his work.   [14] Ibid. 135, 207–8.

with cash. But very little of the money paid into the court was retained by it. Receipts exceeded issues by only £1,400 a year, and
money tended to go out faster than it came in at the beginning of
each term, so the tellers had little scope for the malversation which
was so common elsewhere. For this and other reasons, the Exchequer's capacity to handle cash was well regarded.[15]

In its internal organization, the Exchequer comprised two separate departments: the Upper Exchequer, or Exchequer of Account,
and the Lower Exchequer, or Exchequer of Receipt. The former
was a court of audit which took the accounts of accountants and
debtors within its purview, settled legal disputes concerning the
revenues, and enforced payment of outstanding debts. The latter
was a treasury and pay office responsible for the receipt, safe
custody, and issue of all money paid into the Exchequer, and for
the production of records relevant to its activities.[16] In earlier times
it has been governed in accordance with procedures established by
the reign of Henry II and set down in the Black Book of the Exchequer.[17] According to the view of the 'ancient course' which
developed in the latter half of the sixteenth century—the historical
accuracy of which need not concern us here—the treasurer and the
two chamberlains had been responsible for the king's treasure,
which was administered for them by three subordinates. These subordinates were the treasurer's clerk and the two deputy chamberlains. The former compiled a receipt roll, or pell of receipt, by
which his master was charged, and an issue roll, or pell of issue, by
which he was discharged. The latter compiled counterpells of receipt
and issue to charge and discharge their masters, and to 'control' the
treasurer's rolls. All receipts were entered, as they occurred, in the
three receipt rolls, and all issues, similarly, in the three issue rolls.
The six rolls therefore provided a record in triplicate of all the
transactions of the Receipt and guaranteed the security of the treasure.[18] However, for reasons that were controversial, these arrangements had been set aside, and by 1553 the Lower Exchequer showed
little trace of them. There was still a treasurer of the Exchequer—

[15] Ibid. 185, 187–8, 254, 260.

[16] For an outline of our limited knowledge of the Upper Exchequer, see ibid.
267–72.

[17] E 36/266, fos. 20–47. Johnson's edition of the *Dialogus* is a collation of this
and two other MSS.

[18] E 407/71, *passim*. For a classic statement of the fully developed account of the
ancient course and its reform by Henry VII see ibid. fos. 27–32.

William Paulet, marquess of Winchester—but though he had been markedly more active than his immediate predecessors, he had still played very little part in the running of the Receipt, relying on an appointee, the writer of the tallies, to supervise the tellers for him: there were still two chamberlains, but it was decades since the occupants of these offices had done anything to earn their fees: there were still two deputy chamberlains, and a clerk (known as the clerk of the pells) who produced a treasurer's receipt roll, but they had long since ceased to compile either issue rolls or genuine counterpells. In short, although warrants for issues were still directed to the treasurer and chamberlains of the Exchequer, the three officers were no longer custodians of money and only the treasurer produced records which enabled him—or rather his appointee—to control those who were.[19] Notionally, the Receipt was in the charge of an officer to whom the ancient records made no reference, but who was in fact the descendant of the treasurer's clerk, the under-treasurer. In practice, however, the incumbent, Sir John Baker, was weighed down with offices—among them the chancellorship of the (Upper) Exchequer and of the Court of First Fruits and Tenths —and, like his immediate predecessors, contributed almost as little to the Lower Exchequer as his superior, the treasurer.[20] Real authority was vested in Thomas Felton, the writer of the tallies and auditor of the Receipt. Under the system he oversaw, all money paid into the Receipt was delivered to one or other of the four tellers, who locked it in his personal coffers and made out the documentation necessary to charge himself with it and to secure the accountant's acquittance. All warrants directed to the Lower Exchequer were delivered to the office of the writer of the tallies who, to simplify a great deal, registered them, filed them, and sent orders to the tellers instructing them to make the necessary payments. They then issued the money and made out the records necessary to charge the recipient and to discharge themselves. At the end of each of the Exchequer's six-month terms, the writer of the tallies examined the tellers' accounts—comparing their rolls, or counterbooks, with his own records of issues and the clerk of the pells' record of receipts—with the object of establishing, not the actual contents of their coffers, but their *charge*. This done, his staff concluded

19 Alsop, 'Edwardian Receipt', 2, 24, 59, 62–3, 66, 71–3, 96–9, 116–21, 271.
20 Ibid. 3–4, 61–2, 64–5, 118–21, 269–71, 315–18. Baker's distinguished career is summarized in *HC 1509–58*, i. 366–9.

proceedings for the term by drawing up a heterogeneous assortment of views and declarations of account.[21] In short, the officers who really mattered in the Receipt were the four tellers and the writer of the tallies. The former were severally, but not jointly, responsible for the handling of money: the latter, for the regulation of their activities and the running of the department. This, then, was the position when in Janunary 1554 the Second Court of Augmentations and the Court of First Fruits and Tenths were annexed to the Exchequer, and the first of four new phases of development began.[22]

What seems to have initiated the first phase was the interaction of three events. The first was the unexpectedly early death, on 23 January 1554, of Robert Strelley, whom Mary had only appointed chamberlain in November 1553.[23] The vacancy brought into the Exchequer—on 23 February 1554—a man whose fortunes were strikingly out of line with his birth: Henry Lord Stafford, only legitimate son of the late Edward duke of Buckingham. Significantly for later developments, he was a scholar and antiquarian, a born trouble-maker, and a man painfully anxious to restore the honour and fortunes of his house.[24] The second—which took effect on 23 October 1555—was the termination of Sir Edmund Peckham's appointment as custodian of all cash paid into the revenue courts during the period of reorganization.[25] This meant that the revenues of the dissolved courts were now kept in the Receipt, which became fully responsible for the vast bulk of the cash revenues of the crown. The tellers, who together had handled about £80,000 a year in Edward VI's reign, now found themselves handling about £265,000, never less than 75 per cent and sometimes as much as 95 per cent of the crown's centrally administered income.[26] This had

---

[21] Alsop, 'Edwardian Receipt', 55–74 (the writer of the tallies, 1450–1553), 79–111 (the course of receipts), 111–34 (the course of issues), 138–62 (the audit), 334–7 (Felton's career). I am grateful to Dr Alsop for allowing me to read an unpublished paper on Thomas Felton and his family.

[22] For the amalgamation of 1554 and the background to what follows: Elton, *Tudor Revolution*, 238–57; Richardson, *Augmentations*, 246–70. For the events of 1554–8, I am deeply indebted to Dr Alsop's work, and in particular, 'Edwardian Receipt', 356–62.

[23] *HC 1509–58*, iii. 397–8.

[24] *CPR (1553–4)*, 4; A. H. Anderson, 'Henry, Lord Stafford (1501–1563) in Local and Central Government', *EHR* lxxviii (1963), 225–42. Anderson has exaggerated the importance of Stafford's role in the conflict over the organization of the Exchequer.

[25] D. M. Loades, *The Reign of Mary Tudor* (London, 1979), 191–2.

[26] This is an estimate for the years 1554–71, based principally on: E 407/71, fos. 48–9, 56 (abstracts from tellers' views, accurate wherever they have been checked

profound consequences for the Exchequer and its officers. The former now became the focus of financial administration: the latter benefited in a variety of ways, two only of which need concern us here. As far as its junior officers were concerned, the extra work provided them with an opportunity to enhance the fees they received from the crown and from the accountants and debtors with whom they dealt, though some were better placed to exploit it than others. As for the senior officers, they new standing of the Exchequer gave them an unprecedented chance to improve their status. Whichever of them controlled the Receipt would be a vital intermediary between government and administration, and as such, ideally situated both to influence and implement policy. Control of the cash surpluses—if they were not transferred from the Exchequer—could make him one of the most powerful of ministers. Considerations such as these made it likely that when the many practical problems arising from the amalgamation were encountered, their solution would be the subject of bitter controversy. The third of the events with which we are concerned was the death of Richard Brown, the clerk of the pells, on 8 December 1555. Brown's significance is that he was both quiescent in his minor office and a friend of Thomas Felton, the writer of the tallies: in other words, a man unlikely to challenge the order of the department in which he worked.[27] But his death created a vacancy, and into it, on 18 December, was appointed Edmund Cockerell, a different sort of man altogether.

Cockerell had already served for several years as a clerk or deputy to his predecessor, so he was aware of the disparity between his new position and that of the writer of the tallies. He had probably worked in the treasuries—his master had been an usher—and seen both the voluminous records his predecessors had compiled and the Black Book of the Exchequer. As his actions made clear, he arrived at some time at the conclusion that the negligible office he now occupied had once been a much more important one, and that the writer of the tallies had usurped his authority. As soon as he had been admitted, on 21 January 1556, he started to campaign vigorously to recover what he thought was his ancient place. He adopted the title of clerk to the lord treasurer and writer and keeper of the pells of

against the original views); Northants RO, Westmoreland (Apethorpe) MSS 4. xix. 3, 4. xix. 5, 4. xix. 6; F. C. Dietz, *English Public Finance 1485–1641* (2 vols., 2nd edn., London, 1964), ii. 301–4.

[27] Alsop, 'Edwardian Receipt', 58–61, 70–1, 320–1.

receipt and issue, began to make abridgements of tellers' receipts from entries in the receipt roll, and, at the end of the term, drew up the first of his own declarations of receipts, rivalling those produced by the writer of the tallies.[28]

Exactly why he undertook this course of action it is impossible to say. It is tempting—in the light of later events—to see him executing a stratagem of Winchester's, but the evidence of his patent, which was conventional in content, suggests that there was no thought in the treasurer's mind of breaking with tradition when he appointed Cockerell to his office.[29] In all probability, the clerk of the pells' actions were the initiatives of an intelligent and ambitious man with a grievance, one who could see that the new importance of the Exchequer would considerably enhance an associate's fees and standing, but not his own. In an institution as precedent-conscious as the Exchequer, an appeal to ancient authority was an obvious step to take. But if Winchester did not initiate the first of the post-1554 wars in the Receipt, he certainly participated actively —and on Cockerell's side—once it had begun.

That the man who is usually regarded as a leading light of the 'reform movement' in the mid-Tudor period should commit himself whole-heartedly to the restoration of the ancient practices of the Exchequer is not as puzzling as it may appear.[30] He had excellent reasons for doing so, though these had nothing to do with 'Cromwellian principles'. Initially, it may have been his professional instincts, as an experienced and accomplished administrator, that inclined him to support Cockerell. In 1554, the teller Robert Darkenall had died with over £1,600 outstanding on his account, and subsequent attempts to recover the bulk of the money had failed. Then, early in 1556—when Cockerell was beginning his campaign against Felton—two more scandals came to light. By January, it was clear that £2,500 had been missing from Jerome Shelton's coffers when he had left office, and in March, an elaborate conspiracy to steal money in the charge of Nicholas Brigham, the most active of the tellers, was uncovered. Subsequent investigation revealed

---

[28] Ibid. 356–62; E 36/266, fo. 74ᵛ (Cockerell's admittance); *HC 1509–58*, i. 664–5.

[29] E 403/2451, fo. 146. Dr Alsop concluded the same in 'Edwardian Receipt', 359–60.

[30] It was, of course, Professor Elton who first suggested the need for a reappraisal of Winchester, in 'War in the Receipt', 361, 363, 371, 387. See also *Reform and Reformation*, 358, 390.

that Brigham's coffers had been left unguarded in his own home, that the plot had come within a hair's breadth of success, and that the yeoman usher of the Receipt, William Rossey, had been implicated in it.[31] These events may well have convinced Winchester that there were serious shortcomings in the Lower Exchequer and have predisposed him to sympathy when Edmund Cockerell began to argue, citing the *Dialogus* for authority, that the present disorders were the consequence of neglect of the ancient course. But careful examination of the key texts would have provided him with conclusive reasons for supporting the clerk of the pells. Until his entry into the treasurership in February 1550, the office had been, for some considerable time, an honorific one. He had given it more attention than his predecessors, establishing himself in rooms in the Exchequer and performing in person some of the duties they had preferred to leave to others, but he had not taken over the running of either of the two departments.[32] Nor, in his associated position of lord high treasurer of England, had he succeeded in making himself the first minister of finance. He had established a reputation for hard work and competence: but Northumberland had kept the direction of financial policy in his own firm grasp, relying on Cecil, Gresham, and Mildmay for advice, rather than the treasurer, and using Peter Osborne, clerk to the four principal gentlemen of the Privy Chamber, as a (highly informal) personal treasurer.[33] Mary had been markedly cool towards him, perhaps because he was regarded as a self-seeker who had enriched himself at the expense of the church and of wards and minors. He was only reappointed to the treasurership after a period of acute uncertainty, and as late as November 1553 there were rumours circulating that he would be replaced by Sir Edward Waldegrave. When the revenue

[31] For Darkenall, see Alsop, 'Edwardian Receipt', 186–7, 329–31, and *HC 1509–58*, ii. 16–17. For Shelton, see Alsop, 'Edwardian Receipt', 186–7, 347–9 and 'The Financial Enterprises of Jerome Shelton, a Mid-Tudor London Adventurer', *Guildhall Studies in London History*, iv (1979), 33–50. For Brigham, see Alsop, 'Edwardian Receipt', 318–19 and 'Nicholas Brigham (d. 1558), Scholar, Antiquary and Crown Servant', *Sixteenth-Century Journal*, xii (1981), 49–67, and D. M. Loades, *Two Tudor Conspiracies* (Cambridge, 1965), 190–1.

[32] Alsop, 'Edwardian Receipt', 2, 24, 66, 71–3, 116–21, 271.

[33] D. E. Hoak, *The King's Council in the Reign of Edward VI* (Cambridge, 1976), 210–13; 'The King's Privy Chamber, 1547–1553' in D. J. Guth and J. W. McKenna, eds., *Tudor Rule and Revolution* (Cambridge, 1982), 106–7. It should also be noted that Winchester was not appointed to the most important of the revenue commissions set up to deal with the financial crisis in 1552: Alsop, '1552 Revenue Commission', *passim*.

courts were amalgamated, he was obliged to surrender his lucrative mastership of the Wards to Sir Francis Englefield—a political decision, no doubt, but one which the recollection of the scandals revealed in June 1552 may have facilitated.[34] So Winchester was not, in Michaelmas term 1555, the dominant figure he is often presented as, but a man with his way still to make. His reading of the *Dialogus*—or Cockerell's explication of it—would have taught him two things of great significance to himself. The first was that the treasurer had been the most active and important member of the Exchequer, if not its titular head. A return to the ancient course would, therefore, considerably increase his power in the court, and, in view of the developments of 1554, his standing in Mary's government. The second was that, under the ancient constitution, the undertreasurer's office did not exist.[35] This, in an age when tradition was venerated, was sufficient to justify the view he adopted, that Sir John Baker had no right to his *de facto* position as head of the Receipt: he was an upstart, a jumped-up clerk, usurping the rightful place of the treasurer and chamberlains.[36] So Winchester had good reason to support Cockerell. The clerk of the pells had not simply identified what he conceived to be the causes of the scandals in the Receipt and the steps necessary to remove them: he had provided the treasurer with the justification he needed to embark on a battle for authority. The conflict which followed was not, then, only about the tedious details of accounting procedures: it was also about power, and there was a political dimension to it from the outset.

Once Winchester had absorbed the implications of Cockerell's argument, he gave him his unstinting support. In the Michaelmas term of 1556,[37] he authorized the clerk to move into the former premises of the Court of First Fruits and Tenths, which had been rendered redundant by Act of Parliament in 1555, and to set it up

[34] Loades, *Mary Tudor*, 86–7, 253; M. A. R. Graves, *The House of Lords in the Parliaments of Edward VI and Mary I* (Cambridge, 1981), 24; Joel Hurstfield, *The Queen's Wards* (2nd edn., London, 1973), 198–204, 211–12, 243–4.

[35] Johnson, *Dialogus*, pp. xv, 8–13, 20, 28–9.

[36] My interpretation of the events of 1554–8 and Winchester's part in them is based on Stafford's version in BL Lansd. MS 106, fos. 7–15, which I have collated with the copy in the Staffs. RO, D(W) 1721/1/1 fos. 241^v–244^v. I am grateful to Dr George Bernard for drawing my attention to the latter.

[37] That is to say, the term which began at the feast of St Michael Archangel, 29 Sept. 1556, and finished at Easter 1557. The sources are imprecise and inconsistent in their references to Exchequer and law terms.

as a new pells office. He also gave him permission to transfer the old pells, and possibly a number of other records, from the treasuries to the new office. Cockerell took possession of his new premises early in 1557. According to the yeoman usher's accounts—which were countersigned by both the clerk of the pells and the treasurer —he had the office reglazed, furnished with three writing desks, and liberally provided with stationery. Among the items he purchased was '1 Buckram bag for the new red book containing the old ancient orders of the Receipt'; among the payments he made for work on the room was one 'For fair setting out the names of all the kings since the conquest both within and without the presses wherein the pells of receipt and issue with all such writings as in the same office remain are bestowed.' There is no reason to doubt that by Michaelmas term 1556 Cockerell had convinced Winchester of the desirability of a return to the ancient course, and that by Easter 1557, the treasurer had taken a significant step in that direction.[38]

However, to set up a new office was one thing: to change the practice of the Receipt was another. To make the return to the ancient course effective, Winchester had still to secure the co-operation of the undertreasurer, the writer of the tallies, and the four tellers. It is impossible to discover what the initial response of these officers to the treasurer's new policy was, but their subsequent actions, and the arguments refined by Felton's successors, make it reasonable to assume two things. The first is that they were hostile to this challenge to the status quo and refused to co-operate. Baker, in particular, is likely to have seen it as a deadly insult, as well as a threat to his recently enhanced position. The second is that they based their defence of the existing order on an alternative—and equally imprecise—vision of the Exchequer's more recent history, derived in the main from the office papers of the writer of the tallies. To summarize, very briefly, what later became a complex and sophisticated argument: the Exchequer had indeed been governed according to procedures established by Henry II's reign, but Henry VII had decided that the old practice was inefficient, insecure, and expensive to maintain. He therefore introduced, in the twentieth

[38] E 407/71, fos. 5, 13, 196, 206, 208, 223ᵛ; *Stat. Realm* 2 and 3 Phi. and Mary, c. 4; E 407/68/2—yeoman usher's accounts for Hil. 1557 i.e. the period between 13 Jan. and Easter. (I am grateful to Dr Alsop for drawing my attention to the latter source.) Winchester's patronage probably extended beyond the Exchequer: Cockerell represented Portsmouth in the Parliaments of 1554, 1555 and 1558. *HC 1509–58*, i. 664–5.

year of his reign or thereabouts, a sweeping programme of reform. He relieved the treasurer and chamberlains of their responsibility for money, thus rendering the pells and counterpells obsolete; he transferred the charge to the four tellers, to whom he also confided the custody of the treasure; he abolished the office of treasurer's clerk, and appointed in his place an undertreasurer whom he made responsible for the operation of the Receipt; and he appointed the clerk who then wrote the tallies to supervise the tellers. These changes made possible the establishment of as efficient, secure and cheap a method of accounting as could be devised—one which should on no account be abolished.[39]

This defence, mounted by those who were already in possession of the field, was impregnable and left only one course of action open to Winchester and Cockerell: to prove that the historical foundations of their enemies' case were unsound. This the clerk of the pells set out to do, combing the ancient records for the necessary evidence.[40] He probably enlisted the support of Henry Lord Stafford, the antiquarian chamberlain, who threw himself enthusiastically into the conflict, bombarding the treasurer and barons of the Exchequer with petitions about the corruption of the current course and the virtues of the ancient.[41] But Stafford's contribution to the dispute proved a mixed blessing. It was no doubt advantageous to have the case for the ancient course advanced by a man as eminent socially as he was, but the terms in which it was expressed can hardly have been welcome to Winchester and Cockerell. For the chamberlain did not simply endorse the claims of his colleague. He presented them in a way calculated to enhance his own standing in the Exchequer. He accused his own predecessors of negligence, and listed the treasurer and the clerk of the pells among the authors of the present disorders—the former for usurping control of the treasuries and turning a blind eye to the wholesale destruction of the records in them, the latter for improperly taking custody of the old pells and counterpells and failing to see that the chamberlains' deputies produced their counterpells. It is reasonable to assume, therefore, that Winchester is more likely to have regarded the chamberlain as a rival than as an ally.[42]

---

[39] E 407/71, fos. 1–3, 8ᵛ–9, 13, 24, 28–32, 36ᵛ, 39, 41ᵛ, 115–19, 150–3, 174ᵛ, 183–4, 213, 229ᵛ–230ᵛ.

[40] Alsop, 'Edwardian Receipt', 358.

[41] BL Lansd. MS 106, fo.14.

[42] Ibid. fos. 9–10, 11ᵛ.

By the Michaelmas term of 1557, sufficient evidence had been accumulated by the clerk of the pells to convince the treasurer that the time for the final offensive had come. Winchester therefore took the matter to the Exchequer court and submitted it to the judgment of the barons. Arguing the case himself, he told them that great disorders had occurred in the Receipt because of the neglect of the ancient orders. Tellers had died thousands of pounds in debt to the queen. The present situation was intolerable, and he was determined either to have the ancient course restored or to give up his staff of office. Not surprisingly, Sir John Baker contested the issue, but Winchester was able to demonstrate that there was no undertreasurer in the complement of the ancient Exchequer, only a treasurer's clerk, and therefore no warrant for his position in the Receipt. The barons must have appeared impressed, for Baker took fright and persuaded his friends on the Privy Council to refer the matter to the queen. Mary was told—by whom it is not certain—that the real cause of the treasurer's anger was the continuing sale of crown lands, and the failure of the Exchequer staff to keep what he regarded as a proper record of sums accruing from this source.[43]

This may not have been a complete misrepresentation of Winchester's position—the treasurer was hostile to the alienation of crown land, and probably did object to the recording of receipts arising from it only in the counterbooks of Nicholas Brigham, the teller[44]—but it was a report likely to secure the queen's sympathy for Baker. Winchester had been troublesome about land sales before. Mary had once been obliged to write him a placatory letter on the subject and—perhaps because of his attitude—to exclude him from the most recently appointed commission for land sales.[45] More significantly, she had been using Nicholas Brigham as a personal treasurer since the early months of 1555, and had since diverted an ever-increasing proportion of the revenues into his hands.[46] At the time of Winchester's outburst in the Exchequer court, he was handling nearly 70 per cent of the money accounted

[43] Ibid. fos. 14–15.

[44] Receipts from land sales were passing by tellers' bill, not tally, and therefore were recorded only in the tellers' counterbooks, to which Cockerell did not have access. In other words, they were not recorded in the pell of receipt, which was a register of tallies struck, not a composite record of receipts. (See n. 51 below.) Brigham was the receiver of all money from the sale of crown lands, 1556–8: Alsop, 'Brigham', 56.

[45] Loades, *Mary Tudor*, 302–4, 318.

[46] Alsop, 'Brigham', 55–7.

for at the Exchequer, six times more than any other teller.[47] Our knowledge of his activities is far from complete, but he was surely playing a much more important role in government finance than his modest office in the Exchequer would indicate. The queen may then have concluded—as her advisers possibly suggested—that in raising the question of the ancient course in the Exchequer court, Winchester was transferring to another forum a debate he had already lost at the council board and was mounting an oblique attack on government policy.[48] At any rate, she responded quickly and positively to the undertreasurer's appeal for help, ordering the treasurer not to change the existing order in the Receipt. Her intervention was decisive. Baker kept his command of the Lower Exchequer, Felton his responsibility for the tellers.[49] Brigham was formally vested with even greater responsibilities: over £175,000 passed through his hands in the Easter term alone.[50] Not only the extraordinary receipts from loans and land sales, but also the ordinary receipts from the lands of the former Court of Augmentations, were exempted (in part) from the rigours of the ancient course.[51] Winchester was first excluded from the council of finance, then found a job in the provinces—albeit an important one for which he was well qualified—that kept him away from council meetings. It is hard to resist the conclusion that attempts to locate the 'rise of the treasurer' in Mary's reign are doomed to failure.[52]

To sum up the events of 1554–8: the amalgamation of the Courts of Augmentations and First Fruits and Tenths with the Exchequer

[47] Calculated from E 407/71, fos. 56–7.

[48] There were, in fact, a number of issues on which Winchester disagreed with government policy. One of them was the employment of Sir Thomas Gresham in the Antwerp money market: *CSPF 1560–1*, 137; J. W. Burgon, *The Life and Times of Sir Thomas Gresham* (2 vols., London, 1839), i. 171–2, 190–1, 326–31; Loades, *Mary Tudor*, 410.

[49] BL Lansd. MS 106, fo. 15.

[50] That is to say, the term which began at Easter 1558 and finished at Michaelmas. E 407/71 fo. 56ᵛ; Alsop, 'Brigham', 56–7.

[51] The subject remained a matter of controversy until the 17th century, but in general, receipts from loans and land sales did not pass by tally; receipts from the lands of the former Court of Augmentations passed by tally, but the tallies were not joined in the pipe office. E 407/71, fos. 17, 33, 107, 160, 222ᵛ.

[52] Loades, *Mary Tudor*, 381–2, 388, 409–10; Alsop, 'Edwardian Receipt', 21–2; Penry Williams, *The Tudor Regime* (Oxford, 1979), 202, 387–8, 426. For Winchester's contemporary misfortunes, both political and financial, in Hampshire, see R. H. Fritze, 'The Role of Family and Religion in the Local Politics of Early Elizabethan England: the Case of Hampshire in the 1560s', *HJ* xxv (1982), 268–9. Was Stafford bought off? Graves, *House of Lords*, 13–14.

restored the latter to its historically central position in financial administration and, after the termination of Sir Edmund Peckham's commission, brought a massive influx of cash into the Receipt. They also gave rise to fierce conflicts—at a variety of levels—about the way in which the much enhanced revenues should be handled. On the initiative of a minor clerk, Winchester and Stafford did their best to reintroduce the ancient course, hoping both to improve the efficiency of the Exchequer and to further their own interests. Baker and Felton opposed them because the reintroduction of the ancient course would have deprived them of their authority in the Receipt. When the barons seemed likely to make a ruling unacceptable to them, Baker successfully enlisted the queen's support for his defence of the status quo. As a result, the treasurer and chamberlain were defeated, and the undertreasurer and writer of the tallies were confirmed in their control of the Receipt, which in most respects continued to function as it had done before the amalgamation. The revenues of the dissolved Courts were not subjected to the full rigours of the ancient course. In the Upper Exchequer, a tripartite system of auditing—involving the (separate) use of methods of both the pre-1554 Exchequer and the former Court of Augmentations—was adopted;[53] in the Lower, where the tellers frequently registered receipts which were not recorded by tally and therefore could not be enrolled by the clerk of the pells, a bipartite system of accounting was established. Additionally, one of the tellers, Nicholas Brigham, was employed as a special treasurer to the crown. As such, he received and issued nearly 70 per cent of the cash paid into the Receipt in the last year of Mary's reign—approximately £290,000 between Michaelmas 1557 and Michaelmas 1558.[54] The extraordinary state of his last counterbook, the issues section of which is entirely blank, and the inability of the writer of the tallies to establish his charge within six months of his death, suggest that neither he nor the lords of the Council, who sometimes wrote to him personally for information about the Receipt, were much troubled by the formal rules of Exchequer practice when it came to making payments.[55]

---

[53] The complications of the Upper Exchequer's auditing 'system' are summarized in Elton, *Tudor Revolution*, 254–5. See also Richardson, *Augmentations*, 436–74 *passim*.   [54] E 407/71, fo. 56ᵛ.

[55] E 405/124; E 165/11, fo. 100 (supplied by Dr Alsop, who is continuing his work on Brigham's accounts); Alsop, 'Edwardian Receipt', 132–4, and 'Brigham', 57.

In the winter of 1558, three events brought this period of Exchequer history to an end and introduced another, which lasted until the autumn of 1566. The queen, Nicholas Brigham, and Sir John Baker died, the former on 17 November, the latter two before the end of December.[56] So within a matter of weeks, three of the four principal obstacles to the plans of Winchester, Stafford, and Cockerell were removed. Felton survived, it is true, but with his superior dead, Brigham's accounts in disarray, the barons unsympathetic, and no built-in support on the new Council, his position was a much weaker one. With a new and—as it transpired—more sympathetic queen there was every reason to hope for a successful outcome of a renewed attempt to restore the ancient course.

Stafford, who had been granted his chamberlain's office for life, was able to respond immediately to the new situation, but there is no evidence that he did so. Winchester could not, for his own offices had lapsed with the death of Mary. His first concern must therefore have been to secure a place on the Council, his second to persuade Elizabeth—or, more importantly, her close advisers—to reappoint him to the treasurership. There was no certainty that he would achieve either of these objectives. He was, it is true, an able and experienced administrator, and a magnate of considerable standing in the south of England, but he was also a conservative in religion —as he soon showed by voting against the abolition of the mass in the 1559 Parliament.[57] However, something turned the scales—perhaps the need for some continuity in office in a period of wholesale change, perhaps the fact that the conflicts of 1557 had to some extent distanced him from the discredited government of 1558. At any rate, he was summoned to the Council by 27 November, and regranted his treasurership on 21 January 1559.[58] His reappointment was followed by wholesale changes in the Lower Exchequer, which radically altered its practices and produced a major shift in the (internal) balance of power. It is tempting to attribute everything

---

[56] Baker died on 23 Dec. 1558, *HC 1509–58*, i. 369. The date of Brigham's death has not yet been established, Alsop, 'Brigham', 58.

[57] J. E. Neale's suggestion, in *Elizabeth I and her Parliaments* (2 vols., London, 1953, 1957), i. 80, that Winchester voted against the Act of Uniformity only to strengthen a subsequent use of the royal veto, is unconvincing. For a presentation of Winchester as a leading Catholic, see Norman Jones, *Faith by Statue: Parliament and the Settlement of Religion, 1559* (London, 1982), 175; Fritze, 'Family and Religion', pp. 268–70.

[58] Loades, *Mary Tudor*, 459; Williams, *Tudor Regime*, 453; *CPR* (1558–60), 59.

that happened to Winchester, but it would be a mistake to do so. The treasurer was not free to give whatever orders he chose. At one level, he was constrained by politics, for—to take but one example—the standing of a prestigious office was of great concern to the crown, regardless of the duties actually performed by its occupant, since it helped determine the extent of the monarch's precious powers of patronage. At another, he was circumscribed by precedent and law. For instance, an officer admitted to his place for life was esteemed to be seised in his demesne as of freehold—and a freeholder could not be deprived of his property.[59] Even the orders he could give with some confidence that they would be obeyed were uncertain in their effect. He did not have a sufficient grasp of the minutiae of Exchequer practice to be able to work out the best way of putting them into effect. That had to be left to subordinates, who had both to reorientate their relationships with each other and reorganize their work on the basis of trial and error. As a result, many hands—some reluctant ones—contributed to developments, and for different reasons. Although the general trend of events was clear enough—towards a full reintroduction of the ancient course and the establishment of Winchester's undisputed authority—progress was by fits and starts, a fact obscured by the analytic treatment necessary here.

What, then, happened between 1559 and 1566? The most important developments may be summarized under six heads.

First, the late Sir John Baker's empire was dismembered. His chancellorship of the (Upper) Exchequer was granted to Sir Walter Mildmay, at Winchester's own suit, on 5 February 1559, and his undertreasurership was awarded to Sir Richard Sackville, a cousin of the queen and a personal friend of Sir William Cecil, together with a considerable increment on the traditional fee.[60] The latter appointment may look like a set-back for Winchester, but it was not. Sackville was an experienced administrator—among other things, a former chancellor of the Court of Augmentations—and was actively involved in both the formulation and execution of financial policy under Elizabeth—but he probably played only a

---

[59] E 407/71, fos. 93ᵛ–94, 122ᵛ. It was also held (controversially) that a superior officer with an office in his gift was obliged to observe the letter of the ancient form when making a grant of it, ibid. fo. 90.

[60] *HC* 1558–1603, iii. 53–6 (Mildmay), 314–15 (Sackville); BL Lansd. MS 28, fos. 2ᵛ–4. (The increment was £200 p.a. for life.)

minor part in the running of the Lower Exchequer. That this was so is illustrated by Winchester's correspondence with the teller, Richard Stonley. Not only did the treasurer deal directly, secretly, and informally with his subordinate, but he sometimes ordered him to conceal their highly important dealings from the undertreasurer, as the latter's involvement would only slow things up.[61] It is hard to resist the conclusion that Sackville's office was essentially an honorific one—as Sir John Baker's had been until 1554—and therefore that he was no rival to Winchester in the Receipt. This, perhaps, was why the undertreasurer was prepared to cede the chancellor responsibility for First Fruits and Tenths when they were restored to the crown.[62]

Second, Henry Lord Stafford gained some of the ground for which he had been campaigning in Mary's reign. With the support of his colleague, George Talbot, sixth earl of Shrewsbury, and later of the principal secretary, Sir William Cecil, he was able to revitalize the chamberlain's office. He had both the counterpells of receipt revived and defects in the two series remedied by reference to the treasurer's rolls.[63] This permitted his and Shrewsbury's deputies to participate in the auditing of accounts—of the tellers in the Lower Exchequer, and of officers such as the cofferer of the household in the Upper.[64] Furthermore, he won control of one of the keys to the treasuries, and took on the daunting task of surveying and putting in order the massive collections of records which had accumulated there and in the Tower.[65] More than this he had

[61] Essex RO, D/DFa 04. See esp. Winchester's letters of 29 Jan., 30 Jan., and 3 Feb. 1564; 27 Mar. 1566. I am grateful to Dr F. G. Emmison for persuading me to follow Stonley from Westminster to Essex. For Stonley, see *HC 1558–1603*, iii. 450–1.

[62] Elton is right about the agreement but has confused the offices of the two men, *Tudor Revolution*, 256–7.

[63] BL Lansd. MS 106, fo. 8ᵛ; Staffs. RO, D(W) 1721/1/1, fo. 197ᵛ; SP 12/33, fos. 2–5; E 407/68/5 (showing Thomas Reve, Stafford's deputy, and Thomas Burrow, Shrewsbury's deputy, checking Shrewsbury's counterpells against the pells, 7 Feb. 1565); E 407/68/7 (showing William Stanton, Shrewsbury's deputy, copying from the pells the counterpells neglected by his predecessors, in Trinity 1565). Both chamberlains' counterpells survive until Easter term 1564, E 401/1261, 1262.

[64] E 407/68/5 (17 Nov., 5 Dec., 1564; 13 Feb. 1565); E 407/68/6 (3, 9, Dec. 1566).

[65] For Stafford's labours in the record repositories and the work of the chamberlains and their subordinates see Anderson, 'Stafford', 235–42; C. H. D. Coleman, 'Arthur Agard and the Chamberlainship of the Exchequer, 1570–1615', *Derby Archaeol. J.* c (1980), 64–8; R. B. Wernham, 'The Public Records in the Sixteenth and Seventeenth Centuries' in L. Fox, ed., *English Historical Scholarship in the Sixteenth and Seventeenth Centuries* (Oxford, 1956), 16–23.

no time to achieve, for he died on 30 April 1563. Since neither his colleague nor his successor—Sir Nicholas Throckmorton—subsequently took any personal interest in the chamberlain's office, the last threat to Winchester's supremacy in the Exchequer disappeared.[66]

Third, Thomas Felton, the writer of the tallies, and the treasurer arrived at some sort of *modus vivendi*.[67] This is not as surprising as it may at first appear, for Felton needed the treasurer's good will to exercise and benefit from his office, and Winchester needed the experienced writer of the tallies to help him run the Receipt. The arrangement had three practical consequences for the writer of the tallies. In the first place, it permitted him to continue to work very much as he had done under the old regime, supervising the tellers and auditing their accounts; in the second, it obliged him to defer to some extent to the treasurer's wish to raise the clerk of the pells to equality of office, and therefore to share some of his responsibilities with both his rival and the chamberlains' deputies; and in the third, it obliged him to co-operate with the treasurer in his multitudinous activities as an energetic minister of finance, sometimes, as we shall see, with dire consequences for the accounting procedures of the Receipt.[68] In short, the developments of 1559–66 reduced the standing of the writer of the tallies, though without significantly changing the way in which he performed his formal duties, and brought him into a close personal relationship with the treasurer.

Fourth, the office of the clerk of the pells was transformed by the introduction of a modified version of the receipt side of the ancient course. The process of transformation probably began before Cockerell died in the Easter term of 1560, but it is (as yet) impossible to be certain of this as the sources are flatly contradictory.[69] Cockerell's clerk, William Stanton, testified many years later that

---

[66] The grant to Throckmorton—made fourteen months after Stafford's death—was probably intended to reward his activity as a diplomat. *HC 1558–1603*, iii. 497–9.

[67] See, for example, Essex RO, D/DFa 04: Winchester to Felton, 27 Mar. 1566, asking for his friendship in secret matters he has on hand, and informing him that the queen 'allowed well of' his book (*not* the tellers' views for 1565 Michaelmas) and sent her thanks.

[68] For the chamberlains' deputies see p. 181 above; for the clerk of the pells and the treasurer, see pp. 182–4, 186–7.

[69] Cockerell's fee was paid until 14 April 1560, though he did not collect it himself. He was dead when his successor was granted his office on 30 May. E 405/515; E 407/71, fo. 104.

although his master 'Contended against m^r Felton for some addition to his place', he gained nothing from it; but Chidiock Wardoure, one of Cockerell's successors, found documents in his office papers which, he was convinced, showed that his predecessor had been trusted with a wide range of duties in the Receipt. If Wardoure was right, Cockerell was permitted to make constats from the pell for all those who needed them—for example, the receivers of the lands of the former Court of Augmentations—and to check the weekly certificates the tellers delivered to the treasurer. He was also made responsible for the keeping of the privy seal and assignment books, and for the examination of the usher's *liberate* and the customers' declarations.[70] If Stanton was right, it was Cockerell's successor in office, Robert Hare, who took on these extra duties. The latter, a long-standing servant of Winchester's, and, as it transpired, 'a man devoted to Popery', was appointed to the clerkship of the pells on 30 May 1560. The treasurer used the opportunity presented by the vacancy to redefine the office in his gift: so Hare was granted his new post, not as clerk of the pells, but as clerk to the lord treasurer and writer and keeper of the pells of receipt and issue. He celebrated his apppointment by recording the new patent at the head of the first membrane of the receipt roll for Michaelmas term 1560, and set about expanding his responsibilities.[71] In 1559 his predecessor had introduced a paper receipt book into the tally court, so that the cumbersome and expensive pell roll could be made up carefully and at leisure.[72] This handy record made it possible for him to take on an increasing proportion of the work of the Receipt. By Easter term 1560, he was using it both to assist with the audit of the receipt side of the tellers' accounts, and to make up an abbreviate which was itself the basis of a half-yearly declaration similar to the receipt side of that produced by the writer of the tallies.[73] Access to the counter-books enabled him first to make

---

[70] E 407/71, fo. 223^v; BL Lansd. MS 106, fos. 5–6. A constat was a certificate of a payment into the Receipt, required by accountants whose accounts were not audited in the pipe office.

[71] E 401/1244. For Hare and his earlier service to Winchester see: *HC 1558–1603*, ii. 254–5; E 407/68/2 (26 July 1556 to 5 Mar. 1557); E 407/71, fo. 34^v.

[72] It was begun on 2 Oct., E 401/1794. See also Camb. Univ. Lib. MS Gg. 2. 7, fo. 83.

[73] That the clerk of the pells was examining the tellers' counterbooks is proved by the *deficit billa* notation in the receipt book, E401/1795, E 407/71, fos. 8, 181. For the abbreviate of receipts on which the (missing) declaration book was based see E 401/1795, fos. 140–298.

good the discrepancies in his own records—that is to say, to copy from the tellers' rolls references to payments which should have passed by tally but had not yet done so—then, from Michaelmas 1561, to transform the pell from a simple register of tallies to a comprehensive record of (official) cash receipts by copying the entries of payments intended to pass by tellers' bill only.[74] Thus by 1566 the clerk of the pell was producing four series of related records of all receipts, submitting declarations to the treasurer and undertreasurer, and participating—though as a junior partner—in the auditing of the tellers' accounts. But he was only half way to restoring even a modified version of the ancient course, for Felton somehow succeeded in preventing him from reintroducing the pell of issue.

Fifth, the tellers seemingly fought off an attempt by the treasurer to deprive them of the custody of their cash surpluses and establish a central deposit treasury, but were obliged to submit to some reorganization of their office. As far as we can tell from sources that are fragmentary and confused, Winchester began his campaign to establish a deposit treasury on 2 February 1559—before either Sackville or Mildmay were appointed to office—by establishing Roger Alford in rooms in the Tower and making him responsible for the receipt of spiritualities unpaid at the beginning of Elizabeth's reign, foreign loans, and the proceeds of land sales.[75] When Alford closed his 'foreign' account on 3 February 1562, preparatory to giving up his teller's office, the treasurer procured a letter from the queen ordering him to transfer all four tellers' surpluses to the Tower without delay, and, on the very same day, used his own servants, Robert Hare and Humphrey Shelton, to move the cash from the Receipt to the house that stood before his own in the Tower.[76]

[74] These two points were established by comparing successive volumes of the receipt book with the receipt roll and the tellers' rolls. E 401/1794 (Michaelmas term 1559) is simply a register of tallies struck; E 401/1795, fos. 129–33 (Easter 1560) contains the first *deficit billa* entries; E 401/1250 (receipt roll, Michaelmas term 1561) is the first to record receipts by tellers' bill as well as tally.

[75] E 101/429/11; E 314/1/9 (my thanks to Dr Alsop for supplying this reference); E 407/68/4 (provision of equipment for the Tower in Easter term 1560); SP 12/21, fo. 80; *CPR (1558–60)*, 119–20, and *CPR (1560–3)*, 60. For Alford, a trusted servant of Sir William Cecil, see *HC 1509–58*, i. 306–7; *HC 1558–1603*, i. 339; R. C. Barnett, *Place, Profit and Power. A Study of the Servants of William Cecil, Elizabethan Statesman* (Chapel Hill, NC, 1969), 24–8.

[76] E 314/1/9; SP 12/16, fos. 23–4; ibid. 12/21, fo. 80. It is far from clear what became of this money.

Presumably this was only a temporary expedient, for on 15 April he procured another, this time addressed to Sackville and Mildmay as well as himself. In it, the queen complained bitterly of the improper keeping of the treasure in the tellers' houses and the great losses suffered because of the defalcations of Darkenall and Shelton. She then ordered the three officers to find out what the ancient practice of the Receipt had been and consider how best to restore it. Finally, she instructed the tellers (and others) to obey any orders they might revive or establish in this respect, 'vppon payn of our displeasure and such perill as may fall vppon them for the contrary'.[77] However, the signs are that even this unequivocal letter had little effect on the tellers. At an earlier date—probably before the end of the Michaelmas term of 1559—Winchester had tried to introduce a table of new orders for them, and they had ignored it.[78] If he made another attempt now, it must have suffered the same fate, for the tellers kept up the offices they maintained in their own homes and were reimbursed (officially) for expenditure they incurred about their work there.[79] Neither the reluctance of the tellers to comply, nor their ability to withstand such pressure, are difficult to explain. The large surpluses which occasionally accumulated in their hands were a source of considerable private profit; and their duties, as properly admitted officers, could not arbitrarily be changed. The odds, then, were against Winchester achieving anything but temporary successes in his campaign. But lesser problems faced him in his efforts to tighten up the tellers' practices and to reduce the opportunities for malversation. Here, therefore, the co-operation of Mildmay, Felton, and Sackville enabled him to make some changes. The tellers' accounts were subjected to the scrutiny of the clerk of the pells and the chamberlains' deputies, as well as the writer of the tallies;[80] and arrangements were made for all tellers' bills to be presented in the tally court on their day of issue, so, in theory, enabling the clerk of the pells to produce records that were both complete and up to date, and reducing his and the writer of the tallies' dependence on the tellers' own rolls for information about

[77] SP 12/22, fo. 95.

[78] BL Lansd. MS 106, fo. 10.

[79] In Michaelmas term 1566, Robert Taylor (Henry Killigrew's deputy) was given an allowance of £3. 16s. 6d. for 'iron work about his office done in London', E 407/68/6.

[80] See pp. 181, 183–4.

receipts not passing by tally.[81] Furthermore, the income of the Household and the Wardrobe were guaranteed, though not certainly on Winchester's initiative, by readopting the traditional practice, abandoned in 1540, of making block allocations to them by tally of assignment—a step which had the practical consequence of reducing the cash flow through the Receipt by £40,000 a year.[82] It is unlikely, though, that any of these changes significantly altered the way in which the tellers worked. What did, however, is best considered under the next head.

Sixth, the treasurer achieved most of the real objectives for which he had fought in Queen Mary's reign. Thanks, in the main, to the fortuitous death of his rivals, he was able to establish himself in a position of unchallenged authority in the Exchequer. This enabled him to make some major changes to the practice of the Receipt—not by abolishing the supposed constitution of Henry VII, but by placing a modified and incomplete version of the ancient course alongside it. This had the consequence of raising one of his own servants, the clerk of the pells, to a position of notional equality with the writer of the tallies. The standing of these two officers and their willingness, for very different reasons, to obey him, enabled him to take charge of the Lower Exchequer, though not to divest the tellers of their surpluses. This provided him with what he had been seeking since the amalgamation of the revenue courts: an opportunity to manage the cash revenues of the crown. However, his dealings with the tellers were not always influenced by either 'bureaucratic principles' or respect for the various accounting procedures now established in the Receipt. If anything, he modelled his policy on the practices of the previous reign, promoting first Roger Alford, then Richard Stonley to a position similar to that formerly occupied by Nicholas Brigham. Between Michaelmas 1558 and Michaelmas 1566, the staggering sum of £1,171,050 was channelled into Stonley's hands, about £146,380 per annum, or 52 per cent of all the cash flowing into the Receipt.[83] Much of this money was no doubt received and issued with strict propriety, but

[81] The tellers were obliged to date their bills, and accountants were required to deliver them to the tally court on the same day. The practice was introduced in Michaelmas term 1565 and made effective in Easter 1566: E 402/122, 123, 124, 275, 286, 287, 288.

[82] Elton, *Tudor Revolution*, 406–12.

[83] E 407/71, fos. 48–9, checked against tellers' views where they were available. For Stonley, see *HC 1558–1603*, 450–1.

some was not. The treasurer established a close working relationship with the teller, which enabled him both to borrow money for
his own use,[84] and to bypass the cumbersome machinery of the
Exchequer whenever it was necessary to raise or expend great sums
of money in unusual haste. Their extremely complicated private
correspondence shows that when the public interest was at stake,
Winchester would take whatever steps were necessary to deal with
the situation, with barely a backward glance at the rules of Exchequer practice. Sometimes he would order the teller to make an
immediate payment; on other occasions, he would stay money in
London for disbursement there, and instruct Stonley to acknowledge the receipt and send him the bills for it; more frequently he
would arrange for direct transfers of cash from accountant to
accountant and send to Stonley for the bills necessary to validate
the transactions. But he also took up money and expended it himself.
Well-intentioned these dealings may have been, but 'bureaucratic'
they were not.[85] The consequences of these various developments
were profound. Ready access to cash, authority in the Exchequer,
and a position on the Council enabled the marquess to play a vital
role in government and administration, and, for the first time, to
make his honorific office of lord high treasurer of England into a
real one.[86]

What brought this second period of Exchequer history to an end,
and introduced another which lasted until April 1571, was, once
again, an accident of mortality. Thomas Felton, the writer of the
tallies, died on 4 September 1566.[87] By a coincidence, the undertreasurer's office was vacant, for Sir Richard Sackville had died on
21 April and had not been replaced.[88] So Felton's death presented
Winchester with an opportunity to make a new appointment at a

[84] SP 46/28, fos. 119, 133, 183, 186; Essex RO, D/DFa 04 (undated petition to
Burghley and Mildmay). Stonley was still pursuing Winchester's executors for £700
in 1587, E 192/3, fo. 11.

[85] Essex RO, D/DFa 04: Winchester to Stonley, 7 Aug. 1560; 29 Jan. 1564 (two
letters); 30 Jan. 1564; 3 Feb. 1564 (two letters); 6 Feb. 1564; and Winchester to
Felton, 27 Mar. 1566.

[86] For Winchester's energy and activity in Elizabeth's reign, and also his close
relationship with the rulers, customs officers, and merchants of the City of London,
see G. D. Ramsay, *The City of London in International Politics at the Accession of
Elizabeth Tudor* (Manchester, 1975), 55, 59, 146-55, 161. But Englefield's appointment as general surveyor of the customs in 1558 (ibid. 151) should perhaps be seen as
another set-back for the treasurer in Mary's reign.

[87] E 405/522.

[88] *HC 1558-1603*, iii. 315.

time when he had not even to pay lip-service to the wishes of the notional head of the Lower Exchequer. It also removed Robert Hare's only rival for the position of senior clerk in the Receipt. This meant that the treasurer and the clerk of the pells were able to take their plans for the restoration of the ancient course another stage forward.

The first step was taken on 8 October 1566. On that day Winchester admitted one of his own servants, Humphrey Shelton, to the office vacated by Thomas Felton.[89] The appointment was an appropriate one, for Shelton had been an active agent of the treasurer for years, and had been working for him in the Exchequer since at least April 1560.[90] He therefore brought to his new post considerable experience in financial matters and a willingness to co-operate with Robert Hare which derived from long association in personal service to the marquess. This enabled the clerk of the pells to attain the one significant objective he had failed to achieve in Felton's lifetime: the revival of the pell of issue. Precisely what arrangements the two men made to enable Hare to record expenditure, it is impossible to say, so unsatisfactory are the sources for this period, but it is probable that the important decisions were taken before Hilary 1567. Though no issue roll survives for Michaelmas 1566, Hare was provided with the stationery necessary to produce one;[91] if he did not use it in that term, he used it in the next, and from then on produced a pell of issue every term until he left office.[92] No attempt was made to revive the counterpells, perhaps because the chamberlains' deputies were unwilling to take on so much extra labour and expense to so little point,[93] but one further step was taken to remedy the abuses thought to have been permitted by, among other things, neglect of the ancient records. On 3 June 1568, an outsider, Thomas Lichfield, was issued with letters patent empowering him to search back to 1540 for evidence of improper expenditure. So fruitful did his researches prove that he was kept at the task until his death in 1586.[94]

[89] E 36/266, fo. 76.

[90] Shelton had also acted as a searcher in the port of London and as a collector of the subsidy from the nobility. Alsop, 'Jerome Shelton', 143; SP 12/21, fo. 80; Essex RO, D/DFa 04 (Winchester to Stonley, 30 Jan. and 3 Feb. 1564).

[91] Hare was provided with paper books to write the *exitus* and to enter warrants, E 407/68/6.

[92] E 403/858–863.   [93] Camb. Univ. Lib. MS Gg. 2. 7, fo. 84.

[94] *HC 1558–1603*, ii. 478; E 407/71, fo. 155; SP 12/139, fo. 83 and 12/181, fo. 57ᵛ; BL Lansd. MS 35, fos. 70–6 and 44, fo. 14.

These developments had important consequences for the Receipt and its officers. As far as the institution was concerned, the revival of the pell of issue brought to its conclusion the campaign launched by Edmund Cockerell eleven years earlier to reintroduce the ancient course: his successor, Robert Hare, was recognized as treasurer's clerk, kept pells of receipt and issue in which all sums officially paid into and out of the Lower Exchequer were recorded, and (in theory) used these, and other, records to regulate the activities of the tellers. But there was a world of difference between the constitution of Henry II and that established in 1567. For one thing, the new pell of issue was not an authentic one. The way in which the tellers worked—for example, in a variety of different buildings —made it impossible for the clerk of the pells to record each of their payments at the time it was made. He had, therefore, to borrow the tellers' counterbooks from Humphrey Shelton after each audit and copy their entries into his roll: in other words, to make a duplicate of a record he had affected to regard as invalid.[95] For another, the chamberlains were not provided with any significant role in the Receipt. More importantly, though, the so-called consitution of Henry VII was not abolished: the writer of the tallies was not stripped of the duties associated with his supposedly illicit role as auditor of the Receipt. This meant that, in essentials, Shelton's office continued to function very much as his predecessor's had done. In other words, the consequence of Winchester's 'reforms' was not to replace one 'system' of accounting with another, but to set up a second alongside that which was established already. The treasurer may have thought that there was some virtue in this arrangement, that—as was suggested later—it would improve the security of the Receipt if each of its principal clerks were able to keep a check on the activities of the other; but it is more likely that he saw it as a compromise which suited his own interests very well and enabled him to side-step a hornet's nest of new legal problems. As for the other officers of the Receipt, the appointment of Humphrey Shelton ended—for the time being at least—the long feud between the clerk of the pells and the writer of the tallies. It also enabled Robert Hare to take on Thomas Felton's mantle of responsibility in the Lower Exchequer—not because of the arrival of the ancient course, but because Winchester continued to employ the writer of the tallies as his principal agent outside the Exchequer,

[95] E 407/71, fos. 6, 21; Alsop, 'Edwardian Receipt', 361.

so preventing him from giving his new office as much attention as it deserved.[96] Finally, by replacing Felton with a willing servant, it gave the treasurer as complete control over the Receipt as its peculiar constitution would allow, and one that was in no way weakened by the appointment of his still loyal and over-worked chancellor, Sir Walter Mildmay to the position of undertreasurer, on 17 January 1567.[97] This permitted him, when he wished, to do what he had been hoping to do for over ten years: to take the tellers' surpluses—worth about £31,000 at Easter 1568—into his own hands.[98] It may also have encouraged him to set afoot the massive reconstruction of the Exchequer and other offices at Westminster with which he was occupied in the last years of the decade.[99]

However, the private empire Winchester was—literally—building in the late 1560s was an ephemeral one. In the spring of 1571, a fascinating conjunction of circumstances—which can only briefly be summarized here—brought about the abolition of his course in the Receipt and, for all practical purposes, the overthrow of his authority there.

In the first place, the treasurer's considerable age finally began to catch up with him. He retired to his great house at Basing in the summer of 1570, and, although he probably intended to return to Westminster, was never able to do so. Debility may have undermined his efficiency before retirement: it certainly prevented him from mounting more than token resistance when the storm broke about his head.[100]

---

[96] From 9 Dec. 1565 until 4 Jan. 1568, Shelton was acting as a deputy for Winchester, managing and keeping the accounts of a complex operation which involved the use of money taken up by Sir Thomas Gresham in Flanders to purchase grain in East Anglia for sale in France and Ireland, AO 1/172/493. (Dr Sybil Jack kindly drew my attention to this account.) Shelton's successors mistook him for the clerk of the pells and blamed him for the abuses uncovered by Thomas Lichfield, E 407/71, fos. 4, 155; BL Lansd. MS 67, fo. 25ᵛ.

[97] *CPR* (1566–9), 137.

[98] E 405/423. To judge by the subsequent defalcations of the tellers—discussed below—this step is more likely to have been a response to a particular problem than the first application of a general principle.

[99] H. M. Colvin, ed., *The History of the King's Works*, vol. iii. *1485–1660* (Part I) (London, 1975), 71–86; SP 12/47, fo. 35.

[100] Professor Loades and Dr Alsop have kindly allowed me to read an unpublished paper which suggests that Winchester may have been over ninety in 1570. Whatever his age, he was neither sick nor senile when Stonley wrote to him on 3 Mar. 1571 about (*inter alia*) their likely meeting at the next Parliament, Essex RO, D/DFa 04. For (fragmentary) accounts of his last days at Basing see E 407/71, fos. 4, 14, 34ᵛ–36, 97, 107.

In the second, the Exchequer was shaken to its ancient foundations by a series of scandals that made those of the 1550s seem trivial by comparison. Five of the six tellers who held office between 1567 and 1571 defaulted on their accounts, at the enormous cost to the crown of over £44,000. Subsequent investigation—in one case, years after the event—revealed that Richard Stonley had used £6,100 from his receipts from first fruits to purchase land; William Patten had frittered away £8,000; Richard Candler and Richard Smythe had lost £8,700 between them, speculating in the London and Antwerp exchanges; and Thomas Gardiner had invested £21,600 from the proceeds of land sales in his—ultimately disastrous—farm of the duties on French wines. Even if these men were, to some extent, the victims of a difficult economic climate and the longstanding tradition which allowed them to employ their surpluses about their own affairs, their disgrace cannot but have had serious consequences for the treasurer's reputation.[101] To make matters worse, Winchester's two servants—Humphrey Shelton and Robert Hare— deserted their posts and their master. Shelton surrendered his office in June 1569, and, in the Easter term of 1570, fled abroad, never to return.[102] Hare took himself off to France, leaving an inconsequential subordinate, Thomas Lovell, to regulate issues and represent the treasurer's interests, and in April 1570 sold his office at an inflated price to Chidiock Wardoure, another of the treasurer's servants.[103] But that was not all. Winchester's own finances fell into

---

[101] This is a considerable simplification of the tellers' complex dealings, which are massively documented. For Stonley, see Northants RO, Westmorland (Apethorpe) MS 4. xxii. 1 (containing a certificate of the contents of the teller's coffers, 27 Dec. 1568) and E 192/3 fo. 22 (Stonley's confession and an admission that his debt had grown to £19,000 in c.1578). I am grateful to Ms Margaret Condon for drawing my attention to her important additions to E 192/3, and to Mrs Laetitia Yeandle for her invaluable help with my work on Stonley's diaries, which I hope one day to publish (Folger Shakespeare Lib. V. a. 459–61). For Patten: E 159/357 *Communia*, Trin. 10 Eliz. rot. 229. For Candler and Smith: E 112/26/90 and E 159/361 *Communia*, Easter 13 Eliz. rot. 134. For Gardiner: E 351/600; E 405/423; BL Lansd. MS 13, fos. 111–14. See also *HC 1509–1558*, ii. 187 (Gardiner), and B. O'Kill, 'The Printed Works of William Patten (c.1510–1600)', *Trans. Camb. Bibliog. Soc.* vii (1977), 28–45.

[102] E 36/266, fo. 77ᵛ; *CPR (1572–5)*, 159; SP 46/34, fo. 242. Shelton forfeited the profits of his lands to the crown for carelessness in office. BL Lansd. MS 67, fo. 25.

[103] This is the best that can be made of the following, highly confusing, sources: E 407/71, fos. 4, 6, 21, 97, 107, 155; BL Lansd. MS 67, fo. 25ᵛ. For Wardoure, see *HC 1558–1603*, iii. 581–2; Elton, 'War in the Receipt', *passim*.

total disorder. The complexities of his multitudinous public and private activities have still to be unravelled, but it is clear that in the last year of his life he was in serious trouble. Not only was he embarrassed by his inability to clear his account in the Upper Exchequer for £11,500 advanced to him for the purchase of grain for Ireland, but he was burdened with debts to the crown and private individuals which amounted to more than £46,000, which were an encumbrance to his family for generations.[104] Even without Thomas Lichfield's continuing revelations of corruption, it must have been obvious to those with access to this highly secret information, that the treasurer's management of the Receipt was a disaster and that he himself was no longer capable of putting things right.

In the third, Winchester's standing in the government was transformed by the crisis in domestic politics which followed the seizure of the Spanish treasure in December 1568.[105] How, precisely, he responded to the swift rush of events it is impossible to say, but it looks as though he was horrified by the dangerous and damaging turn foreign policy had taken, and by the shift in the balance of power within the Privy Council which had made it possible. At any rate, he began to act less like the omnicompetent servant of the Elizabethan regime than its stubborn and troublesome opponent. The last of his active years saw him feuding with his long-standing enemy, Sir Thomas Gresham;[106] striving, unsuccessfully, to prevent the farming of the customs; and throwing the whole of his still considerable authority into a successful attempt to smash Thomas Gardiner's farm of the French wines—in spite of the queen's explicit orders to desist.[107] When, in addition, he was implicated in the abortive conspiracy of Norfolk and Arundel to overthrow Cecil in the spring of 1569, the secretary and his supporters on the Council

[104] A01/172/493; Laurence Stone, *The Crisis of the Aristocracy 1558–1641* (Oxford, 1965), 423–4, 542, 554.

[105] W. T. MacCaffrey, *The Shaping of the Elizabethan Regime* (London, 1969), 199 ff.

[106] Winchester's final dispute with Gresham—over £1,000 which one of the two of them had misappropriated—was resolved in the treasurer's favour in 1606, thirty-four years after his death: AO 1/172/493.

[107] The wine importers refused to pay the impost on the grounds that it was not granted by act of Parliament, and that Gardiner, a mere patentee, had no case against them in common law. The customs officers, encouraged by Winchester, refused to hand over the duties they had collected: E 112/26/71 mm. 1–2; E 112/26/93; BL Lansd. MS 13, fo. 113; Ramsay, *London*, 148.

must surely have concluded that it was not only necessary to do something about him, but dangerous not to.[108]

If Winchester's old age, disasters in the Receipt, and political enmities provided the motives for an attack on the treasurer and his disintegrating control of finance, the Parliament of 1571 provided the impetus. It assembled on 2 April, that is to say, within a matter of weeks of the disgrace of Candler, Gardiner, and Smythe.[109] That members of the Lower House had some idea of what had been going on in the Exchequer there is no doubt, for when, on 7 April, the Subsidy Bill was introduced, there was an immediate reaction. John Popham expressed unequivocally what many believed: that the present 'lacke in the prince's coffers' had arisen because treasurers of the crown had been allowed to keep far too much money in their hands, to use it to purchase lands, and to defer repayment by going bankrupt and stalling their debts 'as of late someone hath stalled a debt of thirtie thousand powndes'. His meaning was clear: the Commons were being asked to vote taxes for the crown because of the incompetence of the Exchequer, and something had to be done about it.[110]

The government—or, we might tentatively say, the Cecilian faction within it—was prepared for this turn of events. Indeed, to judge by the rapidity with which it responded, it may even have stage-managed the whole affair. On 12 April, the first of a number of bills which eventually gave rise to the Act for Tellers and Receivers was introduced in the Lords,[111] and on 14 April, when Parliament adjourned and the Exchequer's Michaelmas term ended, the dismemberment of Winchester's empire began. So many were the changes that followed that only the barest outline of them can be provided here.

[108] William Camden, *The History of the most renowned and victorious Princess Elizabeth late Queen of England*, selected chapters ed. and introd. by W. T. MacCaffrey (London, 1970), 105–6.

[109] Candler was imprisoned in the Fleet c.12 Feb. 1571, E 159/364 *Recogs*. Hil. 15 Eliz. rot. 567^v. (I owe this reference, and many others to the memoranda rolls of the queen's remembrancer, to the kindness of Dr Gregor Duncan.) Gardiner's account for land sales, showing a deficit of £24,300, was taken on 10 Mar. 1571, E 351/600. Smythe was suspended from office on 16 Mar. 1571, E 159/361 *Communia*, Easter 13 Eliz. rot. 134.

[110] T. E. Hartley, ed., *Proceedings in the Parliaments of Elizabeth I*, vol. i. *1558–81* (Leicester University Press, 1981), 202, 218, 224; Neale, *Parliaments*, i. 218–24.

[111] Hartley, *Proceedings*, 218, 225, 247–8, 251, 255; *Stat. Realm* 13 Eliz., c. 4.

In the first place, Sir Walter Mildmay exercised his authority as undertreasurer and took control of the Receipt—presumably with the blessing of the Privy Council, of which he had been a member since July 1566. Then, with the assistance of his client Robert Petre, an able younger brother of the former secretary whom Winchester had appointed to Humphrey Shelton's office of writer of the tallies in June 1569, he set afoot a reorganization which was as clearly intended to break Winchester's grip on the Lower Exchequer as it was to remedy the abuses there.[112] In effect, he abolished both the revived ancient course and Winchester's 'system' of divided authority by depriving the clerk of the pell of all his duties but one—the production of the receipt roll—and transferring the whole responsibility for the running of the Receipt to Petre.[113] In other words, he did not attempt to introduce a *new* accounting system, but simply to restore what was regarded as the constitution of Henry VII. He did, though, introduce a number of regulations designed to prevent misconduct by the tellers. The most significant of these dealt with the thorny issue of their surpluses. In practice, it permitted the tellers to retain sufficient cash in their own hands to keep their accounts solvent, but obliged the writer of the tallies to 'chest up' superfluous sums in great coffers whose keys were kept by the undertreasurer.[114] In short, it set up a central deposit treasury, one that was housed in the Receipt at first, but may have been moved to the nearby mansion of St Stephen's, Westminster when the tellers and the writer of the tallies set up their offices there in June 1574.[115]

[112] E 407/71, fos. 25, 107, 170; BL Lansd. MS 67/11, fo. 25ᵛ, and 106/2, fo. 6. For Petre, see *HC 1558–1603*, iii. 210–11 and Elton, 'War in the Receipt', *passim*.

[113] The timing of Mildmay's coup is confirmed by the fate of the pell of issue. It was abolished between 23 Feb., when Wardoure was provided with 60 skins of (expensive) parchment to make up the roll for the current term, and 14 Apr., when term ended without the clerk of the pells gaining access to the tellers' rolls. E 407/68/7 (charges for parchment, Michaelmas term 1570). There is a detailed and near-contemporary description of the Receipt after Mildmay's 'purge' in Trinity College Camb. MS O. 2.20, pp. 19–22. For the effect of these developments on the chamberlains, see Coleman, 'Agarde', 66–7.

[114] E 36/266, fo. 80; E 404/230, fo. 36; Camb. Univ. Lib. MS Gg. 2.7, fo. 87.

[115] The new orders for chesting up the treasure were in effect by 15 June 1572, SP 12/91, fos. 106–11. The mansion of St Stephen's Westminster was acquired by the crown after the death, on 5 Mar. 1572, of Edward Lord Hastings of Loughborough, a debtor. E 407/71, fo. 211ᵛ; *HC 1509–58*, ii. 315. It was refurbished, for the use of the tellers and the writer of the tallies, between 30 Dec. 1573 and 30 June 1574, E 351/3209. There is a minutely detailed description of the coffers in the tellers' offices and their contents, dated 1 Oct. 1585, in SP 12/183, fos. 1–2.

These developments did not go unopposed. The hapless clerk of the pells, Chidiock Wardoure, did everything he could to defeat Robert Petre, the man he wisely chose to blame for his misfortunes, while the old treasurer attempted one last throw, sending Mildmay a letter—now unfortunately lost—instructing him to suspend the new orders.[116] But time and chance were against the ancient course. The marquess died on 10 March 1572 and was succeeded in the treasurership by Burghley who, after taking some pains to familiarize himself with the Exchequer, gave his wholehearted support to the undertreasurer.[117]

Under Burghley, Mildmay, and Petre, the Receipt was managed as efficiently as its constricting constitution and climate of ideas would allow. Relatively favourable economic conditions enabled the queen to build up a deposit treasure of which her grandfather would have been envious: £102,000 at Michaelmas 1573; £150,000 at Easter 1579; £240,000 at Easter 1580; and £270,000 in the summer of 1585, on the eve of the intervention in the Netherlands.[118] Reserves of this magnitude permitted her to govern without recourse to those desperate expedients so often forced on the governments of the 1540s, 1550s, and 1560s: the sale of crown lands and the negotiation of foreign and domestic loans.[119] But if

[116] E 407/71, fos. 41–2, 136, 199; Trinity College Camb. MS O.2.20, pp. 16–22; BL Lansd. MS 106, fo. 6. In Apr. 1571, Winchester began, but did not complete, a letter to the queen about the crown debt (in general). He was not able to leave home, he said, because 'I am so trowbled with the humor upon my nose that I am not able to go abrode.' H. Ellis, *Original Letters Illustrative of English History . . . from autographs in the B.M. and . . . other collections* (11 vols., London, 1824, 1827, 1846), iii (1846), 369–72. Mr Henry James kindly provided me with this reference.

[117] E 407/71, fo. 199; SP 12/91, fos. 106–11; R. B. Outhwaite, 'A Note on *The Practice of the Exchequer Court, with its severall Offices and Officers*, by Sir T. F.', *EHR* lxxxi (1966), 337–9.

[118] E 405/242, fos. 153–67; Northants RO Westmorland (Apethorpe) MS 4. xix. 12; BL Add. MS 34,215, fos. 14–26; SP 12/183, fos. 1–2.

[119] There was no borrowing abroad between 1574 and 1603; no borrowing at home (except in 1575–6, when the sum of £30,000 was taken up) until 1588; no commission for land sales until 1589: R. B. Outhwaite, 'Studies in Elizabethan Government Finance: Royal Borrowing and the Sales of Crown Lands, 1572–1603' (University of Nottingham, unpublished Ph.D. thesis, 1964), 38, 70, 347, 370–1. (I am grateful to Dr Outhwaite for lending me his own copy of this important work.) There was no fiscal exploitation of the English coinage in the Elizabethan period, though the Irish coinage was debased in 1555–9 and 1601–3: C. E. Challis, *The Tudor Coinage* (Manchester, 1978), 257–8, 263, 268–74. Mildmay delivered a glowing account of the achievements of Elizabeth government to the House of Commons in 1576: Neale, *Parliaments*, i. 346–8. (I am grateful to Professor Russell for reminding me of this.)

Mildmay's coup might be said to have inaugurated something of a golden age for royal finances, it was not one that was destined to last. For the undertreasurer had not, significantly, provided the 'forward-looking' reforms one might have expected of him if, as Professor Elton thought, he was essentially the right-hand man of Cromwell's leading disciple.[120] He had not, for example, introduced a device to prevent the tellers from building up their cash in hand to disproportionate levels when circumstances were favourable to them. On occasions, therefore, there were considerable sums 'at large', as, for instance, at the end of the Michaelmas term of 1578, when they totalled about £149,200.[121] Nor had he introduced a regulation requiring the tellers to submit to a cash count at each half-yearly audit. As a result, they retained the liberty to exploit a part, at least, of their surpluses in their own interest, and the writer of the tallies was rarely able to discover, before things began to go wrong, whether any one of them did or did not possess the whole of the sum he was supposed to have in his hands. It would be an anachronism to say that these were problems which Mildmay had 'failed' to solve: he was no more free than Winchester had been to change the whole conception of the tellers' office. But it should be recognized that even under his firm hand the Receipt remained dangerously vulnerable to accidents of mortality and to the imposition of unexpected burdens on the tellers. Furthermore, he and the new treasurer had, in a sense, inherited a poisoned chalice from the old. The use of 'ancient course' arguments in the debates of the 1550s and 1560s had raised serious doubts about the *legality* of the supposed constitution of Henry VII; and the complicated developments of 1554–71 had greatly increased the number of precedents which officers could draw on if they wished to argue that the responsibilities of their office had been improperly diminished and ought to be increased.[122] So Chidiock Wardoure, the clerk of the pells whose career had been ruined by the events of 1571, had never given up hope of recovering his standing in the Receipt, and did not cease to search for evidence to substantiate what was in essence the case manufactured by Cockerell in the

---

[120] Elton, *Tudor Revolution*, 118–19, 223–4, 247–8, 257–8; *England under the Tudors*, 410; *Reform and Reformation*, 390.

[121] Northants RO Westmorland (Apethorpe) MS 4. xix. 12.

[122] Professor Russell kindly reminded me of the latter point.

1550s.[123] When the pressures of war emptied the treasury and, in effect, bankrupted two of the tellers, and death removed Petre's patron and protector, Mildmay,[124] Wardoure was able to persuade the queen to issue, on 5 August 1589, a signet warrant ordering the immediate restoration of the ancient course.[125] Its initial impact was negligible—Burghley either could not or would not put it into effect—but after eight years of argument it was used in the summer of 1597 to inaugurate another major reorganization of the Receipt. In other words, Elizabeth's reign ended as it had begun, with a determined and, in a limited sense, successful effort to put the clock back to the time of Henry II.[126]

The history of the post-1554 Exchequer does not, then, conform to Professor Elton's expectations—and this alone provides grounds for scepticism about the alleged long-term significance of events that took place in the 1530s and 1540s. But it does more than this to undermine his argument. It displays a number of general features which are inimical to the idea that one, inspired hand was responsible for a long-term programme of reform. Three, only, of these can be mentioned here. First, there was, as asserted at the outset of this chapter, no consistent line of development after 1554: the history of the Elizabethan Exchequer was essentially an episodic one, in which there were frequent, but not irreversible, changes of direction. Second, the many changes in Exchequer practice which have been identified were not the product of a reforming ideology, consistently applied, but rather of conflicts between individuals with markedly different interests—conflicts which took place in highly specific, and changing, circumstances, and within an intellectual framework prescribed by somewhat confused conceptions of law, custom, and history. Third, when officers of the Receipt argued about the way the institution should be organized, they did so in terms of competing historical myths. When they wished to

---

[123] Elton, 'War in the Receipt', *passim*.

[124] At the end of the Michaelmas term of 1588, there was nothing left in the deposit treasury but £3,000 in Robert Freke's coffers, and a pile of Sir Horatio Palavicino's obligations, worth about £1,200, in Robert Taylor's: Northants RO Westmorland (Apethorpe) MS 4. xix. 17. Stonley had been in financial straits for years (see n. 101 above), but his and Taylor's accounts were wrecked during the Armada campaign—a fact which Mildmay and Burghley at first concealed from the queen, BL Harl. MS 6994, fo. 146. Mildmay died on 31 May 1589.

[125] E 407/71, fo. 17.

[126] Elton, 'War in the Receipt', 381 ff.

substantiate their views, it was to time-honoured authority they turned: to Henry II, or Henry VII, but never to the man whom John Foxe was busy turning into a hero of the protestant Reformation—Thomas Cromwell.[127]

[127] A. G. Dickens, *Thomas Cromwell and the English Reformation* (London, 1959), 179. Cromwell was probably remembered only for giving the then relatively minor office of chancellor of the Exchequer 'a spell of rather personal importance'. Elton, *Tudor Revolution*, 113–14, 256.

CONCLUSION

AFTER THE 'REVOLUTION'

DAVID STARKEY

So what is left of the Tudor Revolution? Its central arguments were that governmental change was concentrated in a single decade, the 1530s; that it was conceived and executed by one man, Thomas Cromwell; and that it was fundamental, marking the frontier between the medieval 'household' monarchy and the early modern 'bureaucratic' state. Little of this survives. The 1530's have lost their primacy. In the household the crucial changes were earlier, in *c.*1495 and 1518–19; in the Council they were later, in 1540 and 1553; and in finance they were later still, in 1553–4 and 1569–72. And with the primacy of the 1530s goes much of Cromwell's personal role. It was Cromwell's opponents, not Cromwell, who finally set up the Privy Council in 1540; and it was the broad-based Tudor establishment, not the shadowy disciples of Cromwell, who re-established that body in 1553.

But not only Cromwell the planner is in doubt; so is the importance of planning and premeditation in general. Most striking is the case of the royal household. The early Tudor period saw the replacement of a household of two departments—Household and Chamber—with one of three—Household, Chamber and Privy Chamber. But though the outcome was straightforward, the road there was not. The new institutional structure did not spring fully armed from the head of one man; instead much time and many factors were at work: long-term developments in domestic planning and upper-class life style; the powerful and sharply contrasting personalities of Henry VII and Henry VIII; and the immediate pressures of the foreign and domestic politics of 1518, the year of the Treaty of London with France, and 1519, the year of Wolsey's expulsion of the minions from Court. Much the same goes for the Council. Elton saw the Privy Council as being 'deliberately and consciously organized some time between 1534 and 1536'.[1] In fact a

[1] G. R. Elton, *The Tudor Revolution in Government* (Cambridge, 1953), 320.

small select Council, having most of the characteristics and even bearing the name of the later Privy Council, appears at several points in Henry VIII's reign: in 1509, when such a Council ran the country for the careless young king; in 1529, when the Council contained (increasingly uneasily) the faction-ridden junto that had overthrown Wolsey; and in 1536, when the Council temporarily elbowed aside another minister, Cromwell, to offer the broader-based, more respectable form of government needed to surmount the crisis of the Pilgrimage of Grace. There is no reason to give primacy to the 1530s experiment; and neither it nor the others look remotely planned. Instead they were short-term and usually short-lived responses to immediate political circumstances. The result is an interesting reversal. For in rejecting Elton's 'creationist' view we go back to the 'evolutionary' thesis he attacked. This saw the gradual emergence of a Privy Council, culminating, at least for Pollard, in its 'definite organization' in 1540.[2] My only quarrel here would be with the definitiveness of what was done in 1540. Within six years the drafters of Henry VIII's will were playing ducks and drakes with the concept and even the existence of the Privy Council.[3] And the chief culprit (almost certainly) was the Privy Council's first clerk, William Paget.[4] Paget more than made up for his back-sliding later, when he led the Tudor establishment to a discreet victory over Mary's personal following. This victory certainly re-established what we could call the classic Tudor Privy Council. But did it do so, again, definitively? At least as important surely was another political fluke: Elizabeth's accession and her enduring commitment to Cecil and to the rump of the Edwardian Council (or their descendants).

We have already played with the terms 'creationist' and 'evolutionary'. We could go even deeper into modern jargon and claim that we have changed the paradigm. Elton, it might be said, saw Tudor governmental reform rather as an eighteenth-century deist perceived the universe: as the orderly creation of the divine artificer, Cromwell. For this we have substituted the chaotic twentieth-century cosmos that followed the 'death of God'. Cromwell is dethroned; governmental change (we had better not call it reform)

---

[2] Ibid. 318.
[3] T. Rymer, ed., *Foedera, Conventiones, Litterae* (15 vols., London, 1704–35), xv. 111–18.
[4] G. R. Elton, *Reform and Reformation* (London, 1977), 331.

is rarely the result of long-term planning; rather it is the outcome of the most complex interplay of circumstances, over which chance and the luck of the political game preside as often as reason or will.

More down-to-earth language might also be used. Rather than changing paradigms we might only have failed to see the wood for the trees. Contingency is present in all events; indeed it is a precondition of action. So behind the arras of chance Elton's fundamental change could still be taking place. Dr Alsop thinks that it was, though he redates it and reformulates the terms. 'Household' and 'bureaucratic', Elton's key words, are rejected, since, far from representing opposed systems of administration, they are in practice almost impossible to distinguish from each other, at any rate in finance. 'Household' agencies like the Chamber and the Privy Purse employed the same administrative methods as 'bureaucratic' departments like the Exchequer, and an interchange of personnel was common. Men moved from one to the other with apparent ease and even held office in both at the same time. But Elton does not only employ the words in this sense. 'Household' government for him is a government in which the king intervenes directly and frequently as administrator-in-chief; 'bureaucratic', a government in which the king presides over a machine whose operations are directed and controlled by others. In Dr Alsop's view mid-Tudor finance changed from the first to the second of these types. From 1540 the Privy Council took over more and more of the direction of finance, while the reforms of 1553–4 channelled the great bulk of royal revenues into a single, specialist department, the Exchequer. The result was to replace a household finance directly controlled by the monarch with a departmental finance managed by the Council. Once again, this was not the achievement of one decade or a single intelligence; nor did it 'bureaucratize' administrative methods or instantly create 'modern' government. Nevertheless, it was new and was of decisive importance for the future.

This is one way of assessing change and obviously an important one. But there is another and that is to look at change in the context of its own times. In 1598, for example, Robert Barret defined 'modern war' as 'the new order of war used in our age'.[5] It would be worth trying to use the same yardstick for administrative change. The standards for Barret's military 'new order' were set

[5] *The Theorike and Practike of Moderne Warres,* cited in the *Oxford English Dictionary,* s.v. 'modern'.

by the campaigns in the Netherlands. Similarly, the aims of Valois statesmen and administrators will do much to illuminate the concerns of their cross-Channel contemporaries in Tudor England.

In 1523 Francis I issued two edicts which set about an ambitious reorganization of the system of finance. Hitherto finance, presided over by the *généraux des finances*, had been largely decentralized and moneys were raised and spent locally. The Edict of St-Germain-en-Laye of 18 March created a new officer, the *trésorier de l'épargne*. He was to receive all 'casual and unexpected funds' (or extraordinary revenues as the contemporary English jargon had it), and use them to build up a central cash reserve. In December the Edict of Blois extended the new system to all the royal revenues, ordinary as well as extraordinary. Now all income, from whatever source, was to be paid to the *trésorier*. And he in turn would make all payments. Thus for decentralized debit finance was substituted an intensely centralized, wholly cash-based system. That at least was the theory. The practice was somewhat more modest. In 1524 the *trésorier* lost part of his revenues, the *parties casuelles* (mainly income from the sale of office) to another new official, the *receveur des finances extraordinaires*; while as far as expenditure was concerned, in 1528 only a quarter of *épargne* payments were in cash; the remainder were still in *décharges*, or assignments on local collectors.[6] But scepticism must not go too far: the *parties casuelles* was only a subtreasury to the *épargne*, much smaller and paying over its surplus at the year's end to the *trésorier*; while even to handle one quarter of payments in cash was, as Dr Knecht sensibly puts it, 'an advance on the old system'.[7] In short, though achievement fell behind aspiration, finance was moving towards a 'new order'.

In the military 'new order' England lagged behind the Continent; in financial administration, it is now clear, the boot was on the other foot. The fifteenth-century Exchequer bore a strong resemblance to the pre-1523 French system. The Exchequer, like the *généraux des finances*, administered a decentralized structure, which dealt not in cash but in assignments (made in England by tallies) on local collectors. But the Exchequer's ascendancy had been broken in the later fifteenth century, when first the income of

[6] Martin Wolffe, *The Fiscal System of Renaissance France* (New Haven and London, 1972), 78 ff.

[7] R. J. Knecht, *Francis I* (Cambridge, 1982), 131.

the crown lands, and subsequently almost all other royal revenues were transferred to the treasurer of the Chamber. Historians all agree that the 'Chamber system' was novel. Neither before nor since had the king depended on the crown lands for so large a part of his income. But as important (and much less commented on) was that the Chamber knew nothing of assignment. All Chamber revenues were received in cash in Westminster;[8] and all Chamber payments were made in the same way in the same place. So with the rise of the Chamber England had achieved a centralized, cash-based system of finance forty years earlier than France, and had achieved it more thoroughly and completely than was ever possible in the much larger, less closely knit dominions of the French crown.

This sort of finance is not modern in our sense of the word. Rather it combines the attitudes of the piggy-bank and the binge. But it was modern in their sense of the word, which is all that is to the purpose here. Cash eased the ordinary business of government, as there was no need to borrow to keep the day-to-day machine of government ticking over. And it was crucial for a swift response to emergencies, whether war or rebellion. The Tudors had a quick way with rebellion and it depended more on the gold in their coffers than on the overrated quality of their propagandists. These same coffers also explain a long-standing conflict of historical judgement. Recent historians never tire of pointing out that the revenues of a king of England were only a fraction of those of a king of France. On the other hand, well-informed contemporaries never ceased marvelling at the wealth of Henry VII. The different speed of 'modernization' in England and France is the key to the paradox. Louis XII's revenues were indeed vast, but little came to his coffers in cash. Henry VII's income was comparatively small, but almost all of it came to the King's Chamber in coin that was lovingly counted, bagged and coffered. Louis was rich on paper, and that impresses historians; Henry was rich in cash, and that impressed contemporaries.

But at the very moment France was setting up the *épargne*, the English Chamber was beginning its long decline. It was displaced first by the Privy Purse; then by Cromwell's personal treasury, and finally by the specialized revenue courts of the 1530s. The result was that by the 1540s the Chamber was only one of the lesser

---

[8] With the exception of some transfer payments from the Exchequer.

departments of a complex, even chaotic financial machine. And when the chaos was finally reduced to order in 1553, it was by restoring not the Chamber but the Exchequer to its ancient primacy over finance. Such is the way the story is told, and indeed more or less the way we tell it above. Dr Alsop raises the first note of doubt when he argues that early Tudor finance worked reasonably well. It did, and largely because behind the bewildering succession of institutions there was a remarkable continuity of practice and control.

Let us go back for a moment to France. The *épargne* and the whole cash-based system of finance was only a means to an end. The objective was to create a war-chest big enough to enable Francis I to launch a campaign without having to wait for a creaking financial machine to get into gear. The organization of the war-chest, set up in 1523, was elaborated by the Edict of Rouen of February 1532. The treasure chests of the *épargne* were now to remain in the strong-rooms of the Louvre instead of following the Court as hitherto. The chests themselves were also divided between those holding funds for the day-to-day operations of the *épargne* and two special war-chests. The latter had slots, so that money could be got in but not out; they were to be opened only in the presence of a special heavy-weight committee; and they had four separate locks, the keys to which were held by four separate personages: the king, the chancellor, and the two royal favourites, Montmorency and Chabot. Any money that was going spare went into the war-chests, but casual or windfall revenues were particularly marked out: like the money screwed out of the heirs of the vastly wealthy chancellor Duprat, or the dowry of Catherine de Medici.[9]

So another cross-Channel parallel. Just as the *épargne* was the equivalent of the Chamber, so the war-chest was the twin of the English Privy Coffers. The Privy Coffers, like the French war-chest, were kept in palace treasuries (and increasingly in *the* palace treasury at Whitehall); they too were administered directly by the king; and they received similar windfall revenues: the French pension, the early spoils of the church, and money wrung from the estate of another great chancellor, Wolsey. Moreover, while the Chamber declined steadily in the later years of Henry VIII, the Privy Coffers (despite a few hiccoughs) went from strength to strength and reached their peak in the 1540s.

[9] Martin Wolffe, *Fiscal System*, 87 ff.

And it was this fact, strange though it may seem, that gave both continuity and continued effectiveness to English finance. For both the Privy Coffers and the French war-chest were more than windfall treasuries. The war-chest also received the year's end surplus from the ordinary operations of the *épargne*; while the Privy Coffers went further. When money came into a treasury in dribs and drabs—as it did into the Hanaper or the Exchequer in an ordinary year—the king was content to wait to the year's end before transferring the surplus into his coffers. But if (say) the Exchequer received a sudden influx of cash, like the payment of a subsidy instalment, then Henry creamed it off immediately.

In all this Henry VIII may have acted for the worst of motives (he usually did). No doubt he was meanly suspicious of his servants' honesty, and he certainly had a miser's pleasure in handling and hoarding cash.[10] Nevertheless the effect of the Privy Coffers was to help forge a financial system out of the chaos of separate treasuries. It made it easy to know what the government's total reserves were at any one time—knowledge that was as vital as it was otherwise hard to come by. And it imposed a rigorous discipline that penetrated into the most inaccessible corners. The king's insatiable demand for cash meant that every financial department had to operate in cash too. And if you had to hand over your surplus at the end of the year (if not more frequently) you had to keep running accounts that enabled you to calculate that surplus quickly and accurately. Henry VIII was not of course the first to impose the discipline. That was Henry VII's work. But the Privy Coffers meant that Henry VII's achievement survived in the much less favourable circumstances of Henry VIII's reign.

But its survival beyond Henry VIII's death depended on something else. Dr Alsop remarks that the later sixteenth-century Exchequer was fundamentally different from its fifteenth-century predecessor. And one of the key points of difference was that it dealt mainly in cash. The change was largely the work of the founding fathers of the 'Chamber system', Edward IV, Richard III, and Henry VII. Driven by that determination to secure the 'more hasty levy of money', which was the keynote of the new financial order, they set about the Exchequer. Its accounts were simplified and its structure stream-lined. The aim was for the king 'yearly [to] see the

[10] 'Not from the King's coffers' is a recurrent phrase: *LP* VII. 1010, 1587; *LP* IX. 850.

profits of the court',[11] and once having ascertained the profit, to get it, in coin, into his coffers as quickly as possible. The result was that by the end of the first half of Henry VIII's reign the Exchequer was almost as cash-based as the old Chamber. Thereafter, under Mary I and Elizabeth I, the changes became an issue in the Exchequer's increasingly lively internal politics; while these disputes in turn were caught up in the larger political struggles of Paulet and Cecil. The outcome, as Mr Coleman shows, was not only a modified victory for innovation, but a further sweeping reorganization of the Exchequer in 1569–72. Large-scale building works and tightened rules for the administration of cash made the Exchequer what it had not been for many years: a secure deposit treasury. And in the next decade and a half its new capacity was exploited to the full, while a war-chest, eventually even bigger than Henry VIII's, was painstakingly accumulated in the Exchequer's coffers.

It would, of course, be going too far to see the accumulation of a cash reserve as the only goal of sixteenth-century finance. It vanished in war, and above all in the aftermath of war, as in the mid-1550s when impending bankruptcy made administrative retrenchment and simplification the order of the day. Nevertheless, a cash reserve was a goal that recurred: under Edward IV, Henry VII, Henry VIII, and Elizabeth I. And when it did so, the effects were felt far outside the royal treasure-house. The accumulation of cash reserves led inexorably to cash-based finance, to a kind of 'monetarism' in fact. 'Cash-finance' was not, save in the short perspective of its own time, 'new' or 'progressive'. Any medieval king would have understood it, and many, when times were ripe, had built up substantial war-chests of their own. But then, as we have discovered, long-term developments in early sixteenth-century financial administration are not thick on the ground. Probably there are only two. First was the turning once again of the ancient cycle of going out of court as the Chamber was displaced by the Privy Chamber and its agencies. This cycle was never complete and it was more or less the end for household finance. The second development was a beginning: the rise of departmental finance in the Exchequer charted by Dr Alsop. In and between came the fiscal switchback of the 'age of plunder', in which revenue courts came and went, not as

---

[11] B P. Wolffe, *The Crown Lands 1461–1536* (London, 1970), 133–7.

the stages of a developing administrative logic, but largely by MacGregor's law of exhaustion. A revenue-hungry government discovers a new source of supply and a new agency is set up to exploit it. Quickly the source is mined to exhaustion and the government moves on to a fresh field and a new agency.

Nor is finance the only area of sixteenth-century government where a wider contemporary context has much to tell us. Elton sees the emergence of the Privy Council simply in terms of efficiency: the old Council was: 'large, cumbersome and inefficient'; the new was 'small, flexible and effective'. Dr Guy points the way to a different approach when he describes the debate in which the leaders of the Pilgrimage of Grace formulated their demands for a reform of the King's Council. They talked not in terms of the Council's efficiency, but of its representativeness, and revived the medieval claim of the nobility to the leading place on the Council as '*consiliarii nati*'. This raises exciting possibilities. The most likely date for the emergence of the Privy Council is in the crisis of 1536–7 provoked by the Pilgrimage itself; other select councils had come to the fore in 1509–12 and 1529–32, while the new Council finally assumed the full dress of institutional formality in 1540, when it was given its own secretariat and records. All of these dates have one thing in common: they are periods of unusual noble activity in high politics, when a handful of peers took the lead in Court and Council. 1526, when Wolsey produced the blueprint for the Privy Council in the Eltham Ordinances, appears an important exception. But it is at least possible that this chapter of the Ordinances represents one half of a bargain. Wolsey, we know, had got a free hand over the royal household; in return, perhaps, his fellow politicians demanded a properly collegiate Council as some check on his otherwise untrammelled power. Be that as it may, the general thrust is clear. We can no longer think simply of the Privy Council as the crowning achievement of the great ministers' endless search for efficiency and tidiness. The Privy Council also incorporated a large dash of aristocratic conciliarism. And the fact showed. For the formal institution of the Privy Council in 1540 inaugurated a series of regimes more narrowly aristocratic than any England had known since the first half of the fifteenth century.

The Pilgrims' debate of 1536 is important in another way as well: not for what was said, but for the fact that it took place at all. It was an open, reasoned critique of royal policy, and it forced out of

Henry one of the few public defences of his government he ever had
to offer. But the incident is isolated. On no other occasion does
governmental change seem to have been an issue of public political
debate. Bearing in mind the claims that are made for the 'Tudor
Revolution' the fact is surprising; and in contrast with the fifteenth
century the silence is deafening. Then governmental reform was the
subject of intense debate in Court, country, and Parliament, and
the new language of 'common weal' was formulated to express it.
Not only does the early sixteenth century offer no parallel to the
fifteenth-century debate, it also changes the usage of the word
'common weal' itself. In the fifteenth century 'common weal' and
governmental reform go hand in hand, and indeed in 1536 the most
substantial written contribution to the Pilgrims' debate harks back
to this position when it calls for a 'Council of the Commonwealth'.
But once again the occasion is unique. Otherwise governmental
change and 'common weal' go their separate ways. Change in the
machinery of state is discussed, if at all, as a technical question in
the corridors of power, while 'common weal' ceases to be a
political and governmental slogan, as it had been in the fifteenth
century, and becomes instead the banner for *social* improvement
and reconstruction. The conclusion is inescapable. Government in
the sixteenth century, unlike government in the fifteenth, did not
need and did not get radical overhaul. Within its limits it worked
very well; some modifications were of course required, and they
took place. But they happened *ad hoc* and without great drama. It
is always a pity to drive a great idea, Coriolanus-like, off the stage,
but it must be done: Tudor readjustment in government indeed, but
no revolution.

INDEX